Italy,

A Love Story

Edited by
Camille Cusumano

SEAL PRESS

Italy, A Love Story:
Women Write about the Italian Experience

Copyright © 2005 by Camille Cusumano

An excerpt from *Rome and a Villa*, by Eleanor Clark, published 2000 by
Steerforth Italia, an imprint of Steerforth Press, Hanover, NH, is reprinted
by special arrangement with HarperCollins Publishers, Inc.

"Rome, the Art of Living" was previously published in *Italian Days*, copyright
© 1989 by Barbara Grizzuti Harrison. It is used by permission of Grove/Atlantic, Inc.

Published by Seal Press
An Imprint of Avalon Publishing Group, Inc.
1400 65th Street, Suite 250
AVALON Emeryville, CA 94608
publishing group incorporated

All rights reserved. No part of this book may be reproduced or transmitted in
any form without written permission from the publisher, except by reviewers
who may quote brief excerpts in connection with a review.

Some photos and illustrations are used by permission and are the property of
the original copyright owners.

ISBN 1-58005-143-X

Library of Congress Cataloging-in-Publication Data

Italy, a love story : women write about the Italian experience / [edited] by Camille
Cusumano.— 1st ed.

p. cm.

ISBN 1-58005-143-X

1. Italy—Description and travel. 2. Women travelers—Italy. 3. Travelers' writings.
I. Cusumano, Camille. II. Title.

DG430.2.I843 2005

914.504'082—dc22

2005007646

9 8 7 6 5 4 3 2 1

Cover design by Jacob Goolkasian
Interior design by Domini Dragoone
Printed in Canada by Transcontinental
Distributed by Publishers Group West

For my grandparents, Giovanna Franciamore,

Salvatore Catalano, Maria Federico, and

Vincenzo Cusumano, who put Italy in my blood.

Contents

Introduction

I was born into a Little Italy, an Italian enclave called Peterstown, in Elizabeth, New Jersey. My parents and the first seven of their ten kids, which included me (number five), lived in the flat beneath two of my four Sicilian grandparents. Beyond the standard-issue diet of macaroni, meatballs, tomatoes, garlicky greens, and pizza, I recall customs that came through Ellis Island with my grandparents and distinguished my Italian side from my American side. While my classmates celebrated St. Patrick's Day on March 17, in my home we celebrated St. Joseph's Day (March 19); we also celebrated the feast of Santa Lucia, a huge patron of Sicily, on December 13, and sometimes Pasquetta (the day after Easter). Instead of rushing us to the doctor or applying Bengay, my grand-mother healed us with her hands and olive oil: She rubbed my dislocated shoulder back into its socket and soothed my sister's foot when it was mangled in bicycle spokes. There was this: I knew the ultimate profanity was to take the name of the Madonna (*Madonna mia*) in vain. And there were these habits: A loaf of bread was never, ever allowed to rest upside down—it was and still is sacrilegious; if you spilled olive oil, you threw a little salt in it.

Our weekly socializing often took place on Saturdays at an outdoor market where Italian was the reigning tongue. We bought vegetables and greens (some of them gathered in the wild by the vendors)—*cucuzza*, *scarola*, dandelions, *carduni*—that Americans in general would not even think of eating then. Long before I learned their English names, I knew the Sicilian for many common items— like *gupina* (sauce ladle), *gobbagul'* (spicy ham—today I know it's *cappacola*), and *mullinjohn* (eggplant, or *melanzana* in Italian). My parents had more *goombas* (*goomas* if they were female) than a Scorcese film.

Even though I was born on American soil, I have very proprietary feelings when it comes to Italy. I was raised to own with unstinting pride my Italianness (uh, make that Sicilianness—or my father will dance the tarantella in his grave). All of which is to say that even though I didn't set foot on Italian soil until I was twenty-one, I know from things Italian. So it's a tribute to the keen observation and storytelling power of the twenty-eight writers selected for this anthology that they not only command my attention but move me to tears, laughter, or outrage over a culture that's mine through blood, breeding, and parental decree.

Introduction

Italy, *il Bel Paese,* is a storied land that tells its tale in every medium, from Mediterranean foodstuffs to Carrara marble. Magazine and newspaper travel sections abound with articles on Italy—from Venice, Tuscany, and Rome to the Dolomites, Amalfi coast, Sicily, and Sardinia. You read of villages where old men whisper secrets of the simple life and women speak in clipped proverbs. All of this sweetness is there for the visitor—I have seen, tasted, and breathed it in. It's as if there is some ancient sustenance in the food, wine, air, language. I have traveled to fabled corners, walked the entire Via dell'Amore in Cinque Terre, soaked in the art of Florence, cycled the thigh-hardening routes of the hill towns in Umbria, and encountered a mountain village full of "my people" in Sicily.

I can promise you that you won't find the composite portrait of the Italian experience contained within these pages anywhere else. There was a defining moment when I knew this book would be great, that these literary essays would transcend the typical travel article, would rise far above all other books on Italy and contain writing that penetrates beyond the facile stereotypes of Italy. That moment came as I read Rachel Dacus's piece, "Venice and the Passion to Nurture," while my mother rolled out enough pizza dough to feed the four generations of our family, who would drop by for some pre-Thanksgiving conviviality. Dacus was taking me to Venice on Mother's Day, where she was anguishing over the possibility of being infertile. Meanwhile, with the same nonchalance with which she bore children, my mother shoved pies into the oven and pulled them out, all the while trying to console my niece, who was awaiting her first, slow-in-coming pregnancy. At first I tried to tune out their conversation in order to concentrate on the essay, which is grounded in Venice, where architectural masterpieces are "born" out of lagoons. But the author's personal need to bear her own masterpiece to nurture awakened me to the painful dimensions of my niece's dilemma. Dacus's stirring meditation on the Madonna, the role of mothers and children in Italy, and the universal desire of women to nurture was as relevant to me as to my niece and mother. In one goose-flesh moment, I understood how I, who chose not to have kids; my mother, the Sicilian matriarch of ten kids, twenty-six grandchildren, and eleven great-grandchildren; and my niece, who aches for her first child, shared more than we knew.

I also understood more clearly the merits of the distinctly female nature that unites the stories in this collection. They may be universal in dealing with death, love, identity, the environment, culture shock, and the like, but they are specific and focused in the way they inform women's lives. And Italy, with its deep-rooted devotion to the Madonna (and its pagan forerunner, goddess worship, highly in evidence among pre-Christian ruins in the south), offers a unique proving ground for female self-discovery.

In compiling this anthology, I read a few hundred stories on Italy, many of them graced with sparkling travelogue, funny anecdotes, or witty commentary on the Italian persona. But I realized I wanted more than that. I wanted stories, like Dacus's, that stir the soul, raise goose flesh, awaken something deep, and deliver this sort of universal epiphany with an "Ah, that could only happen in Italy."

Take the story by Holly Smith Dinbergs, a cancer survivor. There is no dearth of literature on how Italy appeals to all the senses. But I have never read an account of how Italy opened one's heart by way of one's nose, which had been "retuned" by chemotherapy treatments. Having had one too many loved ones stricken with cancer, I cry and laugh upon every reading of Dinbergs's Florentine adventure in "Aromatherapy, Italian-Style."

We know by the numbers—Italy receives more visitors than any other European country—that Italy is loved. Its people are loved. And love is a difficult subject to write about without resorting to clichés and sentimental language. And yet Susan Tiberghien's touching portrayal of the wise and eccentric Emilia, for example, shows us that unspoken love isn't any less powerful than when "I love you" is said aloud. And sometimes love comes as a surprise, as with Elizabeth Asdorian, who is determined to have a fairytale travel romance—but soon wisely drops the *chooch* (that's East Coast Italian for "clueless boy") like hot potato gnocchi and gives her heart to his Nonna, who cheers like a Milanese Ma Kettle in front of the TV for her favorite skier. And there's Kate Adamek's crone: Just when you've had enough of the stingy, officious Signora, Adamek reveals a tender side, where both narrator and protagonist are redeemed in one uniquely Italian moment. Adamek, like all of these writers, is not afraid to illuminate the *scuro* (dark side) as well as the *chiaro* (light side) of Italian culture.

There are many moments of comic relief: At dinnertime, the fatally overstylish women in Deanna David's action-packed essay sing and bark orders while the kids play with Power Rangers in the war zone beneath the table; a carful of nuns and a lone businessman banter over the best way to cook artichokes amid a traffic jam in Sicily in Natalie Galli's story; and the blond-worshipping Romeos trail Julianne DiNenna's fair-haired travel companion as DiNenna searches for her roots.

And there are moments of discovery and introspection: Terez Rose visits tranquil Matera, a once-shadowy corner of the boot that until just decades ago was racked with unspeakable poverty; sitting in her stalled car in Bergamo, Beth Schommer contemplates the notions of home, family, and identity.

Yes, like my father before me, I may be a *capotosto* (hard-headed) *siciliana*. It's tough to tell me, with my lifetime of received wisdom, about Italy. But here I present to you twenty-eight writers who have humbled me and opened my heart to my *paese*, my people, in twenty-eight new ways.

Camille Cusumano

San Francisco, California

March 2005

Holly Smith Dinbergs

Aromatherapy, Italian-Style

I'm standing near a weather-beaten wall beside the glittering pool at Villa Casalecchi, an elegant four-star hotel outside of Castellina in Chianti. An olive-skinned waiter wearing a crisp white shirt open at the throat and pressed black pants tight in the right places bounces by, having just delivered iced drinks to the only other people there: a silver-haired British couple soaking in the afternoon sun. The waiter's dark eyes flash in my direction. He obviously thinks I'm daft, or that I need a doctor, since I seem to be manifesting an odd respiratory ailment. Well, the man *is* Italian, so he might conclude that I'm doing nothing more than expressing grief for *amore* gone wrong. What could he think? There I stand, wrapped in a blue-and-yellow striped towel, head thrust in the middle of white jasmine blooms, making loud sniffling sounds.

I had ended a second round of chemotherapy in 2001 with a bald head and one burning ambition: to go to Tuscany. I don't know why or how Tuscany entered my dreams. I've wondered if, under anesthesia during one of my surgeries, I had absorbed a conversation between doctors and nurses chatting about blinding sunlight on rolling hills, quilted vineyards, and rows of cypress trees guarding fields of wheat. Maybe I had fallen under the spell of Diane Lane's sweetly triumphant smile in the publicity for *Under the Tuscan Sun* as I perused DVDs while choosing a Friday night's excitement.

I had been to Italy only once before, as a university student, in the late '70s. At the end of my junior year in France, my roommate and I redirected our grocery money to buy cattle-class train tickets to Florence. During a long weekend, we stayed in a cheap *pensione* (which meant no bathing facilities) and divided our time between reading menus in search of inexpensive meals and combing markets on the lookout for cheap gifts to impress our parents and friends on our return.

Thirty years later, at the end of my slash-and-burn cancer treatment, Italy called me again, so loudly, so clearly, that it seemed a matter of life and death. I answered that call by treating myself, on the occasion of my fiftieth birthday, to a weeklong walking tour starting and ending in Florence, the city of *David*, the Ponte Vecchio, and the Duomo. I went looking for many things: the warmth of sun on my skin; the quiet dazzle of fading frescoes in crumbling churches; the cool strength of white marble; and the heat of steaming pasta, for which I relaxed my strict no-carbs rule.

While I found all of those things, something unexpected marked me more: the smells.

Arriving in Florence a little past three on a hot June afternoon, I stepped off the climate-controlled train into the airless station. As the cacophony of diverse languages exploded around me, the steamy smell of unwashed bodies hit me in the face like a cast-iron frying pan.

I did a slow 180-degree turn, looking for the Italian equivalent of WAY OUT. With an eye on the exit sign, I politely pushed my way through tourists and glass doors to enter Tuscan airspace. Trudging along, map in hand, trying to find my hotel, I smelled summer in the city: clouds of exhaust; whiffs of urine wafting from hidden corners; the perfume of ripe cheeses pouring out of shop doors. None of these odors was disagreeable—I interpreted each as proof that this city was alive and so was I, far from hard hospital beds, bleached linoleum, and disinfectants masking the metallic smell of fatal illness. Dragging my red duffle, I smiled as I navigated narrow streets and dodged tiny cars, a vintage Vespa, a man pulling dogs, grandmothers carrying groceries, and young mothers pushing strollers.

My hotel room was what I can describe only as very brown, with a view of the Medici chapel and a closed-in smell. I threw my duffle on the bed, cracked the window, and rushed back out to experience the last hours of the famous Florentine open-air market. Vendors, chatting like my new best friends, tried to hawk red leather purses, green silk scarves, pink sunglasses, and pottery glazed in yellow, blue, and white. I bought only postcards. Stepping into a kiosk for stamps, I walked into the dark fog of cigar smoke emanating from the man sitting innocently behind the counter. Normally, cigar smoke in an enclosed place would be immediate cause for leaving. Instead, I patiently paid for the stamps and left, no hard feelings. All normal reactions were suspended. This was Italy, the newest planet in my universe.

For dinner I ordered grilled prawns and a glass of house red. Did the waiter cringe, or was that my imagination? Should I have ordered a glass of white with prawns? I knew as much about wine as I did about building a lunar landing module (and I'm no rocket scientist). When I buy wine, I choose bottles based on price and label design. My father was a teetotaler, and with my medical history, alcohol is high on my list of "things to avoid." But as part of my week in Italy, I decided to enjoy red wine. When the glass came, I sniffed it, because it seemed the right thing to do. After several thoughtful sniffs, I decided that the watery red liquid smelled like . . . well, like . . . wine. Weak, but wine, all the same. That was about all the nasal discernment I was capable of. The rest of the week changed that.

The next morning, I met the other walkers on my tour: one Canadian, a pair of Welsh sisters with a Swiss husband attached, an American from the Corn Belt, and me, an American living in Switzerland for almost a decade. We began our Tuscan tour by walking around the city with an officially licensed Florentine guide, a diminutive man who, judging by his personal scent, did not spend much time fiddling with the faucets in his bathtub. He led our small group from one tourist attraction to the next, stopping to shout at us in heavily accented English. I caught about 30 percent of what he said (picking up key words, like "church" and "Michelangelo" and "doors"), but it didn't matter. He was polite and knew a lot about Florence. I respected that.

Our first group dinner was in a noisy restaurant that had served as stables centuries earlier. The smell of horse dung had been long washed away by clouds of garlic, fried onions, and grilled beef. With the salad came olive oil so seductive, I almost dabbed it behind my ears and other pulse points. I remained intoxicated by that smell until a new fragrance caught my nose: coffee. The steam rising from my dinner companion's snowcapped cappuccino attracted me like a Max Mara half-price suit sale. I finished my herbal tea but fell asleep that night dreaming of cappuccino with a white peak as large as the one sighted by the lookout on the *Titanic*.

The next morning, we were bussed to Montefollónico to begin the day's walk to Montepulciano. This glorious hilltop town boasts a trove of Renaissance treasures and one of Tuscany's most famous red wines, "noble wine," which sounds more impressive in Italian: *vino nobile*. Before lunch we meandered up to a white, stucco, box-like structure on the edge of a vineyard. As we entered the building, a woman appeared behind a counter lined with glasses and bottles of the regular and reserve vintages of this famous wine. I participated, reluctantly, in this tasting opportunity by timidly sniffing the glasses of crimson-colored wines our Dutch guide stuck in front of my nose. The sniffs gave way to tiny tastes, and I was astonished—not that I could tell the difference, but that there was such a profound difference. The regular version of the *vino nobile* exuded a rich smell of cherries. As the wine lady behind the counter explained how the wine was made and how it *should* smell, I sniffed hard, trying to distinguish the smell of vanilla (yes), then violets and blackberry (maybe).

The bouquet of the *riserva* was more intense, and I am proud to say that . . . I think . . . I picked up a faint scent of oak (or some kind of wood) from the barrels in which it's stored. We sniffed and tasted; sniffed and tasted; sniffed and tasted. No spitting in this group. Afterward, half of us needed a nap and it was not yet noon. My eyelids felt heavy and my nose hairs tingled.

Day Three, our most eventful day, was divided into two acts. The first act, "Pig Shit, Pecorino, and the Pope in Pienza," was followed by a madcap Act Two called "Looking for Harvey Keitel." We began our day, leaving the environs of San Quirico for Bagno Vignoni. We walked and talked; we admired rolling hills and distant, ancient skylines shimmering in bright sunlight; we snapped pictures of sheep that seemed paralyzed by our friendly greetings.

We smelled the pigs before we saw or heard them. Pork is a staple of the Tuscan diet, and where there's pork, there are pigs. Glimpses of massive pink-and-white porkers behind bars brought us, cameras in hand, to the edge of the muddy pigpen. Although they lived in mud, these pigs gleamed, as if they'd been conveyor-belted through the local Pig Wash in preparation for tourist photo ops. The larger pigs grunted mightily, flaring nostrils so enormous that I thought I could probably stick my head in one. The piglets squealed as they played hide-and-seek with our cameras. We snapped away, breathing in the strong smell of healthy farm life. I left understanding why Charlotte felt compelled to save Wilbur from someone's dinner plate by spinning her infamous web, pronouncing him "Some Pig." We returned to the road, where the tour van picked us up for the long uphill ascent to Pienza, birthplace of Pope Pius II. On the drive, we discovered a village that was blocked off with out-of-place modern cameras and movie-caliber spotlights at strategic locations. Members of the film crew told us that Harvey Keitel was in town filming. The eyes of our Dutch guide lit up, and after pointing out that the only tape she listened to was the soundtrack of *The Piano* (in which Harvey had starred alongside Holly Hunter), she proposed we try to find him. No takers, for the moment. It was starting to rain and we were hungry.

We arrived at the gates of Pienza as the rain turned cold and violent. For shelter I darted into the church. The noisy rain amplified the chilly dampness of the dark interior, but with one delightful outcome: Striking a match to light a white candle released a few seconds' worth of sulfur, enhancing the spiritual experience of everyone who entered, even if it was only to escape the downpour. Small, flickering lights exponentially increased as the rain pounded above.

Since walking outside meant being cold and wet, I went into every open shop, including the pharmacy, where I checked out Italian toothpaste. In one of many cheese shops, I tasted the cheese

7

for which Pienza is famous: pecorino, made from sheep's milk. It has a gentle, milky smell with a mild but tangy taste. The crust of the black pecorino, treated with oil and ashes, is dark brown; the red variety owes its name to the fact that it's treated with tomatoes and oil. Dinner that evening was a large bowl of hot soup. To drag out the pleasure, I raised my spoon slowly, inhaling the steam of the white-bean broth flavored with olive oil, pepper, garlic, and chopped onions. My smiling waiter knew instinctively to leave me alone to enjoy the perfume of the soup, which I am sure would out-perform Love Potion Number Nine in a controlled test.

We returned to the hotel around ten, and our guide asked who wanted to try to find Harvey Keitel. I was game to go along for the ride. Driving along in the bright yellow minivan emblazoned with the tour group's logo, we talked about where to go. After a philo-sophical discussion regarding where a Hollywood actor would stay while on location, we came to a logical conclusion: the nicest hotel nearest to where we saw the cameras. After multiple wrong turns in the dark, we found the only five-star in the area: Hotel Adler Thermae, a luxury hotel and health spa. On the ten-minute walk from the parking lot to the door, we fixed our strategy for what we would say if we actually found Harvey: Shake hands and say "Mr. Keitel, I really love your work." Our only concern was that every time we practiced saying it, we'd break into peals of laughter, which somehow diminished the sincerity of the message. We sauntered into the hotel, trying to look bored and affluent, like normal guests in a five-star rather than movie star stalkers. The reception area was perfumed by lilies in an extravagant floral arrangement. No Harvey in the ultramodern bar, but plenty of cigarette smoke. No Harvey in the splendid outdoor heated pool, but the smell of warm water made me wish I'd worn my bathing suit under my jeans. No Harvey in the lavish ladies' toilet, but a light, fruity air freshener. We returned to our hotel Harvey-less but content in the knowledge that at least we tried.

Day Four took us to Castellina in Chianti and introduced me to a life-changing fragrance: broom, the scent which moved me more deeply than the musty smell of the many empty churches we visited. For hours, we traipsed through field and forest along a winding path amid broom's spidery, green stalks topped by bright yellow flowers. As the daughter of a florist and a resident of Europe for almost a decade, I was shocked that I had never known broom as anything other than a tool for sweeping floors. The sweet scent of this flower—think wisteria cocktail laced with grape juice—rivaled gardenias, long at the top of my list of Favorite Flower Smells. My walking ritual became: walk, stop, sniff; walk, stop, sniff. After a few hours, we arrived at the Abbey Sant'Antimo (which I think of as the Abbey in the Middle of Nowhere, or better yet, the Abbey in the Middle of San Somewhere). The stone abbey, built of local travertine, is an extraordinary example of Romanesque architecture, but when I recall that visit, I don't remember the bas-relief or the bell tower. I recall the mild mildew scent of the dark crypt, the whiff of match-smell as I lit a candle, and the calming fragrance of lavender, growing in spectacular silver-green clumps near the main door. We finished that day in the shops of Montalcino and tasted a robust ruby-red brunello, one of the most famous Italian wines. Was my nose becoming more sophisticated or was it wishful thinking? Did I really smell bits of licorice?

The next day, we walked through more fields of broom. I breathed deeply, deliberately, profoundly. Just before I passed out from hyperventilation, we arrived at another sumptuous structure, the Abbey of Monte Oliveto Maggiore. Its sheer size and strength and its tower, carved woodwork, and world-famous cycle of frescoes telling the tale of St. Benedict took my breath away. So did the souvenir shop, filled with an astonishing array of herbal creams and potions, like a Sacred Body Shop, complete with testers. While my walking mates perused postcards and religious souvenirs, I unscrewed lids, sniffing sage salve, calendula ointment, and lavender balm. I considered asking the monk sitting behind the cash register if he had any Balm of Gilead, but I didn't suppose he'd find it as hilarious as I did.

Later that evening, our last night at the four-star near Castellina in Chianti, I went to the pool for a swim but spent most of the time inhaling the fragrance of the profuse jasmine covering the old stone wall. I had never seen jasmine that thick and lush, and I couldn't resist filling and refilling my lungs with the fragrance. I inhaled so hard, tips of flowers entered my nostrils. I tried to memorize the smell, ignoring the waiter as he darted by.

On the penultimate day of this fantastic week, we had free time in the shops of Siena. I explored pottery stores, looking for the perfect red-poppy-on-white pattern I had seen in Florence. When I learned that a traditional Florentine pattern was not to be found in Siena, I turned to leather for consolation. The smell of the leather-goods store was as intoxicating as a new car's leather interior. I met Marco, the shop owner, who assured me that the black leather, three-quarter-length jacket I tried on was 1) made for my body, 2) much cheaper here than anywhere else in the world, and 3) made me look ten years younger and ten pounds lighter. As I admired my silhouette from various angles in the mirror, I decided it would be cheaper to buy a bottle of leather juice, suitable for sniffing before putting on my favorite woolen coat. I bid Marco farewell and left empty handed to join the others for a drink at a table on the edge of the magnificent Piazza del Campo (known by tourists for centuries as The Big Empty Place in the Center of Town Where All the Restaurants Are). Back at the hotel that evening, we dined alfresco and drank red-velvet chianti, intense with hints of violets. I will never smell violets in the same way, now that I know so many of them give their lives for our drinking pleasure. Dessert was an individual pudding, sprinkled with confectioner's sugar and oozing with molten chocolate like a miniature Vesuvius. I bent my head over the plate, in prayer, as I inhaled that steaming chocolate and gave thanks. For chocolate. For my nose. For life.

On our last day, we walked the streets of San Gimignano, one of Italy's most famous artistic centers. We navigated worn stone stairs, cobblestone pathways, and narrow alleys. I spent my last hours on this miraculous trip buying a red-poppy tablecloth, modeling different leather purses to see how they felt and looked on my shoulder, and eating gelato before getting ready for our end-of-tour feast. Leaning back in the enormous tub (water, very hot; soap, very lavender), I watched sunbeams dance outside the window.

I gave our dinner, a cavalcade of Tuscan specialties, the highest compliment possible: I ate it. All of it, without asking for any variations to appease my dietary restrictions. I ate the fresh pasta in creamy saffron sauce, topped with truffle shavings, then the grilled steak, then the lemon cake. To finish the meal on a majestic note, I ordered the object of a week's obsession: a cappuccino, which came with the faint but recognizable outline of a powdery chocolate heart atop its milky foam. True to my pattern, I sniffed and sipped, sniffed and sipped.

The next afternoon, a mere five hours by train later, I was back in my husband's arms in Switzerland, entertaining him with details of the trip. Unfortunately, olfactory memories, among the most powerful we can have, are difficult to describe. To help him experience my wonderful week, I have since tried to expose him to various smells: I pushed him toward a large jasmine plant at a local nursery; I stuck a glass of chianti classico under his nose; I whisked a cappuccino in front of his face. In each case, I announced jubilantly, "*That* was Italy."

I didn't realize, until the end of my week in Tuscany, that the healing I went looking for arrived in the form of a weeklong aromatherapy—broadly defined as using fragrant essential oils to balance, refresh, and relax the mind, body, and spirit. But the benefit was much greater than a simple, yet profound, sense of harmony and well-being as I boarded the train back home. Sniffing my way through Tuscany kept me in the moment. It's not possible to worry what might happen ten minutes down the road if you're reveling in the scent of coffee or olive oil or jasmine (or, yes, even pig shit). A passionate desire to stay present to the moment is one of cancer's greatest gifts. One moment at a time, one fragrance at a time, the perfumes of Italy entered by way of nose, reopened my eyes and heart to the beauty of this world . . . well, at least, of Tuscany.

Next time you're there, if you see Harvey Keitel, shake his hand and say, with a straight face, "Mr. Keitel, I really love your work." (And let me know what his cologne smells like.)

Elizabeth Asdorian

Falling in Love in Milan

He had warm, soulful, brown eyes and thick, wavy hair that curled slightly at the nape of his neck. He was shorter than I remembered, but even in the dreary February air, his face was the same glowing olive color. He smiled broadly as I made my way toward him through the crowded Milan Malpensa Airport. His teeth were gleaming white, his lips the color of young sangiovese.

We had met four months earlier in Oludeniz, on the Aegean coast of Turkey. Under a brilliant sun, in a bay of aquamarine water and alarmingly bright sand, we had shared rough Turkish wine and stories. He was riding a motorcycle across the Middle East. I was trying to decipher my life and plan my next move.

He had an easy manner and a calming presence. His words

were carefully chosen; he was not outspoken or full of bravado. His shyness made him intriguing, mysterious.

We spent my twenty-ninth birthday on a yacht, sailing from cove to cove and lamenting the skies that had turned dark and menacing, threatening the three-day voyage. But the final day dawned bright and clear. We toasted the last year of my twenties and parted ways. I assumed I'd never see him again, until I got his letter from a bedouin camp in Kuwait, inviting me to meet him in Milano.

"*Buon giorno,*" he said, with a perfect Italian accent.

"*Buon giorno,*" I replied, with the farthest thing from a perfect Italian accent.

He smiled again and kissed my cheeks, one, two, three, in the familiar greeting. His breath smelled of fresh mint, his skin vaguely of lavender.

We stood back and looked at each other, then laughed nervously. We were complete strangers, united only in a brief travel experience, months and worlds away. It was exciting, exhilarating, wildly romantic, if just a little uncomfortable. The next week was full of possibilities.

He pointed up to the gray, misting Milan sky. "Again, the weather," he observed. "Please, this is not an omen," he said reassuringly.

"Of course not!" I laughed.

He paused. "Well, welcome to Milano, Elizabetta," he said, using the Italian version of my name, as he took my hands in his and looked deeply into my eyes.

"Thanks, Alex," I replied shyly. I lightly touched his arm, feeling the luscious silk of his perfectly tailored shirt. True, he was American, but everything about him felt intrinsically Italian.

"Are you ready to go?" he asked softly.

"Of course."

"Great. I'll show you which bus to take to my grandmother's house. I'm going to ride my motorcycle."

And like that, the spell was broken.

One hour, three transfers, and two soaked socks later, I finally made it to the stop where I was to meet Alex. I practically threw my backpack at him as I lurched off the orange MM streetcar. I hadn't slept in thirty-six hours, and the bile had been brewing in my empty stomach the entire trip from the airport.

"Here, carry this," I practically hissed at him.

"How was the ride?" he asked.

"Just peachy. I only had my ass pinched twice," I replied snidely. "And yours?"

"Great. I love riding my bike through the streets of this city. It's invigorating. Then I stopped for a cappuccino and biscotti. Nothing like it." He was either a clueless clod or maniacally cruel; I was the big loser either way.

I winced as I bit my tongue. If I knew him better, I would have unleashed the full fury of Crabby Travel Girl. Cappuccino? Biscotti? The closest I had been to food was stepping in gum. But there were six days and eighteen hours left of this tête-à-tête, and I needed to step back and readjust my jet-lagged attitude.

"It's just a short walk to Nonna's house," he said. "*Andiamo.*"

That we were staying at his grandmother's house was not news to me, but it began to take on more significance. Gee, this was going to be fun—me, Mr. Insensitive, and a doddering old Italian woman. I pulled my coat tightly around my neck as the wind blew cold and strong.

We walked through the mazelike concrete structures of what I could only assume were Milan's suburbs. I had no idea where I was, which left escaping a difficult proposition. Alex walked ahead with my backpack, turning around occasionally to flash me a broad grin. Why is he so damn happy? I thought bitterly. Oh yeah, he's loaded up on caffeine and sugar.

"I'm so glad you're here," he said.

"Yeah, well . . . me too," I lied.

"Here we are. My grandmother's going to love you."

He showed me to the door of a building that looked like every other building we had walked past: dingy gray cement, devoid of personality. The only difference from address to address was the assortment of sad little potted plants that sat outside. It looked a little like a prison. This was definitely not the Italy of frescoed ceilings and ornate architecture I had imagined.

We walked inside and climbed the stairs. And as I took each step, I began to feel better, lighter, happier, *hungry*. A smell wafted in the air and soaked into my pores, down into my soul, and into the pit of my stomach. Food. *Italian food.* And it was coming from apartment 2D.

Alex fumbled with the keys and opened the door. And there she was. She couldn't have been more than five feet tall, with white, wispy hair pulled back in a calm little bun on the back of her small head. Her skin was pale, but brazen, rosy circles gleamed defiantly on her tiny cheeks. She was dressed in a severe black dress, an "I'm not in mourning anymore, but I've given up on wearing anything else" sort of look. Her legs sported thick woolen tights that bagged gently around her ankles. Her thin, delicate hands shook as she reached toward me and made a long, passionate statement in Italian.

"Nonna wants you to eat," Alex interpreted. "She's made a light lunch and she thinks you look hungry. Then she thinks you should take a nap and possibly a bath. She assumes you like gardenias and prays deeply that you brought enough warm clothes. She doesn't speak much English."

I was learning that Alex had an uncanny ability to state the obvious. But I maintained my composure and managed a weak smile at the grandmother. I threw an even weaker one in my lame companion's direction.

Nonna grabbed my elbow, the easiest part of me to reach, I guess, and, with surprising strength for someone who looked so frail, scooted me to the dining room.

A place was set at the rectangular table, a sensible placemat, sensible napkins, and china and silver that had seen better days. In fact, the entire apartment had a seen-better-days-in-Wichita-Kansas feeling, definitely not the urban chic I would have equated with the fashion capital of Italy. A grandma is a grandma is a grandma in every part of the world, it seemed.

That is, until Nonna went out on the small outdoor patio and returned with a large jug of booze. This was different. I didn't know many grandmothers who kept a big bottle of hooch on their porch, although my own Nana was prone to drinking a tremendous amount of it (kept, politely, in the kitchen cupboard, behind the vegetable oil and Carlton 100s cartons).

Nonna motioned me to sit and poured a hefty glass of ruby wine. I took a small sip and nodded appreciatively. Nonna looked a bit put off and ranted again in Italian.

"She says you must not like her wine because you took such a small drink, and she's going out to get you something you'll like better. She's going to get her coat and walk to the neighborhood store and get you a nice chianti. She says it doesn't matter if it's a mile away and she's an old woman; no guest of hers will be forced to drink wine she doesn't relish."

Great, I had been here no more than ten minutes and I'd already offended my hostess. And the fact was, I loved the wine—I was hard pressed not to love any wine. I was the granddaughter of an Irish lush, and all booze was good booze in my book. But this was really good booze.

I struggled to say something appropriate, but all I could manage was *"Vino muy magnífico!"* I had no idea if it was even Italian; I suspected it was Spanish.

Nonna put down her coat and gave me what must have been a smile, although it looked more like a tiny burst of gas had just passed through her esophagus. She poured Alex a glass and herself a healthy portion, then chugged it in one gulp. It was mesmerizing.

She waddled into the kitchen and left me alone with Alex.

"So, the last time I saw you was in Turkey." Again, the obvious.

"Yep. That's right," I managed to spit out.

Pause.

"I liked Turkey."

"Sure, there were some good parts."

Pause.

I poured myself a big refill and drank it, like Nonna, in one gulp, hoping for a little liquid small talk. Nonna returned just as I set the glass down. She was carrying what I can describe only as heaven in white crockery. The aroma of garlic and cheese and spices swirled around me. I felt faint from hunger. Or was it love?

The next few minutes were a blur of forks and spoons and heaping helpings of the most amazing pasta dish I have ever had the privilege of bringing to my unworthy mouth. I must have eaten a good amount; Nonna actually registered a true smile as she pulled away my plate and waddled back to the kitchen.

"Oh my God. That was amazing," I said to Alex. It was ironic that I was saying those words to him in this context. A few hours ago, I would have predicted a completely different scenario in which to utter that statement.

"Good. Then you'll like the next course."

"There's . . . more? I don't think I can eat another bite."

"Elizabeth, in Italy, we eat three courses. That was just the first. And Nonna is a stickler for three courses."

So I ate. I ate chicken drizzled in olive oil and rosemary, with a crusty skin and the perfect touch of sea salt. I ate zucchini with roasted garlic and chanterelles. I ate a salad of baby spinach and toasted pine nuts. I ate a simple sorbet of winter pears. I had never had a meal quite like it.

"Would it be wrong to hug Nonna or, better yet, kiss her full on the mouth?" I asked Alex, only half-joking, as we retired to the small living room.

"Well . . . um . . . she's not too affectionate." He didn't get it, but I didn't care. I was done with his sorry ass. I was smitten with the woman who had made me the most incredible food in the world. I was an easy, easy girl—just make me a fantastic meal and I'm yours forever. I almost swooned when Nonna came in, sat down on her threadbare La-Z-Boy, and lit up her pipe.

She grabbed her 1980s-style remote control and turned on the small TV that sat perched on a tall wooden knickknack cabinet. We all craned our necks to look up at the screen. A large, robust man was on the ski slopes, being interviewed by a gorgeous, leggy brunette.

"Tomba!" yelled Nonna. "Tomba! Tomba!" She looked at me and repeated the word again, this time as a question. "Tomba?"

I scoured my limited Italian vocabulary for its meaning, but could find none. Alex jumped in.

"Tomba is Alberto Tomba. He's a national hero in Italy—a champion alpine skier. They call him Tomba the Bomba." Nonna said something to me in her rushed Italian. Alex laughed and even blushed a little. "Nonna says he could charm the pants off of anybody. Including her."

I laughed so hard, I blew grappa through my nose (not something I would recommend doing—it burns your nasal cavity as much as it burns your throat). The thought of little Nonna with her knickers around her ankles was too funny for words. I looked at her and saw the sparkle in her eye. I think she may have winked. Oh, that Nonna.

We watched Tomba ski the same mountain for the next hour. Slo-mo, fast speed, from the right, from the left, aerial view—there must have been a camera poised at every angle. Nonna never tired of watching her beloved Tomba. And weirdly enough, I never tired of watching Nonna.

The next few days played out in much the same way as the first. Nonna and I would have breakfast, then watch a little *The Price Is Right* or *The Simpsons* dubbed hilariously in Italian. Nonna found Bart hysterical and would snort loudly every time he got into some mischief. Homer she thought brutish, and she'd glare angrily at the television and clear her throat every time he ate a donut or fell asleep at the nuclear reactor.

Midday, Alex would drag me off to see some castle or a fancy shoe store. I would eagerly return to the apartment and have a cappuccino and another shot of sturdy grappa with Nonna. She'd fix me some sort of amazing snack: homemade biscotti or a hot, fresh loaf of crusty bread with a slice of chunky country cheese. We'd watch skiing, always in search of Tomba. Then Alex would force me out to ride his stupid motorcycle to Padua or to see some ridiculous German soloist at La Scala. He tried, I give him credit, but his chance was over.

When he schlepped me to Chamonix to ski, all I could think of was Nonna and Tomba. When we went to a fancy French restaurant, I compared it—unfavorably—to Nonna's cooking. And when Alex asked me why I seemed so quiet and withdrawn, I couldn't answer. But I knew what it was; I'd rather be back in Milan with Nonna.

The week in Milan flew by. And when it was time to leave, I didn't want to say goodbye. The image of Nonna waving her bony hand from her small porch, surrounded by bottles of delicious table wine, was imprinted on my mind.

Alex asked if he could ride the bus with me to the airport. "No," I told him. "I'd rather go alone." I pecked him on the cheek, got on the MM, and headed for home. He seemed flummoxed by the whole week. Perhaps he had been hoping for something earth-shattering that simply didn't pan out. But I knew I'd never be the same again.

"Did you fall in love?" begged my girlfriends breathlessly when I returned from my trip, desperate for that quintessential Italian love story.

I thought back to Nonna's manicotti and the joyful hours we spent together, joined in our admiration of *Gilligan's Island* and Ginger's pretty ball gowns. I thought of the sparkle in her eye as she watched her beloved Tomba race down another hill. I thought of the jugs of cold chianti she had stored on her balcony and the soft gray hair pulled back from her tiny, wrinkled brow.

"Yes," I told them. "I fell in love in Milan. But not with whom you'd think."

Mardith J. Louisell

Toccata
and Variations
on Venice

Venice, Venezia, Serenissima.

Serenissima, the name with which the Venetians christened her, most clear, most bright, most fair. Glittery but grounded.
The word most like Venice, so long, so slow. So many *s*'s, a little *m*, a
little *r*, but mostly the *s*'s swishing along, gently, gently, like the
lagoons of Venice.

"It is truly a city of appearances," wrote Mary McCarthy in
Venice Observed. Vistas everywhere, but small, tiny, limited vistas.
Narrow passageways, crooked, broken spokes at the rim of a *campo*,
the small plaza of Italy, literally, "ground." If you stand on any one
of the dozen openings at the edge of the "ground" and peer near-
sightedly down a corridor, you see a church across a square with
what appears to be a false front; then you follow a gnarled alley

until, after many twists and turns, you're on the *fondamenta*, the long breezeway of the city. Sinuous turns behind you, limitless water before you, islands floating like cakes in a swamp. Broad space and nagging closeness at the same time.

Line and surface. Things in their proper place. *Please do not touch the fruit*, arranged just so—red, orange, red, orange, red—*nor the window*. I can with persistence prevail upon the shopkeeper and lightly brush the fruit, but never the window.

Glass: blue, pink, coral, ruby, translucent Murano, crafted on the island across the lagoon, echoing itself. Medallions, necklaces, and earrings arranged in small mounds inside halls of mirrors so that the insides of the shops reflect the maze of cramped narrow alleys in which Venetians pace their days.

Lost always. On the other side of the Rialto, so far west that the buildings actually look new. Too far. Lost is a more or less permanent state here, a turning around to an "aha" of found, only to twist again and lose oneself. No whisper of a grid wafts over this city. A short man in his seventies, dressed in suit and tie, finds me one evening after I have followed a trail of people thinking they were strolling to the center of Venice; instead I have followed them home to their little doors and large smells of dinner. Frederico walks me out of his neighborhood, across a large bridge, under a cramped archway, up a higher bridge, under brick walls, beneath umbrellas; in the dark and rain of a November night he murmurs soft, misty hellos to people he knows. He knows the whole city. Then, after a dreamlike time, both forever and an instant, I find a place I know.

He bows, nods, smiles, and turns to backtrack the miles to the comforting odors of basil pasta and wine where I found him.

Do not bother to talk about directions in Venice. Do not bother to tell a friend where the Filippi poster shop is, where to find roasted red peppers, where the Pesaro family resides. It is not possible. Talk submerges quickly into surrealistic patter, and you find yourself in a Beckett play. Even guidebooks limpidly succumb to the futility of directions. "Off Piazza dei Frari" is as specific as you get. Then you're on your own, and you can't remember if the Frari is the place where you found the love of your life or where you collapsed with exhaustion because you couldn't find your cappuccino.

Room XX, quite by chance. I race through the stone maze of the Accademia, a frantic woman gasping for breath. Guards close the gates behind me, turn out lights as I run around curves, into rooms and out, under paintings, around sculptures, voracious, American to the core, my eyes devouring what art they can scan in seconds. Against the will of the guards who are crying silently, *Leave. Go home.* I am running from imprisonment in the 12C when I trip upon whole rooms, whole walls, frescoed, painted, temperaed with scenes of Venice as she was when other merchants lived here, parading in their pageants, costumed in their long carnelian and cerulean gowns. Carpaccio, Bellini, two minutes to gobble it up. Veronese, Giorgione, Vivarini, Della Francesca, Mantegna, Tintoretto, Memling. Memling? How did he sneak in here?

Constant angles, here, there, under, over. The one-oared boats must navigate canals as angular and tricky as the sidewalks.

Changing directions is hard; whether maneuvering a gondola or hobbling home, it demands preparation, split-second timing, and care—no simple turn to the left and switch of lanes. Venetians are accustomed to making quick turns, to moving deftly in small spaces. Even in the arts. *The Last Supper*, crafted by Veronese, in the face of Church opposition to the secular appearance of the tableau and the presence of Germans in the scene, turns into *The Feast in the House of Levi*. An about-face. Nothing wasted—a few strokes here, a few strokes there, and the masterpiece is useful once more. Venice is, after all, a city built on commerce.

Clarity of sound. Metallic tinkles. Every so often a song or a prayer drifts through streets from the next *campo*, around a corner, down an alley, clearer for being so far. The boats lap, footsteps trudge or scurry on bridges. Gates close, wooden doors shut, brass knockers ring, arguments echo. No wind here—wind lacks clarity through leaves or grass. No leaves or grass.

Rainy season. Thirty meters high at 7:00 AM. It's *acqua alta*, the routine swamping of the piazzas, stores, and homes that happens every November. Venetians turn out in one body with their brooms and sweep the water out of their stores. First floors are tiled, not carpeted, part of the Venetian's precautionary respect for the Adriatic. They sweep and the water swishes, obeying the shopkeepers, out to the street, into the canals. After all, this is a city where people and water have struck a truce. We stay here and you stay there, except for the *acqua alta*. Have your yearly tirade but then get out!

It's during *acqua alta* that you see rubber boots in unequivocal color, yellow, red, and blue, hanging from the tops of hardware store windows, gaiety in the face of the routine swampings. Fashionable Venetian women are now up to their knees in outlandish color, while above the knees their torsos remain swathed in brown and beige suede coats. Ugly and rough wooden swampwalks appear in the night—the snowplows of Venice, they allow commerce to continue. Venice, always pragmatic, always in touch with the necessity of accommodating the elements, knows that there are times when beauty cannot prevail and it is prudent not to argue.

Water protocol is finely developed. Umbrellas, at least one million of them, float through the narrow streets, bobbing along, disembodied. Hold them straight up, straight across, do not slant. If I tilt my umbrella, the whole city loses its balance. Balance is everything, analyzed and synchronized centuries ago. Like the gondola and the harmony of life in death, the rainy reason has been sorted through. When I make a mistake, when I angle it sideways like *Singing in the Rain*, a chorus of Italian erupts and I quickly get in line.

Please use the umbrella stand in cafés. When I neglect water protocol, the owner points to the umbrella stand with his long fingers, and a peremptory nod indicates what I should do. When I accidentally lay a wet blue umbrella on his chair, he picks it up silently, cigarette in hand, and puts it in the umbrella stand, then wipes the offending chair. I feel as though he would wipe me if he could. I am trailing water into his shop, water which the Venetians agree belongs in the lagoon.

A huge puzzle, Venice. Thousands of islands creaking on piles, temporary artificial legs, a soggy jigsaw puzzle sitting on poles, easily separated. The stones "strain, / Crack and sometimes break, / Under the burden, / Under the tension, slip, slide, perish / Decay with imprecision, will not stay in place, / Will not stay still."* You see how precarious it is.

The all-consuming algae have upset the balance between water and stone, contributing to Venice's dehydration. Gnats nibble at the algae as Venice dehydrates; they swarm, constantly, overwhelming the brain with their sheer numbers, like the paintings and the churches, the Byzantine tiles, the lace and glass silhouetting the air, Escher and Gaudí magnified to city size.

No one can see where they are, who is with them, or where they are going, not in the dark streets, snaky walkways, and deluge of umbrellas. I think Venetians find their way with radar, as if bats after sunset, not too fast and hurried, not too slow—at the water's pace.

At night in the mist, muffled voices, the *clackety-clack* of shoes on pavement. I light upon a restaurant and feel I have discovered a hut in the middle of a night in the Alps. I am grateful, crazy with warmth, bubbling from wine.

There is regularity, even for tourists. I go to the same *caffè* bar, Piccolo Martini, whenever I can find it, three times to Malibran's for ham and marinated red peppers on white bread, to the same *pasticcerie* where the same people serve me. To Harry's Bar in '83 and '87, the same waiter both times. Obsessive sameness, infinitesimal changes. I return to the same places inevitably. I must concentrate with all my might to find them, but I do because I need the certainty they provide, that I am here and haven't floated off into some interminable eel-shaped alley leading always to nowhere.

Restoration is the business of Venice. *Memento mori.* Remember that you must die. Everything is passing, peeling, and patched, but the city plods along, preens, and on occasion drops off a bit. Craftspeople work for restoration, commemoration, and magic. A Jewish artist at work in the ghetto says, "I work from the Bible and from my imagination." From form and image. The imagination, always present in Venice, near the surface, intruding, extruding, suffusing, stretching its tendrils into reality, making us pay attention.

Du Maurier's *Don't Look Now* takes place in Venice. In Nicholas Roeg's movie of the same name, as the husband and wife glide on Venice's gondolas, their dead child seems to appear, then disappear; they hear the click of her footsteps, the slapping of her mackintosh against stone. The husband won't admit that the séances and spirits he doesn't believe in affect him in Venice; because he doesn't admit this, he is caught, fatally, unaware. The city is a phantasmagoria, insinuating the imagined whisper, the word left unsaid, the boat, almost seen, slipping around the corner.

"The things of this world reveal their essential absurdity when they are put in the Venetian context. In the unreal realm of the canals . . . the real world with its contrivances, appears as a vast folly," writes Mary McCarthy. Venice is funny, a cackle. There are few streetlamps, no traffic lights, and no stop signs. No cars, no buses, no bicycles, nothing on wheels. My *bicicletta* sits on its haunches in the parking lot adjacent to the train station outside of the city, waiting to whiz off through Mestre, a less silly place, toward Ravenna, Bologna, Firenze. What could you do with a bicycle in a city where a bridge interrupts your straightaway every few yards? The specter of a ten-speed careening around Venice is funny and horrific at the same time. And because there are no cars, no street needs to be broader than the widest human being, so the large delivery trucks that we are used to must shrink themselves to human size.

The frenzy that is me finds perfect recourse in Venice. I try to run tearing through the stone streets, rubber tennis shoes on my American feet, but I can't go far without running into a person, steps, a bridge, or an abrupt dead end at a *rio*. And I can never dart quickly into and out of my hotel because I'm never dropped at my door, but always at the vaporetto dock. From there I must walk. I wonder, what happens to the old, the infirm, the wheelchair-bound, the dying? Where are the ambulances? Even what Venice lacks stimulates obsessive thought, worry, and giggling. The hearse I can picture—hearses move slowly—but not the ambulance. In a city of death, a hearse appears often.

Because there are no cars or bicycles to watch for, everyone is uniquely free—at the same time, uniquely confined.

Confinement on islands constrains. *Isola*, Italian for island. Walking up up and then down down, go a few feet and do the same, go farther, again up and then again down. "The way up is the way down, the way forward, the way back." Now I've crossed into the Jewish ghetto after a walk over a bridge, *Sotoportego de Ghetto Nuovo*.

The world's first ghetto. In the sixteenth century, the first naming of the act of isolating, the Venetian love of clarity again. How fitting that these island dwellers would turn to isolation as a solution for those they wanted to control.

"Ghetto" seems to have meant a foundry for artillery when the Venetian Republic placed the Jews here in 1516, having forced them to leave the fertile island called La Giudecca due to the usual real estate imperatives: The land was beautiful, and more powerful people wanted it. The Jews were plopped down here in limited space. Venice doesn't expand, but the Jews did—their buildings grew higher and higher. In the ghetto the height between floors is smaller than in the rest of Venice—more people had to squeeze in, so there wasn't room for the luxury of air or tall people. Guards watched the bridges at night to ensure no Jew leaped out the windows to passing gondolas.

The Campo Ghetto Nuovo is very small, women in black, children so tiny they pass unnoticed. Hugging the northeast wall are seven small bronze reliefs, each the size of a painting you might hang on your den wall. They seem to grow out of the wall, mottled and chipped, white and brown and beige and ash in decay. They are memorials to the Venetians who were boated away to concentration camps during World War II and didn't return.

". . . Old stones that cannot be deciphered . . ." What is compelling, mysterious, eerie; what we love about old places, is the sense that many lives have passed through, millions have been here before, and they are watching, rising up from the water, their spirits hovering, slightly damp and wrinkled, an eye lost to the fish here and there, but still clear sighted, thoughtful, attentive.

The city lends itself to the neurotic. The water, its hypnotic changes, the labyrinthine besotted alleys mirroring the waves, always changing, always the same. I obsess in Venice. I must. I can't not. This is Venice, this trying every which way with slight variations, losing yourself so deeply that you don't remember where you started from and where you hoped to end.

I too like to get lost. I like to get lost in my mind, to follow each path around and down and over to dead ends. I like to take a question, big or small, and tease it to its very marrow, chew it down to its skeleton. An Irish friend tells me this is the essence of Americans. We devote the same attention to everything, whether it's a funeral or buying a pair of shoes. Lack of perspective makes us dizzy.

Remembering, reexperiencing, retelling a drama of love: Each time I relive it in my mind I find a new detail, a nuance neglected in the previous telling, a reminiscence with new meaning. All the obsessions that slither and slime around in my mind, that slosh in and out of the blood vessels in my brain, are externalized in Venice.

Every so often a square opens up, lets in the light, gives me breathing space before I am off again to the mire, the subconscious elucidating just long enough to keep me above water. The next step, and I am plunged again into the subterranean landscape of my soul.

But to prove they know the beauty of light in space and form against sky, in addition to glass, water, and lace, Venetians give us

Piazza San Marco, a huge square where the light never stops, where there is more space than any city has a right to. The orchestras, the cafés, even the millions of tourists don't fill it up. The pigeons in San Marco's square, as many pigeons as there are tiles in the Byzantine mosaics of the story of Job in the Basilica di San Marco, can't darken it. Their millions of shadows, Escher reflections, constantly ebb and flow on the stone floor of the square.

How brilliant to have a square like this, so large, so full of light that it easily accommodates the irregularities of obsessive detail and at the same time measures God.

Frame anything against water and it pleases the eye. Laundry hung out between buildings, colored and white, is strung like chunky Navajo jewelry above the canals. I wonder how many pale blue shirts, plum-colored skirts, pairs of pink underwear fall into the canal, how you find them, whether they smell, if neighbors know exactly whose they are. Impossible not to be a great photographer in Venice. Like her glass, mirrors, and water, she welcomes the camera as a good friend dedicated to her reflection. Despite this, Venice is always a double or triple exposure.

Portraits of the *doges*, former presidents of the Republic, lined up on the ceiling in the Palazzo Ducale, look down on me as, my neck cramping, I crane upward. A veil blackens one painting. A *doge* betrayed the Republic, high treason, the veil a potent sign of what happened to those who did not fear the Republic. It remains covered today, chillingly clear what these water people can do.

Is Venice a place for lovers? I haven't done it, but I think not.

Venice is for intrigue, for mirrors, for looking through a microscope in greater and greater depth to the tentacles and terrors beneath the surface, the crack in the stone, the intricacies of the waves. It's a place to plan, plot, and perhaps consummate an affair or a liaison, but not a romance.

On the surface it seems a likely place, but "seems" is what Venice is about. In no time, with a few steps in one direction, a few errors in another, your romantic notions hit a bridge, or an unknown alley, or a stony dead end, or the perilously seductive water—and the chill sets in.

The glitter of Venice is built upon its antitheses: water and stone. The tensions of these, the fight as to what will endure, is the lure of Venice. Venice is not a happening; it's carefully planned, diagrammed, and measured. Very real materials constitute the show of Venice, glass, tile, and stone, and the whole chimera wages a constant battle not to lose ground for its existence. That battle is more than any romance could sustain.

---

*This and all subsequent unidentified quotations are taken from T. S. Eliot's "Four Quartets."

Laura Fraser

An Affair to Remember

The most romantic way to get to the Aeolian Islands, the rugged volcanic archipelago north of Sicily, is by overnight boat from Naples. Bring dinner to eat onboard, pass Capri in the disappearing light, and be lulled to sleep by the sea. Set your alarm clock for 5:00 AM, then crawl out of your bunk and onto the deck, face in the wind. The night is so black the stars of the Pleiades are as distinct as the seven islands themselves.

Then, out of nowhere, a flare of blood orange lights up the sky, shooting sparks like shooting stars. It is Stromboli, the volcano that stands as a sentry to the islands, at once warning visitors of the fierceness of the place and proclaiming its wild beauty. Homer was the first to mention these islands, which Americans refer to as the Aeolians. Here, Aeolus, the god of the winds, greeted Ulysses with a bag of breeze to ensure his safe passage. But when Ulysses's crew, curious, opened the bag, they were blown from rocky shore to shore, left to fend for themselves in the most treacherous waters of the Tyrrhenian Sea. These are dry, inhospitable islands, where all living things—figs, capers, apricots, rabbits—struggle so for survival that they are bursting with the intense fragrances and flavors of a brief but concentrated life.

I am returning to these islands after three years to satisfy a hunger I've had ever since I last left—for the spicy perfume of pale pink caper flowers, for fish that swim in turquoise waters, for sweet cherry tomatoes that explode in your mouth like Stromboli, for pasta with fennel and sardines. I'm returning to simply do nothing—*il dolce far niente*, as the Italians say—in a place where there are only rocks and sea and the happy prospect of your next meal.

As the sky lightens, the island of Stromboli comes into view, its whitewashed houses stacked up by the port. I once made the arduous climb up the volcano to see it erupt red against the orange sunset, booming down a black lava slope into the ocean. There are some things so magnificent they can't be repeated, not without being spoiled—in this case, by the lines of tourists you were too enchanted to notice the first time. So I don't disembark. But I remember Stromboli's charm, its narrow streets, and its nervous atmosphere in the shadow of the volcano. And then there's the carnation-colored house with its plaque commemorating the place where Ingrid Bergman and Roberto Rossellini had an affair while filming *Stromboli*. (Previously, Anna Magnani, who had been living with Rossellini and was promised the lead, overturned a bowl of bucatini with red sauce on his head before fleeing with the crew to another island, Vulcano, to make an equally forgettable film by that isle's name.)

If there were a plaque somewhere in the Aeolians to commemorate a love affair of my own, it would be on Filicudi, one of the remotest and most desolate islands. There, for ten days, I stayed with a French professor in a white house at the top of a steep hill overlooking the port and the other craggy islands beyond. We did nothing but read, swim, make love, and decide where we wanted to eat that day. I always voted for Villa La Rosa, for the pasta of wild fennel fronds and sardines, which tasted exactly like the island's aromatic sea breeze. As with Stromboli, Filicudi was a place where I could never return for fear of spoiling the memory of those magical days.

That still leaves five other islands to explore, though, each with a unique personality. Panarea, small and precious, attracts chic Italians and honeymooners but is all tranquility in the off-season. Lipari is the largest and most industrialized island, with a fascinating museum filled with relics from all the ships that have sunk in these violent seas since before the first Greek settlers arrived. Salina is sleepy and agricultural, covered with vineyards that bear grapes for the region's distinctive malvasia wine. Vulcano, the island closest to Sicily, is heavily touristed on its hot, bubbling shores, but the mountain's uplands are home to pastures that yield some of the world's best ricotta cheese. Small, outlying Alicudi has no cars, few tourist facilities—really, nothing at all.

I've come to the islands this time with my Italian friend

Giovanna, a Giulietta Messina look-alike with the same impish flair. Giovanna isn't content to *far niente* on the islands but wants to explore all the tastes, sights, and activities I had missed before. "*Zampetta, zampetta*," she says, meaning: "A little paw here and a little paw there, and we'll try everything." *Va bene.*

Pulling into the tiny port of Panarea, we're met by a golf cart to take us to our *pensione*. (On Panarea, even the police drive golf carts, since no cars are allowed.) We pass traditional, square Aeolian houses—magenta bougainvillea climbing the white walls and dripping over the pergolas—with wooden doors as blue as the sea. The air is perfumed with a profusion of flowers—wild pomegranate, purple acacia, daisies, lilies, birds of paradise. "*Da delirio*," says Giovanna. Absolutely delirious.

We check into our simple room, wander along the path to the rocky beach, and come back in time for dinner. Like its rooms, the food at La Sirena is simple and clean. We have sea urchin pasta with parsley and tomatoes, and *mille gusti spaghetti*, with all flavors of the island represented in the dish.

In the morning, at exactly the same time (Italians have a strict sense of the order of a day), everyone on the island finishes their coffee and goes to the beach. With only a few square feet of sand, the beachgoers, mainly Italians, spread out on the rocks, wading waist deep in the water with their cell phones. To avoid the weekend crowds, we take a steep footpath to a farther beach and swim in a magnificent blue cove—until I am stung, painfully, by a jellyfish. On closer look, the place was infested with the little monsters—*meduse*—which make swimming like strolling through a minefield. These islands, I am reminded, are full of discomforts and mild dangers.

On Panarea, we do everything but *far niente:* We climb the mountain until our trail gets lost in the sticker bushes. We find a deserted beach and go skinny-dipping. We eat pizza from a wonderful *panificio* for lunch, scout for jellyfish at the beach, and stop by La Sirena to try to pry away the recipe for *mille gusti* but end up with some of the owner's salt-cured capers instead, as consolation. That evening, as we sip prosecco on our terrace at the cool, white Hotel Raya, the morning seems like a distant memory. We watch Stromboli in the distance, smoking like an Italian, a pack a day.

On our last night, we eat dinner at Da Pina, with its lemon-painted and blue ceramic-top tables outdoors. We try fillets of eggplant rolled with olives and capers, and the lightest eggplant gnocchi imaginable. Then I am introduced to *totani*—a large, yet perfectly tender, squidlike creature, this one stuffed with grilled radicchio. If I had to be stung by a jellyfish every time I ate *totani* (flying squid), I'd call it a fair deal. We finish up with a soothing rosemary *liquore*, inhaling the island's nighttime aromas.

Lipari is an hour—and a world—away by hydrofoil. The islanders consider Lipari a town, not another island, and by local standards it's as busy as Milan. With its ten thousand inhabitants, pumice mining, and fishing fleet, Lipari is the center of Aeolian industry. And with its castle and archaeology museum, it's the center of culture too. Some people will tell you Lipari has the best restaurants on the islands, but Giovanna and I decide they are just the most formal; like everything about Lipari, much of the food is overworked and industrial.

At Lipari's castle museum, we spend an afternoon contemplating a collection of Greek terra-cotta theatrical masks, which have a vast array of human characters—there's the chatterbox, the gossip, the flatterer, the crotchety old man; there are characters from Greek plays, lost to time except for their faces, full of unspoken expression.

Eventually we find some small, authentic restaurants on the island: At Ristorante La Nassa, we have an exquisite caponata in which the flavors are distinct, playing off each other, rather than homogenized. Ristorante Nenzyna is smaller and simpler, and the dishes are traditional—fish in olives, capers, basil, and onion; a fish stew made with tomatoes, capers, and dried bread. We agree we'd be happy eating at that little restaurant every day of our lives.

Yet for all those good meals, a corner of my hunger remains unsatisfied. I haven't tasted pasta with fennel fronds and sardines yet. Nor will I find the dish on Lipari. For that, we have to go to Filicudi.

As we check the hydrofoil schedules for the next day, I am reluctant to return to Filicudi for fear of spoiling the bittersweet memory of my first visit there. But I am more afraid that I would never taste that fennel pasta at Villa La Rosa again.

To my relief, nothing has changed on Filicudi—its rocky beaches and hills terraced with ancient stone walls are still there. After a quick coffee at the port restaurant, we hire Giovannino and his blue and white boat for a tour around the island. As someone who makes his living from foreign tourists but would rather not, he is happy to speak Italian and regale us with stories—though Giovanna has to keep translating his dialect into my schoolgirl Italian. He tells us he was born on the island, pointing to a limestone ruin by the beach—"in that house." After World War II, when most inhabitants emigrated to Australia, he was one of only sixty souls left; now there are two hundred forty residents. As we circle the rocky island for an hour, he tells us how they survived by catching lobster for Christmas in Naples, and by growing capers, hiking all over the steep hills to collect them. He describes the *mafiosi* who were interned on the island in the 1970s and the shipwrecks he's seen over the years. Life on these dry, remote islands has always been tough.

After the boat ride, Giovanna and I hike the steep path cutting up the side of the hill to Villa La Rosa, perched above. *"Magnifico,"* Giovanna says when we pause to catch our breath and stare out at the sea. Finally at the villa, we sit at a cool table on the airy, colorful terrace. The waiter warns us they have only two pasta dishes that day. One with almonds—I hold my breath—and *maccheroncini ai finocchietto.* "It's made from the wild fennel growing around here," the waiter explains. Ahh.

The aroma arrives first, the sardines of the sea mixed with the fennel fronds of the island. With the plate in front of me I pause, my desire mixed with a fear of disappointment. But the pasta is perfectly al dente, with grated breadcrumbs on top and a few raisins peeking out; the fennel fronds and sardines have a wild, simple taste that satisfies me to the soul. I am in the very restaurant where I realized my affair with the Frenchman would come to an end, but no trace of sadness lingers. I am back with the fennel pasta, with a friend, and I am utterly content.

"That is your pasta," says Giovanna, refusing more than one bite. She looks around. "And this is your island." She herself would pick Panarea.

After the pasta comes grilled *totani*, stuffed with breadcrumbs. There should be a plaque up at Villa La Rosa for the best lunch I've ever eaten.

We leave that evening, but on the way to the boat, I notice a sign for another restaurant, another La Sirena, which boasts that it's Michelin-rated. How could I have missed it? Giovanna urges me to ask a man on the boat, who looks like he knows how to eat, about the restaurant. "*Sì, mangia benissimo,*" he tells me. "You eat very, very well there. Tell the chef that Sergio sent you," he says. "*Va bene,*" I say. "*Grazie.*" Maybe next time, if I ever return.

Giovanna leaves for home the next day.

I can't help it: I have to go back to Filicudi to try that restaurant. I go straight to Pecorini a Mare, the fishing village, and take a modest room at La Sirena overlooking the fishing boats pulled up onto the beach. In the evening, a Monday night in the off-season, I am the only diner at the restaurant. I mention the bit about Sergio to the waiter, who couldn't care less but brings me some raw swordfish—in olive oil, pepper, and lemon—that is practically still jumping. Then comes a light pasta with almonds, cherry tomatoes, and garlic. Finally, a piece of tuna, with tomatoes and capers, served on a plate decorated with flowers. I am self-conscious eating alone, but one by one several islanders join me, helping me drain my pitcher of white wine—the guy who rents the fishing boats, his nephew, the proprietress, and finally, the chefs themselves.

I rent a kayak the next day and head back to the blue grottoes, carefully navigating in that jellyfish soup. There is no one in sight. Occasionally, on some invisible cue, two thousand tiny, slivery fish arc in the air. I paddle to an empty beach for a swim, then, hungry, make my way back to La Sirena.

An islander is finishing his pasta when I come down for lunch, a beatific smile on his face. "*Buon giorno,*" I say. "What did you eat?"

"Spaghetti with swordfish eggs, and it was divine."

I tell the waiter I'll have what he had.

The waiter, suddenly enraged, argues with the islander. "How could you tell her you ate something special like that?"

"It was the most innocent thing in the world," he protests. "The signora asked, and I told her. What do you want me to say? That it was a *schifezza*? Disgusting?"

The waiter—actually the owner and head chef, Antonio Pellegrino—relates this outrageous story to the cooks. One tries to calm him, arguing that perhaps the signora could have just a little taste. "*Perchè no?*" I say, offering my vast appreciation and whatever the dish costs, but he waves me away. No American tourist is getting swordfish eggs, apparently, no matter how much charm she is slathering on in Italian.

After the scene, the islander looks at me and shrugs. "He's

cracked, but the food here is great," he says. I eat a pasta with *finoc-chietto* and sardines instead, this one with cherry tomatoes. It might be divine, but I am too busy thinking about the swordfish eggs to know for sure.

After lunch Antonio is cheerful again, and we chat. I remember what a friend had told me—that the islands' cooks are fiercely independent and will only cook well for you if they like and respect you. So I tell him about the time I was bitten by a moray eel on Filicudi, almost losing a finger. I show him the scar, and he warms up to me. Everyone on the island has heard stories about someone losing a finger to a moray eel, but for an American tourist to be bitten on a short visit is spectacularly bad luck.

"The next time I encountered a moray eel," I tell him, "I ate him. Grilled." Antonio appreciates that act of culinary revenge and approves of my method. Piero, the chef, sidles by and offers that he was once so mad at the jellyfish for biting him that he wokked them—but alas, they had no taste whatsoever.

I give Piero and Antonio my profuse thanks for the meal, compliment the food, the weather, the island, and Italians in general, and tell them I'll be back. Piero kisses me on both cheeks, which is a good sign.

The Aeolians are a difficult place to get to and a difficult place to be. But I will indeed return to Filicudi. I'll eat at La Sirena every day, until they insist I try the spaghetti with fresh swordfish eggs, until they want me to eat it as much as I do. And then I may just stay, doing nothing all day but deciding: Villa La Rosa or La Sirena?

Deana David

The Trouble
with Tiramisu

My sister called me from a pay phone. Traffic buzzed
in the background, Italian voices raised, horns honked, and
motor scooters revved impatiently.

"They're crazy here!" she told me. I pictured her curled over the
phone, a prawn in profile inside the cramped phone box, cupping
the receiver and glancing nervously over her shoulder.

"Who? Your host family?"

"Yes!" she hissed with such venom I wondered whether a
forked little black tongue darted from her lips.

"Who? The mother or the grandmother?"

"Both!"

"Come on, Joan, they can't both be crazy. Maybe it's you," I
teased. Having been the recipient of a string of gushing postcards

exalting the colors of the Puglian sunset and the wonders of a Limoncello gelato, I found it difficult to humor her theatricals.

"They are as nutty as two deeply disturbed fruit bats! You'll see," she smugly snipped. "And you should see what they feed me!"

"Fish-eye soup and monkey brains?" I asked sarcastically.

"No. I'm talking about the volume. I'm ballooning up into a big fat . . . oh God. I gotta go. I think I see Antonia's big hair at the check-out. Oh, oh! There's Filomena hobbling out the automatic doors."

The line went dead. I looked at the ticket in my hand. One week from today, I'd be there to investigate the reported craziness, the accused lunacy, and criminal overeating. I closed my eyes and imagined a small Italian kitchen with a tiled floor and cramped counters overflowing with antipasti and bread. I could clearly see the bottle of olive oil in the center of the dining table and the heavy block of cheese resting solidly on a grater like a fakir on a bed of nails. What was Joan talking about? She always made her host mother sound like a warty witch with a basket of poisoned apples— except substitute the apples for balls of mozzarella, hunks of bread, and tubs of gelato. Her dream of restoring the peeling frescoes of Pompeii and freeing Madonna statues in every piazza in the land from the insults of passing pigeons was coming true. She had already toured the treasures of Vatican City with her host family. She'd run ghoulishly through the soggy streets of Venice with her eager eye on fading portraits, buckling murals, and sagging ceilings. Really, she must be the only girl in teenagerdom who could complain about spending an exchange year studying in sunny Southern Italy.

On my first night in Bari, Joan's middle-aged host mother, Antonia, arranged a party of friends and family at a nearby restaurant to honor my arrival. Being the guest of honor, I rode shotgun beside Antonia all afternoon as she sped through town like a comet in a tinny, impossibly tiny car. Antonia seemed to be the human version of a fool squirrel who darts in and out of frighteningly close traffic disasters without appearing to have noticed she was ever in danger. The massive gold knot of medallion-style necklaces she wore may have been blinding other motorists. She pointed out the various churches, the florist, the best butcher, the place where she works (sometimes), the places where her friend works (sometimes), and the many restaurants and cafés, each one rated with a "no good" or a "so-so." I could see Joan's face in the side mirror. Under the weary and haunted-looking gaze, there was a flicker of amusement.

We parked in a garage about five blocks from the apartment. I remembered Joan remarking about their curious habit of parking so inconveniently far from home. Three ferocious hounds barked and bayed as we killed the ignition. Antonia, clearly heedless of all dangers, strode past the slobbering hellhounds while Joan and I carefully skirted the wall.

Sounds of chaos and struggle greeted us as we entered the small, unexpectedly grand apartment. Filomena, the adorably barrel-shaped grandmother, kissed me continental-style while Antonia's sister, Elena, waited nearby with her two young boys, Marco and Berto (the source of the clamoring). They peeked out from behind their mother's legs, their little fat hands filled with plastic action figures. Of the daughters, Elena was younger and more chic, although far more harassed looking. The snug jacket she wore over jeans gave her a silhouette like one of Botticelli's nymphs. With her head soberly cocked to one side, she may have easily passed for a denim Venus posing precariously on a seashell. She'd somehow avoided coiffing her sandy bob into a sculptured helmet the way Antonia had. Antonia's beautiful blond hair, so fatally overstyled, looked more like a wig.

Filomena was in the kitchen preparing a snack before dinner. She had tied an apron over her navy dress, and her ultra-shiny black shoes looked like two flat tires beneath her thick, black-stockinged ankles. The espresso bubbled on the stove while she gave the floor a perfunctory mop. The rest of us waited in the doorway as Filomena circled the little dining table with a mop, singing "Like a Bridge Over Troubled Water." She barked the title over and over, that being the only lyric she knew, giving the tune a marching-band quality. It ended up sounding like military propaganda and completely unrecognizable.

"She wants you to know she knows some English," Joan explained.

"Like a bridge over troubled water . . . like a bridge over troubled water . . . like a . . . "

"Yes!" Joan interrupted. "That's all the English she knows."

Filomena finally slammed a plate of fruit and an assortment of cheese down on the table. Having been given the signal, the women rushed in and took their places at the table, yapping loudly. Filomena unscrewed the lid from a jar of strawberries swimming in syrup and slammed that down, too.

"What's that?" I asked.

"Strawberries marinated in liquor," Joan smirked, shaking her head hopelessly. "I bet you anything that before we leave here, Elena will let Marco drink the liquid out of that jar."

"Which one's Marco?" I asked.

Joan nodded toward the younger of the two boys. Right on cue, Marco reached for the strawberries, and all the women lunged forward to assist him. Filomena forked the strawberries onto a dish and pounded the jar down in front of Marco. He grabbed it greedily with two fat hands and started chugging. The women chattered animatedly. The other boy, Berto, received a slap on the back of the head.

"What's that for?" I whispered.

"He's not supposed to have his toys at the table. He always does though. Okay, in the next . . . " Joan glanced at the clock, ". . . in the next ten minutes, Marco will start to feel sick and disappear under the table."

"No wonder he's sick. He just drank a liter of booze."

"I know that, and you know that," Joan said sagely, "but we're in Southern Italy." She smiled and sipped her coffee. "Logic and common sense don't necessarily come into it. He's acting like a little savage, so he'll get his head slapped again." She winked. *"Semplice."*

Every once in a while I heard my name being pronounced with such exotic panache, I straightened in my chair and beamed around the table, nodding and pretending to understand. Suddenly, the head of a fearsome-looking warrior peeked over the edge of the table. He looked like a madman, surveying us all from the trenches. And then a slap and a stream of loud Italian. Berto howled and slid underneath the table to join an ailing Marco, who'd already made his slippery descent, unnoticed. Elena continued shouting and rambling, seemingly to herself and the ceiling.

"What's she saying?" I needled Joan.

"She's saying 'No toys.'"

Oh, oh! The action figures were indeed active. I felt some kind of war going on around my shoes. And then some plastic person ran up my shin, bruising my bone with every superhuman footstep.

"What is it?" Joan asked.

"The Power Rangers are engaged in battle," I whispered, my eyes beginning to tear up, "And one of them is using my leg as an escalator."

Joan discreetly lifted the tablecloth and peeked under.

Filomena saw her, and did the same. "Ay!" she yelled under the table, followed by lots of percussive head-slapping. Joan calmly translated as the room exploded into chaos.

"Filomena's saying to the boys, 'Don't eat that,' and Elena's saying to Filomena, 'That's not food—it's the stupid Power Rangers.'"

"Do the Power Rangers look like food?" I joked.

"No. Not to mention they have this same exact conversation

every time the boys come over. It's scripted at this point, right down to the number of slaps and strawberries."

Antonia stood up suddenly, her chair flying backward. She shouted a stream of conjectures in my direction and gestured as if she were brushing dirt off her palms. I rose, utterly confused but smiling expectantly.

"We're getting ready for dinner," Joan told me, also rising. "It's time."

Filomena rushed everyone out and mopped the floor madly with an under-the-breath dialogue of potential curses that suggested the terra-cotta tiles were filthy beyond description. "Like a bridge over troubled water . . . " she chanted as she marched about the table in her shiny flat tires.

"I thought we were getting ready for the restaurant," I whispered, full of confusion when I noticed Filomena nodding off in an overstuffed armchair.

"Well, yes," Joan confirmed, "But napping is built into the plan. Antonia sets her alarm clock, and in twenty minutes or so we'll be making a move." Joan yawned. I looked toward Antonia's bedroom and saw two crocodile mules with feet inside them pointed up toward the ceiling, as if fatigue had suddenly flattened Antonia the way the airborne house had flattered the Wicked Witch of the West. I turned back toward Joan and saw her disappear into her own bedroom.

Standing beneath the stucco archway, I studied Filomena, warmed and sleeping inside a shaft of light running like a sunny seam where the two curtains met. Her thick, black eyebrows looked like two fuzzy caterpillars, her blanched face framed by a halo of soft white curls. In the quiet, I could see her as a young woman, a wife, with hair as black and glossy as the feathers on a crow. Her eyes, shining and alert, were full of love and fierce with family devotion. In the shadows by the thin, graceful ankles encased in wooly black stockings, I saw two little girls, soft and silly, giggling and hanging from Filomena's lap . . . Antonia and Elena, on their way to becoming the two strong and passionate women they now were.

The alarm in Antonia's room screamed through the apartment. Filomena's eyes shot open as she propelled herself out of the yawning armchair and back into action. The seam of sunlight burst into a flood of color and noise as the curtains were pushed open. The shadows slipped under the furniture and sank into far corners as the sound of motors and horns filled the room.

Although a hazy opal sky had smothered the sun, the air still hung heavy and awkward. It blanketed me the moment we stepped outside, perching heavily on my shoulders and dewing my skin with a light sweat. The long walk to the parking garage didn't help. Filomena had the right idea. She refused to go near the parking garage on account of the vicious hellhounds. She waited in front of the apartment building in the shapeless rosebud shift she had changed into. She stood looking like a little floral barrel with shiny black shoes.

"Get in! Get in!" Antonia yelled as her mother fumbled with the passenger door. Joan, Elena, and I were crammed into the tiny back seat. The two boys alternated between sitting on our communal laps and standing in the space between the front seats. There was not a seat belt in sight. One appeared to have been cut with a pair of scissors, and the others were just plain gone. Antonia nearly killed us a number of times, but it wasn't until she nearly mowed down an elderly pedestrian at a crosswalk that she was forced to take notice. The ancient, frail-looking little man hammered on the hood with his fists, then took to beating the shit out of the car with his cane. He glared levelly inside at Antonia, raining curses (not swears but actual curses). Filomena yelled back from the passenger seat and pounded back on the inside of the windshield with her handbag.

Apparently Antonia had learned nothing about defensive driving from this experience. We pulled out onto the motorway and quickly turbined to over a hundred miles per hour. The boys giggled and poked at Filomena in the front seat. Freakishly quick for a senior citizen, she was able to catch Marco's hand like an iron trap each time and nearly pull it from its socket. I remembered the poor child was drunk, which explained his willingness to repeatedly bear-bait Filomena.

With all the noise and activity in the car, Antonia missed the exit. Enraged, she beat the steering wheel and thought fast. Bringing the car to a complete stop on the motorway, she swung an arm over the passenger seat and began reversing, also at roughly one hundred miles per hour. Deeply shocked, I glanced at Joan for an explanation.

"She missed the exit," she said simply. "She always does."

"We're not allowed to drive in reverse!" I choked, paralyzed with fear.

"No, we're not." Joan looked out the window, rather disinterested. "I feel like having seafood," she mused.

What had been a light misting of perspiration beneath my ponytail and along my spine had turned into a river of sweat. I could feel my makeup dripping off my petrified countenance and guessed that my face had twisted into a mask of intense horror, fear, and confusion. Cars were hurriedly changing lanes and swerving desperately to avoid hitting us.

"These people are crazy," I whispered.

"Uh huh," Joan agreed.

Amazingly, we arrived alive. Antonia's boyfriend was waiting for us. With gentlemanly ease, he took my hand and pulled me from the backseat. My knees, exhausted from their savage knocking, gave out, and I fell onto him. I felt conscious of the ivory-colored lace skirt I wore, showing too much of my wobbly, newborn-deer legs as I struggled for balance. Naturally, I played it off as a misstep, when in actuality, I'm convinced that my brain had already sent this message to my body: "Prepare to die." Then my body sent back this message: "Ten-four, good buddy" and quickly began to shut down.

Gianni, the fatherly boyfriend, hooked me with one arm and Joan with the other. The restaurant overlooked the sea, and I vaguely felt salt breezes sniffing at my skin and drying dapples of sweat as we tiptoed over broken seashells and gravel to reach the entrance. Little

Marco tripped and fell several times as we crossed the parking lot. His "inexplicable" clumsiness overshadowed my sudden inability to stand, and I was grateful to him. Elena and Antonia each grabbed one of his arms and literally towed him to the door, his shoes dragging on the gravel like, well . . . like a drunk.

A large banquet table, laden with food and surrounded by strangers, was awaiting us. The already obscenely noisy room became impossibly loud and raucous as introductions were made and kisses dispensed. Present at my honorary feast was everyone from Elena's manicurist to an elderly gent who resembled the man Antonia nearly ran over earlier that day. Tucked into a far corner was the gaggle of friends and family members with whom Filomena had active vendettas. I was placed at the head of the table, Joan on my right and Filomena on my left. Joan looked fretful and shot me meaningful looks every time I glanced her way. I ignored her. Filomena, humming a marching tune to herself, tore the soft centers from her rolls and balled them up between her fingers before tossing them into her mouth.

Conversation moved like a speeding automobile to talk of coming days. Antonia began spewing with more effervescence than the Trevi Fountain, and Joan scrambled to translate. Gentleman Gianni deftly took the reins from my sister and bravely talked over Antonia's dictatorial rant. He described an ancient city built into a hillside, where crumbling stone steps wound up to long-abandoned villas—hundreds of old villas stacked on top of each other and nestled into the jagged rock of the landscape.

"It's a place where cats rule," Gianni joked. "They are the only ones who've lived there since the plague, when all the residents left." I imagined myself climbing the stairs to the empty shell of a once-grand home with mosaic floors and fireplaces in every room. I saw myself like Guinevere, wearing a golden gown, the point of my conical hat erupting like a smokestack with pastel netting and getting caught on the overgrown ivy of some long-forgotten courtyard while an army of cats toured me through their kingdom.

"It's an incredible place," Joan attested. "You'll think you're walking through a movie when we get there." She sounded as excited, and nearly as loud, as Antonia. My memory flashed to Joan disappearing into her bedroom for an ill-timed nap. Her cardigan hung from her shoulders the same way that Filomena's did. She was holding her fork like a surgical instrument, the same way Antonia was. I noticed she was reaching for the wine and barking remarks into the sandstorm of conversation in a manner that the shyer, paler Joan would have never done. *She fits right in here,* I realized with a surge of contentment.

Plates of appetizers appeared. Thrilling pizzas with gaudily bright toppings, salads glossy in their oily baths, pastas tossed with pink meats and cream fantastically gruesome like nettled squids, succulent fruits, and a dish of black and green olives swimming in seasonings were all placed before me. And then a plate of deviled eggs, peppered and paprika'd to perfection. I began sampling. Delicious! Everything was delicious!

"*Delizioso!*" I announced giddily, draining my wineglass. "My

God, Joanie, the olives, the eggs . . . this is amazing!" My fingers deftly found the button at the side of my skirt and freed it from the straining buttonhole.

"Pace yourself," she warned, slapping at my hand as it plucked greedily at the olives. "Remember what I told you about the food. You're not used to eating like this." I closed my fist meanly over the olives and snarled, suddenly vicious and territorial. "You'll be sorry," she crowed, rolling her eyes. "There's another round of appetizers before they even start bringing the real food out." Belligerently, I hid my hand under the table and capped each fingertip with a pitted olive, revealing it every few minutes for nibbles (which served the dual purpose of taunting Joan).

Sure as shit, an hour later I was marooned in the ladies room while the party raged outside. The guest of honor was well and truly ensconced on her throne.

"Didn't I warn you?" Joan whispered into the doorjamb every few minutes.

"These people are crazy," I rasped in a sickly whisper.

"Antonia wants to know if you want dessert. It's the famous tiramisu."

"Can I have it in here?" I asked.

"Probably," Joan said, as she shuffled off to locate a paper plate and a plastic fork.

From inside the confines of a marble lavatory, I savored the famous tiramisu, tracing tiny highways of mica in the tiles. I pictured our little car, jetting forward and then suddenly reversing along those little veins of mica. Filomena, seatbeltless, with nerves of steel, beside Antonia, swerving and reapplying lipstick in the rearview mirror as we threaded our way from ruined cities to bustling market towns and back again to a parking garage five blocks from home. When a prickly ocean breeze whistled through the open bathroom window, my fingertips felt cold without olives. Despite the tumultuous state of my stomach, I longed to be eating again and hearing the children getting slapped underneath the table. I ached to hear Filomena shouting *"Basta!"* and to see Antonia leaning lovingly against gentleman Gianni's lapel, sporting a dandruff of crispy crumbs. "Am I becoming one of them?" I wondered with rare excitement.

Rachel Dacus

Venice and the Passion to Nurture

The Most Serene Republic greeted Mother's Day with a shifting fog that barely glimmered with the hope of burning off. We were heading toward Piazza San Marco for a Mother's Day Mass that our hotel concierge said would top all masses if the city turned on the new electric lights Sony had installed to illuminate the fabulous Byzantine gold mosaics on the inside of the domes of the Basilica di San Marco. They had first turned them on at Easter, but as with all things in Italy, there were no guarantees for today.

After three days in Venice, we could surf the uncertainties and even stand firm legged in the vaporetti without holding on. These were about the only similarities we shared with the rest of the passengers, a crowd of children and parents also heading toward Piazza

San Marco. We could feel Venice's famous church hovering behind the mist, ready to be born yet again from the lagoon, improbable and perfect. Its eighth-century builders must have gasped when they first saw the completed domes, arches, and mosaics—gasped like any new mother as she checks her infant's toes and fingers.

Birth metaphors seemed to be all I had left of prospects for motherhood. I had begun to believe I was one of the 10.1 percent of women of child-bearing age who are infertile. I was sure it was my fault, not my husband's, though our doctor had said that men and women are equally likely to be infertile. He also said we were no longer ideal candidates for in vitro or its variations, GIFT, ZIFT—not even for fertility drugs and surgery. Our one failed foray into the world of open adoption had painfully emphasized statistics I had read: In 1992, 127,441 children were adopted in America, and 20 percent of those adoptions had been "disrupted," that is, had failed before being finalized. Ours had failed before the child was even born. After the birth mother read our letter, she chose another couple. My way of meeting these facts and statistics had been to do some scream-crying, but I succeeded only in scaring my dogs.

As a remedy, David suggested we head out on vacation to Italy. We signed on for an extravagant tour, complete with preparatory classes in Renaissance art history. By the time we reached Venice, we had had three weeks of basking in Renaissance glories. Walking through churches, piazzas, and hill towns had softened the blow. David and I had reached no decisions about what to do next in our quest for a child, but we had reached some peaceful moments in serene places like Assisi and Venice. Italy's beauty was powerful therapy.

We held hands on the boat, in the sea of kids, like refugees. I had awakened with cramps, ballooned with a kind of tension hardly covered by the term "premenstrual." Naturally, this would not make me romantic company. I felt like nothing so much as The Rotten Womb, diminished to an all-important but nonfunctioning organ. For a loss of this kind, no one sends sympathy cards.

But here I was at the Grand Canal, Venice's sinuous liquid freeway. It made me gasp. If you don't gasp when you ride into Venice, someone should check your pulse. Filigreed and fantastic Renaissance palazzi rose straight out of the water in shades of ochre, melon, pink, and white. They glared proudly in what was now beginning to look like sunshine. They shimmered in their watery reflections. Adorned with rows of columns and round- and pointed-arch windows, they resembled palaces in a Persian fairytale. You could imagine a wedding-cake Juliet calling from one of these sugar-craft balconies to any Romeo with a gondola.

If I thought the boat was crowded, I was unprepared for Piazza San Marco. It was mobbed by hundreds of uniformed children, who, someone said, were here to sing in children's choruses in a service to be televised across Italy. Our hope of squeezing in dwindled. Cameramen roved the crowd, swinging cameras this way and that at the perfect kids; the scene resembled a toddlers' fashion shoot.

We waded through children toward the door but were stopped. "Sorry, no room," said a smiling policeman with a submachine gun.

"We're tourists," David said, stating the obvious in case the policeman was blind. We had been told Italians can instantly spot Americans by their clunky shoes. "We want to see the church with the electric lights on."

"Not without a child who sings," the cop said, so wryly I thought he must be Florentine.

Because we weren't parents, we had to wait for another trip to Venice. I wanted to hit him or grab one of these kids and attempt to go through a different entrance. I breathed, raised my camera, and stole only a shot, of a tiny girl playing horsey on a stone lion.

David pulled me away, saying, "Let's forget it and go shopping. These kids are giving me a headache."

He had no such pain. "There's Santa Maria Gloriosa dei Frari," I said. "We haven't seen the Titian. They probably have a big deal on Mother's Day, too."

Why did I suggest that? Did I need more Mother's Day?

"Maybe the Frari also turns on electric lights," David suggested.

"Quit cheering me up. They don't have golden mosaics. Why would electric lights matter?"

Mass was in progress when we entered the Frari. We sat in folding chairs at the back. Even looking down the length of the nave, Titian's altar painting was breathtaking. Twenty-two feet high and eleven feet wide, it had three orders of figures. Apostles on the ground marveled at Mary as she soared into Heaven. Peter kneeled, Thomas pointed, and Andrew stretched forward as if to catch hold and get a lift from an ethereal Mary Poppins. She swirled up in the classic *contrapposto* pose that makes all Renaissance art figures appear to be ballet dancers. She was one of those Renaissance perspective tricks, like Michelangelo's *Pietà*, whose Mary would be twelve feet tall if she stood up. This Mary's arms would achieve an eagle's wing-stretch if unfolded. As she is portrayed in this painting, a mortal lifted *bodily* into Heaven, her rising suggested the metaphor of motherhood as a return to Eden.

I gazed at her and scores of Italian Madonnas reeled through my brain: Della Robbia's terra-cotta rondelles of mother and babe cheek to cheek, Martini's golden Mary in the Sienese altarpiece; Michelangelo's liquid and mournful *Pietà*. Every other Italian street had a Mary church, an Our Lady of Well-Being, Our Lady of the Angels, Our Lady Triumphant Over Minerva. Everywhere a Mary, a Venus, a Minerva. Why was she so important to Italians?

I was probably never going to be a mother. As I looked up at Titian's transcendent Mary, I felt physical details imprint on this sober thought, embossing it with people who came and went, whispering until a susurrus rose through the vaulted space like an approaching storm. Old women in black dresses and white lace veils mumbled private prayers, becoming part of my childlessness, as did young women in blouses with plunging necklines as they held their infants and gossiped. Men in suits of that peculiar avocado color fashionable that year in Italy gazed up at Mary, and I could feel them thinking of their mothers, as we all were thinking of our mothers and children, feeling both wounded and embraced on Mother's Day.

The liturgy's Latin chant ended, and the real attraction began.

Little girls in white dresses and little boys in dark suits went up to the altar and recited short texts into a microphone held down to them by the priest. Proud parents stood up and lights flashed. Some children were tongue-tied and forgot their lines. Others were letter-perfect. The flashes accelerated like strobe lights at a rock concert. It was a family photo op of the first order. Fathers popped up to videotape their darlings, and then they sat down and wept on their wives' shoulders.

At the end, we all cried, shook hands, and wished our neighbors well. David and I left the church holding hands, anchoring each other.

"If I can just sit beside the water for a while, I'll be fine," I said, knowing he was worried from his sidelong glances, the way he steered me too firmly.

Just to show him I could, I got into my seat in a waterside trattoria, selected scampi from the menu, and took a sip of wine before turning weepy. I didn't want to embarrass him, but feelings were mounting and volcanic. I kept thinking of those kids reciting their texts. A door of tenderness nudged open, and I had to keep slamming it to be able to eat. Then, with a surgical twinge, a menstrual cramp seared off my last hope for a little Francesco or Clare from this vacation.

This crushing certainty was accompanied by an unexpected surge of relief. I fixed my gaze on the floating palazzi across the canal, palaces whose ambition reminded me of the ambition of our new-dollhouse suburbs, sprouting alongside California freeways for all my new-mother friends. I had endured several years of pregnancy announcements, but at the most recent one, I felt not the usual envy but a rebellious sense of escape. So what if they all were obsessing over strollers instead of shoes? Or buying tiny, perfect clothes for each other's baby showers? We could afford a trip to Italy. We might be way down on the Boomer social scale, as childless urban condo-dwellers who maneuvered between fleets of new SUVs that sported PRECIOUS CARGO bumper stickers, but we had freedoms our friends could barely remember. And no college educations to save for.

After the love-fest at Mother's Day Mass, though, there was that word again: "precious." An absurd image came into my head of a couple in my neighborhood who wheeled their cocker spaniel around in a stroller. Later I realized the dog probably had an injured leg and they were just getting him some air, but at the time I was filled with disgust for a society that could shame you into surrogate child-strolling. We all had to have a "Precious" of some kind. I made myself remember the way my brilliant counselor had used the word when she introduced to me the Inner Child and the concept of a tribe of beings buried within the subconscious. My counselor had said I should talk to my Inner Child—and call her "Precious." I was trying, but this phantom child was elusive.

My walking partner, Adell, loved to quote Maria Montessori: "The Child is my driving force." Adell, who had no children of her own, had spent a year in Perugia studying with a student of Montessori to become a teacher in this extraordinary method. Montessori never married and had only one child, but she spent her life changing the lives of children, first as a physician—Italy's first woman doctor—and then creating a revolutionary school in Rome's worst slum. She created an entire system of education by the simple act of observing how each child learned. Montessori, a quintessential Italian nurturer, devoted herself to carrying respect for the Child around the world, ultimately establishing schools in her method as far away as India.

I had tucked a small book into my purse before leaving for Piazza San Marco. I was struggling through *The Mother* by Indian poet-sage Aurobindo Ghose. Its theme was a principle of compassion he called "the Divine Mother." Aurobindo's Mother embodied a very different concept of God from the Jehovah of my childhood. I didn't quite grasp it but was drawn to his tantalizing description of her "calm wideness," "splendid strength," and "secret of beauty and harmony." These attributes of the Mother seemed unusual until I came to Italy, where every Mary had something of Aurobindo's Mother about her: more sanctified than a saint yet more approachable than a god—the mother in whose velvet embrace we all want to be enfolded.

I recognized some of these qualities springing forth from my pregnant and parenting friends, a quality I thought of as the passion for nurturing. What else is it but passion when you neglect your own interests so fully in serving another human being? I did not feel this innately feminine passion. Was it a biochemical product of pregnancy? Women like Adell had it without benefit of biology. Adell devoted herself to her classes. She probably was among the lowest-paid people with advanced degrees in America, and yet she adored her work. All she ever talked about were her kids. What inspired such passion in Montessori and Adell?

Montessori reported seeing something in a single child that kindled and directed the course of her lifelong passion. On her first visit to the site of a proposed new school in the slums of Rome, she saw a child sitting alone in a dark room, making no effort to come out and explore the daytime world outside. From that grim glimpse she inferred how neglect and indifference thwart a child's unfolding, and she was inspired to try to ensure that no child would be left alone in the dark when they might be brought into the light by education. She understood two facts: that children need love to grow, and that every adult has a responsibility to help them.

Where was my inspiration for the passion to nurture? Or did I have something wrong with more than my reproductive system? All these ideas passed through me while David was tearing off hunks of bread and dipping them in herbed olive oil.

"What's wrong?" he said sharply.

"I've got cramps," I said.

I was doing it again, dwelling on infertility as though it were my loss alone. David was reasonably enjoying his lunch, an architect surrounded by his dream city.

"Look at that palazzo, at the porthole windows," he said. "They're symmetrical but not exactly. You see?"

I nodded, feeling a little like a child being distracted from crying about an owwie. The palazzo in question was unusual, rising in tiers of arches on its left side; on its right, the stories were delineated by unusual porthole oculi, large circular windows surrounded by a ring of smaller circular windows; and the whole building was topped with round, flaring chimneys like a steamer's smokestacks. The palace looked as if it were ready to sail away with a puff of smoke.

"The guidebook says it's Palazzo Dario," David said. "Fifteenth century. You could never do anything like that with standardized building materials. It's what's wrong with everything built after 1915."

"Would you want to do anything like that?"

"It's the principle. Your eye is accustomed to standardized proportions, but if you look at this, the 'asymmetrical symmetry' is really very lovely."

Of course he was right. Venice enthroned difference, not standardization. One size did not fit all here. Nor did it fit me. I realized my own ambivalence toward motherhood after a friend had blamed me for my childlessness.

"Why didn't you write a better letter to that birth mother?" she asked me after the adoption fell through.

"Why didn't you write sooner? Why didn't you put more emotion into it?" my friend asked. "If you had, you might be a mother today."

Her choice of words was interesting. She didn't say "have a child," she said "be a mother." To her the being was everything. I gave her a little time off from our friendship after that—five years—

but the question returned today. Why hadn't I tried harder? I dug down to the bottom of myself, in that glorious Venetian sunshine, and discovered a memory of panic. I had panicked when faced with writing to the birth mother, panicked at the prospect of taking on the most despised job in America: full-time motherhood. It took several days to get over the panic and write the letter, to find words like: "I will cherish your child. There's nothing I want more in life than to take care of her." But motherhood in this century seemed fraught with compromise and paradox. I might go through the hard, uncertain work of adoption, finally become a mother, and then, like my peers, be expected to abandon the role to paid caregivers so as to go back to "work." What was the point of it all, from the perspective of children—just to own a child?

And why should I know how to nurture? I had had no real training. My mother, my role model, was ill equipped for motherhood. She had been distracted from the learning curve of new motherhood by daily verbal abuse from my father—the verbal knife being much worse than any fist. She numbed out, became absent, and resisted her children's demands. From her I learned that mothering was a burden atop a pile of burdens. No wonder I panicked.

On this trip, however, my feelings about the role were shifting. The Child had been with me everywhere, on streets, in restaurants, in parks and churches. Everywhere we went children were adored, even by strangers like waiters and airplane pilots, shop clerks and priests. Everyone reached for the nearest child to give a hug or kiss. Italians are naturally generous people. I saw evidence of that generosity almost every time an adult saw a child. "Give" seemed to be a gestural Italian verb, locating itself in the physical heart, arms extending the impulse. I saw motherhood here in a way I had rarely observed it at home.

We finished lunch and decided to rejoin our tour group for the afternoon. We collected at Piazza San Marco with our resident tour guide, Ira, who said we'd go to a church not originally scheduled for today. Because of unexpected scaffolding, we'd visit a different Venetian landmark, Santa Maria della Salute. This architectural marvel, dedicated to health, was built after Venice was struck by the plague in 1630. The desperate Venetian Senate made a bargain with Mary: Venice would build a church to honor her if she would avert devastation. The Venetians kept their bargain and, in thanks for being spared, built the church. Thanksgiving is still an enthusiastic habit in Venice. Each November 21, city workers construct a bridge of boats across the canal from San Marco to the Salute. Venetians walk across it. Gondoliers even bring their oars to be blessed by a priest on the church steps. Those who enter the church pay their respects and give thanks to the city's real patron saint, the Virgin Mary, represented by the Byzantine icon on the church's altarpiece.

A short boat ride brought us to the small campo and a white, octagonal church whose dome was encircled by triumphal arches. Neoclassical entrances were flanked by composite columns surmounted by massive scrolled volutes. The features and the starched whiteness gave the building a prissy gâteau look, like something whipped up for the window of a bake shop. It sat on a plinth of beautiful marble steps. Sculptures atop the entrances had a windswept, Olympian saintliness, as if their robes were rustling in a strong breeze off the water.

Venetian lunch breaks can be extensive and unpredictable. The church was unfortunately not yet open. There was no predicting when it would be. We waited in the brilliant sunshine, the wind salty and refreshing, while Ira mentioned that this church was devoted to the Divine Mother. I felt in my purse for the little Aurobindo book, a touchstone.

At last the church opened. We entered a dim, tall space whose walls were white and unornamented, but which had all the richness needed in an ornate gilt and white marble altar and an intricate floor of marble mosaic. A huge gold lamp suspended from the dome hung low in front of the altar. We walked around the perimeter and found another Titian painting in a chapel, a painting of the "plague saints." Sebastian was depicted, with arrows sticking out of what Ira said were the traditional spots on the body where plague lesions erupted. The "doctor saints" were also represented: Cosmas and Damian conferred, while a shaggy Saint Roch looked balefully up at Saint Mark enthroned, his head in shadow as if to represent the danger to the city. In contrast to his glorious *Assumption*, Titian's painting here was sober.

The carved marble altar swirled with sculpted figures of Venice bowing to Virgin and Child, but I hardly noticed it. I was distracted by a small, riveting painting that hung above the altar, an ancient Byzantine black Madonna. She was the source of Venice's healing, their miracle-maker. Her dark face was grim, and she stared rather belligerently out with mournful eyes, like an overburdened mother. Yet something bright poured from the painting in a way the gold-leaf background could not account for. I was flooded with thoughts of the Child, the Mother, and the passionate mystery by which we create the future. I found myself praying to this powerful, mysterious Mary to help me. It was a leap for someone not given to begging for divine favors, but my request felt . . . invited.

David's leg pressed against mine. What was he thinking? He was probably glad I was calm again. Perhaps he was thinking about volutes and their proportions, not about divine mothers.

It was the moment to cast aside prejudice against superstition and open myself to whatever healing might reside here. A last-minute save, a physiological miracle that would enable us to conceive, seemed such an Italian ending to our story. A wonderful relief rushed through me as I felt assured that motherhood would somehow be a part of my life. The Madonna's eyes seemed to burn away my grief. The tears that surged were those of gratitude, though I could not have said for what.

It was time to go. David and I rose and linked arms and began walking back around to the door.

"I'm not ready to give up yet on little Francesco," I whispered.

"Me neither," he said. "Did you feel the atmosphere? What was going on?"

So he had felt it, whatever it was. We stood at the entrance, looking back to the altar, past the gold lamp, at Mary. She beamed darkly across the space and seemed to me to raise her hand—an odd sensation in my mind's eye, a little motherly wave.

We went out into the piercingly bright sunshine and down the steps to the water. Posing together for a photo, our little group hugged as a family while the wind messed our hair.

At dinner that night we sat with Ira. David mentioned our love of the Salute church. Ira said he found the church's atmosphere that day amazing. "It seemed as if we had an appointment of some kind there."

David and I exchanged glances.

We confessed to each other as we rode home on the plane that we had both felt a healing in Santa Maria della Salute on Mother's Day. I showed David Aurobindo's book and suggested we mark our own day of thanksgiving as Mother's Day, the day on which we stumbled upon the Divine Mother's healing presence. We found new ways to honor the Child, the Child we had lost, the Child within, and the ones we saw every day in the world around us.

Italy gave me the knowledge that my own passion to nurture had been there all along, as had the Child. And the Italian verb for "to mother" translates very well into English, as does the verb for "to give."

Rachel Hosein Nisbet

Volare,
Oh-Oh-Oh-Oh!

It was Patience Gray's description of the Salentine Peninsula in her cookbook *Honey from a Weed* that drew me to the heel of Italy. More precisely, it was her portrayal of the people who inhabit this southern region of Puglia, and their symbiotic relationship with the local countryside, that captivated me. Rocky promontories along the Ionian coast have acted as both a seat and a mallet for fishermen since the Bronze Age, allowing them to relax by the sea, bashing open sea urchins in order to feast upon their sweet yellow ovaries. I wanted to taste for myself this feral heritage, which the sea has held in trust for generations.

So early one day in May, my husband, Dave, and I hulked two large cardboard boxes toward a Swiss railway station in time to catch the dawn train for Milan. At the Milan airport, we lied about the weight of our luggage and flew southward to Brindisi. At 4:00 PM we arrived, unpacked our boxes, greased our pedals, and screwed seat posts into place on our bikes. By 4:30 we were ready for our Italian odyssey.

Dusty heat and the tumble of mauve bougainvillea greeted us as we emerged from the air-conditioned airport. To the east we could see the calm waters of the Adriatic. But our afternoon ride to Lecce followed a schizophrenic route. We passed knotted olive groves parceled behind limestone walls, which gave way to grid-locked villages filled with three-wheeler trucks, maniacally barking dogs, potholes, and exhaust fumes. It was an overwhelming intro-duction, and I soon found myself plastered on the hot tarmac.

Fortunately, the fall was not too hard, as Dave was carrying most of our baggage. I hoisted my bike and myself up, my left elbow very much alive with pain. The Italians frankly acknowledge the fraught nature of modern life in Puglia by posting large triangular signs reading DANGER! at every crossroad. This did not inspire my confidence.

The hot, salt-thick air stuck to us as we traveled south, a reminder that the sea was ever close. After two hours of riding, all I could think about was our hotel. A marbled bathroom, cool bed linen, and crisp writing paper bearing the establishment's insignia awaited us—if we were deemed admissible guests. It was twilight when we arrived. Flocks of swallows wheeled above the narrow streets as we entered Lecce. At first I thought they were bats, but the doorman corrected us as we negotiated our bikes through the revolving entrance of the Patria Palace Hotel. After stowing our bags in our liberty-style bedroom, the porter threw open the heavy curtains in front of our window to show us the floodlit baroque facade of the Basilica di Santa Croce across the square. We unpacked quickly, since the two large panniers of camping equipment that formed the bulk of our gear were redundant that first night. We showered, dressed in our finest clothes, descended the seventeenth-century palace's staircase, and found a restaurant in which to celebrate our second wedding anniversary.

The next day, we crossed the square to the Santa Croce, a church that seemed to be sculpted in celebration of the region. Carved into a single pillar were grapes, pomegranates, palm leaves, and the faces of men staring out from the gnarled bark of an olive tree. The artists seemed to have derived great joy from their detailed observation and replication of this teeming countryside. Having dawdled most of the day in Lecce to enjoy the work of these imaginative stonemasons, we arrived late at our coastal campsite that evening. We pitched our tent, cooked dinner, and went down to the beach—better to paddle in the Adriatic at night rather than not at all.

We left early the next day, tracing the shoreline around to the town of Otranto on the Ionian coast in time for breakfast. Dave was still carrying most of our physical baggage as we set out, but my job as communicator and store master was becoming an increasingly heavy load, now that we were fending for ourselves. Unfortunately, my linguistic kit was flimsier than our gear. I had a small phrase book, but my vocabulary was derived from the lyrics of three opera arias: one from Puccini's *Gianni Schicchi*—"O Mio Babbino Caro" ("Oh My Daddy Darling")—and two from Mozart's *The Marriage of Figaro*. Therefore, the phrases that I knew were of dubious utility: "I'm going to throw myself in the Arno" was hardly practical, even if Florence, where the Arno is the principal river, was our final destination.

Despite my limited communication ability, I managed to load Dave up with market provisions. We stopped at a collection of stalls that straddled both banks of a small stream, which ran straight out into the azure waters of the Ionian Sea. I have never shopped in a more magnificent setting, and everything I bought was beautiful: baby zucchini, sweet cherry tomatoes, little wild mushrooms preserved in oil, strawberries, fresh herbs, and mini-balls of smoked mozzarella. Later, when I went to order two cappuccinos and some local pastries from a nearby bakery, I was on such a high that I did not notice I had been given too much change until I rejoined Dave outside. After some deliberation, I realized that I had misused the word *caro* as "I would care for" when ordering; it really means "darling." An excitable young Englishwoman wearing tight cycling shorts and effusively calling out, "Darling, two cappuccinos, thank you" must have been too much for the poor waiter. He had given me a twenty-euro note as change when I had paid with a ten-euro one!

We biked off naughtily without owning up. I made a mental note to take more care in the future, but with the scent of fresh basil singing from our bike bags, it did not seem too serious. We were bound for Taranto, the Salentine Sea Urchin Mecca. The heavily industrialized town is located to the north of Gallipoli, a two-and-a-half-day bike ride from Otranto. We broke up the long, hot journey around Italy's heel with visits to caves, picnics on the beach, and dips in the cold, clear sea. One night we simply pitched our tent between sand dunes. The pictures of me walking into the Mediterranean Sea at sunset look quite idyllic, but they do not convey how sticky I felt putting my sandy cycle shorts back on the next day. There were, of course, no showers or toilets, and we hardly slept a wink, as the local soccer team won that night and the victorious fans drove around beeping their horns for hours.

We had planned to arrive in Taranto by lunchtime on the third day of riding, but we were, as usual, a little late. The single-lane coastal road, which undulated around sweeping bends overlooking the ever-tempting sea, suddenly morphed into a deadly two-lane highway as we approached the town. Fear brought on a sugar crash, and I hunkered down on a curbstone to scoff pistachios while Dave eyeballed a fast four-way intersection. My confidence was not restored when an Alfa Romeo hurtled into a concrete pole on the overpass opposite us. The driver got out, stamped his foot, got back in again, and then reversed so fast that gravel spun out from underneath his chassis. It took a while for Dave to persuade me to get back on my bike, and even then I had to concentrate resolutely on the prospect of sea urchins for lunch.

When we finally found a nice-looking restaurant in a pedestrian part of town, I realized that neither my opera arias nor my slender phrase book contained the Italian for "sea urchin." Taking great care not to say *caro*, I tried to explain what I wanted. I drew a round blob with some spikes on a napkin and started to mutter something vague about *il fondo del mare* (the bottom of the sea). The waiter shot to the kitchen and reappeared shortly, holding a slim red fish with a few little spines on its brow. I shook my head miserably, Dave looked hungry, and the waiter pointed meaningfully at the menu. We might have cycled for three days to arrive at Italy's sea urchin capital, but I could feel the clock was ticking, and if I wanted to eat any lunch I better order *rapidamente*, and preferably by point-ing. What we ate in the end I think might have been risotto. We definitely drank a whole bottle of white wine under the hot after-noon sun, and this restored enough confidence for me to tipsily order tiramisu for dessert. I was on my best behavior, enunciating my Italian vowels as my singing teacher had taught me: *ti*, with the *i* as in "green"; *ra*, with the *a* as in "amen"; *mi*, with the *i* still as in "green"; and *su*, with the *u* as in owl hoots, "hoo, hoo." In spite of my efforts, the waiter continued to look irritated. He returned to our table after dessert, but when I said, *"Volare due cappuccini,"* he could no longer hold himself back. He spread his arms into a T-shape, and tilted from side to side whilst bellowing *"volare, oh-oh-oh-oh, volare, oh-oh-oh-oh."*

Oh-oh-oh-oh? I didn't understand this musical onslaught, until I recalled that we had flown to Brindisi using the airline *Volare Web*. After the confusion over *caro*, I might have looked up the verb "to want," *volere*, in my phrase book, but hadn't. So I subsequently mixed it up with the verb to fly, *volare*. Once the waiter logged the note of embarrassed comprehension in my eye, he shot off for our bill. Meanwhile, I began to go through all the things I must have asked "to fly" in the last few days: apricots, cherries, tomatoes, and bread. Now I understood the weird look I received from the man selling roasted chickens.

After lunch we passed through Taranto's port on our way to the railway station. Still tipsy from our lunchtime wine, I sensed this was my last chance to fulfill my Salentine Quest and started asking random fishmongers if they were selling sea urchins. My Italian obviously needed brushing up, but I was determined. When they could not understand what I wanted, several good-natured men let me peruse the contents of their cold cabinets. At the fourth wholesaler, when I began to mime what I was looking for, the fishmonger cried out "*ricci, ricci!*" We were both relieved to be put out of our misery, and I went out of his shop following the direction in which he was pointing as quickly as I could. Sadly, the stallholder across the road told me that the boats had not gone out that day because a storm was in the offing, and there would be no *ricci* for sale until tomorrow.

At least Dave was doing a good job of carrying all our baggage, and we had a hotel booked for that night in Matera, a town protected by UNESCO as part of our world cultural heritage. I was eager to stay there, firstly because I had not slept in any sort of bed for three nights, and secondly because all the hotel bedrooms were in caves.

I was enthusiastic to search on for *ricci* in Taranto. I had also been enthusiastic to ride to Matera so that we could clock more than one hundred kilometers of cycling in one day and be wonderfully fit. Fortunately, Dave, the voice of reason, had at least persuaded me to take the train to bypass Taranto's industrial suburbs. But it would have been better to buy a ticket straight to Matera, because when we alighted from the locomotive in a small hillside village, it was suddenly late in the day, and a wind had picked up. As we progressed, large trucks constantly squeezed us onto the side of the road. To compound our distress, I was growing tired and saddlesore. Dave had bought me a very narrow bike saddle as a present since he had deemed my old padded one, designed for women with bottoms, as unstylish. Dave, being a very fit cyclist without a bottom, easily carries two people's baggage for a three-week trip while remaining cheerful. Therefore, thin saddles are perfect for him.

The fact that Dave had changed my saddle began to rub on me as much as the seat itself as I struggled on. We proceeded at a miserable pace, with me standing up on my pedals every three turns, freewheeling on the fourth, and practically coming to a stop after the fifth. I would then repeat the sequence or get off my bike to go to the bathroom or put on more underwear. Both of these activities were performed behind a roadside hedge while fervently praying that a large truck would not pass at that moment.

Dusk arrived rapidly and with it, a light drizzle. We had not gone very far, and Dave, in desperation, suggested that he might attach a bungee cord to my bike and tow me. I told him, as politely as I could, that he might not. Shortly afterward I was able to breathe a sigh of relief as we finally began our descent toward Matera. Seven kilometers were added effortlessly to our cycle odometers, and we found ourselves at the foot of the town. Well, that was the only hitch: The town was perched one hundred meters above us. With my last strength, I swung my leg over my crossbar and dismounted. There was no way I was cycling up anything more that day! Just then an Italian cyclist on a feather-light road bike flashed past us, and Dave, loaded as he was with baggage, felt compelled to chase after the athlete to save his sporting pride. He called back to me something about finding where the hotel was and then disappeared from sight. I, meanwhile, plodded upward on foot, too tired to even fantasize about the nature of the town, the room, or the food that might await me.

I certainly was not expecting, on the crest of the hill, to meet Giuseppe, the cyclist whom Dave had chased. The two of them had chatted away in English like a pair of old wives, and by the time I joined them, a plan had been formed. First Giuseppe took us to meet an old man who ran a cycle shop from a garage. To my surprise, he negotiated with me in German before selling me a soft, large saddle. Giuseppe explained that the man had been in the region since he arrived with the occupying forces during World War II.

Giuseppe led us through the slippery cobblestone streets to a small semicircular plaza with a bar. Our guide entered the bar and emerged with a thin man dressed in black who appeared to be in his seventies. This was the father of the owner of our hotel. He would take us to our room in a cave, or *sasso*. Giuseppe handed us his cell phone number so we could arrange to dine together later. We gratefully said goodbye to our friend and entered a narrow passage, which led to a long flight of stairs cobbled with limestone. It was raining now, and the bikes bucked and bounced as we descended five, ten, twenty, fifty, a hundred steps. I was beginning to wonder why we had bothered to cycle uphill to get here when the old man doubled back down a passage and then opened a gate onto a small courtyard. In front of us, a canyon appeared from nowhere, a steep bank of lights clinging to its far wall; to our left was the arched door of our hotel.

We went inside the warmly lit, cream-stoned lobby, collected our room keys, and installed ourselves in our cave. There was a double bed, a telephone, French windows leading out to a veranda, and a subcave with a shower, toilet, and heated towel rail. I stripped naked and blissfully washed several days of human and sea salt from my skin with hot running water. Once we were clean and dressed, we reclimbed the steps to meet Giuseppe and his girlfriend, Patricia, for dinner. Pizza was on the menu, and they assured us that it was the best we would taste, garnished with local, sweeter-than-sweet mozzarella cheese. While we ate, they told us how Patricia's family had managed the bread ovens in the old town for generations, and how the strain of natural yeast that leavened the bread and the pizza crust was unique to Matera. The culture had developed in the cave environment of the old town and had been passed down from generation to generation.

When we finished eating, we went to a viewpoint that over-looked the dark canyons containing the illuminated *sassi*. Here, Patricia and Giuseppe quietly explained how their community had been closely knit when they inhabited the old town. Extended families lived together in a single cave, with a donkey and its manger installed at the back. These living conditions had fostered a singular social network. They had also engendered deplorable living standards: When the sister of Carlo Levi visited Matera in the 1930s, during the writer's political exile, she drew a parallel between the steps we had descended to our hotel and those described by Dante in *Inferno*. Carlo Levi wrote of his sister's observations in *Christ Stopped at Eboli*, putting Matera on the world stage.

Giuseppe and Patricia have never lived in the old town, as before they were born a government project relocated all of Matera's inhabitants to new, sanitary housing in the 1950s. Today, old family nicknames like "Bari Vecchio," meaning "the old one from Bari"; the ability to locate the right person in the right bar; a special strain of yeast; and a desire to share their story comprise their cultural inheritance. We were therefore incredibly lucky to walk the old streets of Matera with them and to listen as they articulated their relationship with a place once labeled a netherworld and now morphing into a tourist destination.

I went to the Salentine Peninsula in search of a heritage that had linked man to the natural world since antiquity. I thought such a heritage would be held in trust by the sea, and I worked terribly hard with my legs, my mouth, and my brain to find and then savor it. Still, Dave and I left Taranto without having slurped on a single sea urchin like a Bronze Age fisherman, and I thought I had failed in my quest. Yet when I stopped searching for an inheritance and stopped trying to speak in foreign tongues, I chanced upon what I was looking for: not a spiky shellfish living below the waters of the Mediterranean, but rather, a beautiful twenty-first-century baker-pianist and her geophysicist boyfriend who live near their ancestral canyon, suspended between limestone cliff tops. Through discovering how unique their heritage is, I could go home and nurture my own.

Constance Hale

Cutouts

On nights when there was a moon, Aldo and I would
leave Poggio al Grillo without a lamp. It wasn't hard to pick
our way down the dirt road, and anyway, Aldo knew its twists and
turns by heart.

Some nights we walked as far as Vito Lippini's. There we might
see, through a door cut into the stucco walls of an outbuilding, the
family's *nonna* sitting on a stool in a golden rectangle of light, wearing a black dress and headscarf, as silent as Whistler's mother,
staring down the vat of red wine. Some nights we would run into
Ernst, the Swiss farmer, on his bicycle, hurrying home to his wife
and children from a tryst with the Englishman's wife. Other nights
we stopped in on Nino, who came from Milan only on weekends
and brought his mistress with him.

Only a month earlier, it was I whom Aldo had stopped in on. I had just finished dinner and was cleaning up when I heard a deep voice outside, holding up one end of a conversation. *"Cosa succede qui? Chi abita in questa casa scura?"* (What's happening here? Who has turned on the lights in the dark house?) I opened the door to find a tall, fit man with gray hair, black eyebrows, and a neat, gray beard, accompanied by a silent German shepherd.

(Upon hearing that I would be traveling in Italy, a Milanese couple—friends from a theater class in Berkeley—had given me their country place in Tuscany for the fall. They hadn't warned me of this ad hoc night patrol.)

"Sono amica degli Riccardi," I heard myself blurt out. *"Non parlo italiano."*

"Benissimo!" the man replied. "I leeved two years in Feelahdellfeeah."

And so we became friends: the twenty-six-year-old American girl, feeling very alone in a sprawling house in the Tuscan hills, and the fifty-six-year-old painter from Milan with his dog, Doc. It didn't take long before we were eating dinner together every night.

After dinner we would walk, leaving the red traces of our wine-glasses to seep into the new beech table ("It is too new, too perfect," Aldo complained) and leaving dishes to soak in the sink (*"l'acqua calda soltanto nella mattina,"* no hot water till morning.) Often we didn't stop in on anyone. We just wandered.

On a night when there was just a sliver of a moon, I was taught an Italian children's rhyme:

Cutouts

Gobba a ponente,
Luna crescente;
Gobba a levante,
Luna calante.

In Tuscany, apparently, the man in the moon was a hunchback. If his *gobba* protruded to the west, the moon was swelling; if his *gobba* protruded to the east, the moon was diminishing.

On another night, I fantasized about the people of the town, Castagneto Carducci, imagining them as giant blue nudes. Aldo was going on and on about how they were "cut out," their isolation leading not just to poverty, but also to provincial pettiness. Only later did I realize that he was translating *tagliati fuori* a bit too literally: he meant "cut off," not "cut out." His mistranslation took me to Matisse and the cutouts that the aging artist made in his last years in Provence. It didn't matter to me that these hills were a palette of ochre, umber, sage, and sienna; that night I imagined the townspeople as cobalt cutouts against an all-white background.

On another night, I learned that those same townspeople had taken to calling me *la ragazza molto in gamba.* "What did they mean," I asked, "that I had big thighs?" Aldo laughed. To be very much "in one's legs," he explained, was to show pluck.

This had come in one of our conversations about my writing. At the time, I dreamed of becoming a writer; I scribbled in a journal and suffered from dark self-doubt. I didn't have a clue as to how to "become" an artist. I had not so much as tasted the kind of success he took for granted. He, after all, was a renowned painter. His studio at Poggio al Grillo (Cricket Knoll) included not just his own land-scapes and nudes but also a Warhol lithograph of Marisa Berenson, a Magritte, and a Picasso—all acquired in trades with other Italian artists. Aldo even prided himself on having once wittily put De Chirico in his place.

"What could you understand," I jabbed defensively, "about my predicament?"

"Ah," he consoled. "I know too tenderly the swing of the pen-dulum. One day: I am a genius! The next: I am a nothing."

I never called him my lover. It's not that we didn't share a bed—in this case, a modernish wood frame of his design that held two independent twin mattresses firmly together. It's just that that term failed to describe what I found in Aldo. It was as though I had met the person I would have been if I had been born exactly one generation earlier, and in Italy, and a man.

Aldo had the nerve to live ideas I was only beginning to flirt with. He had never doubted that he was an artist. Not that he didn't take risks: He had grown up in a bourgeois Milanese family and had forsaken the family legacy for a deeply nonconformist life. He was still a communist, long after that party had gone out of favor. He had never married. In 1969, at forty-two, he had fled to Philadelphia when he found himself hopelessly in love with his brother Cesare's wife. The exile didn't work; Aldo returned to Italy and helped his sister-in-law raise his niece and nephew. The rela-tionship with his sister-in-law eventually foundered, but he stayed close to his brother's children: During the fall of 1983, when I was with him, he was fretting over the niece's husband, a heroin addict, and giving the nephew his half of La Gallinella, a stone house he owned with Cesare. (In the kind of symmetrical justice only possible in Italy, by this time Cesare was living in town with a former consort of Aldo's.)

The subject of freedom—creative, sexual, political—dominated many of our walks. Aldo was militantly opposed to many things. Like monogamy. Like complacency. Like violence. In the bedroom, a small ragged window was set into the wall beside the bed. Aldo had built the stone house by hand, and during a hiatus in the building project, a spider had spun a web in the valley between two stones. Aldo couldn't bear to destroy the web, so he placed a glass behind the spider and kept building. From the bed, you could stare through the web window, over several ridges covered with olive trees, to the Mediterranean beyond.

One day over lunch, I noticed a very thin steel wire that extended horizontally over my head from one wall of Aldo's house to the other. Thinking it might be for hanging underwear on a rainy day, I asked about it. "After I built the house," he explained, ever the maestro, "I realized that there should be a beam there for aesthetic reasons. The wire represents the beam."

Despite the aesthetic attractions of his house, I maintained my own quarters at the Riccardis'. I would go there during the day to write and to play with arrangements of the paintings Aldo kept bequeathing me. They were all watercolors featuring the hills and the sea, or lithographs of black-ink nudes on bright white paper. As I moved them from bedroom to living room, from the seats of chairs to ledges built into the walls, I examined them for flaws. Imperfection, Aldo insisted, was the soul of art. To him, a perfect painting was merely decorative. A bit of watercolor out of control— or the self-doubt I couldn't escape—suggested Truth, Life, the Human Condition.

On nights when there was no moon, not even a *gobba*, Aldo would grab the huge Panasonic lantern that stood sentry next to the front door. We would follow the beam of the massive flashlight down the gravel drive, watch as it animated the pocks in the dirt road, feel ourselves cradled in a roofless room as the light picked up dusty banks cut into certain curves. I'd be transported to the dark courtyard of an ancient villa, or to the eerie majesty of San Galgano—the ruin of a Cistercian abbey in the Val di Merse whose ceiling and windows had long ago been carried off by the wind, whose walls enclosed a grand abbey now consecrated only to Space.

On one particularly dark night, shortly before I was to leave Aldo in search of my own truths, the beam stretched indefinitely ahead as we fell uncharacteristically quiet, each lost in thought. Suddenly, in that tenantless night, there rose a porcelain-like tinkle. Aldo jerked the lamp ninety degrees, into the black emptiness. There to our right, frozen in the beam and almost near enough to touch, was a flock of sheep. Hundreds of pairs of eyes glazed red-gold. All of us—the flock, the painter, the lamb of a writer—all of us stood frozen for a few eternal seconds. The wonder! Then one sheep turned its head, sharp hooves made the bone-dry grass rustle, and, in a symphony of bells, they were gone.

Melissa Secola

The Opera
Singer's House

The opera singer's house was made of stone and sat
upon a grassy knoll overlooking the mountains, vast and
majestic, like gods watching with reserve. I looked once more at
the green bus and called out to the driver, *"Grazie."* *"Arrivederci,
signorina,"* he answered before driving back down the dirt road. I
pushed open the old cedar gate and walked beneath the wooden
trellis, from which wisteria dangled and touched my hair. I curled
my fingers around the heavy brass knocker, which hung from the
mouth of a lion's head staring back at me, its expression whimsi-
cal and strange. The front door suddenly burst open, and she
appeared. Her silvery hair was wild like the lion's, but her eyes
were tamer, not as piercing as I had imagined. She was draped in a
very plain housedress splattered with paint, her only ornament a

string of large, old keys that she wore around her neck. "*Buon giorno!*" she exclaimed ebulliently. She didn't look anything like an opera singer, but the ghost of her once-commanding posture still lingered.

"Signora Regina?" I asked, uncertain if I should roll the *r* in Regina.

She nodded and said in English, "You must be the young American who answered the advertisement for a room, yes?"

"Yes, *sì,*" I answered. She soon took possession of my things and ushered me in with such warmth that my apprehensions about staying with a stranger were quickly forgotten.

We entered a dim room full of paint cans, open electrical sockets, oil lamps, cardboard boxes, dusty picture frames propped against the walls, and seven cats. The house was undergoing some minor renovations, as it had been abandoned for several years. Signora Regina led me down a hallway. "I lived in Milan for more than sixty years before purchasing this house," she said.

"That must have been exciting."

"I had a little apartment near La Scala."

"The opera house?" I asked. Signora Regina nodded.

"I met one of my greatest loves there," she said.

"What was his name?" I asked inquisitively. When there was no response, I asked, "When did you decide to move to the country?"

Signora Regina didn't seem to be in any hurry to answer my questions and instead reached for one of the large keys around her neck. "This will be your room," she said as she unlocked the door. I ducked under the low doorway, made of wooden planks dug into the walls, and found myself in a small room with an uneven floor. An antique chandelier swooped down from the ceiling, and a canopy of tulle hung above the bed. On the wall just under the window was a trail of ivy that had somehow crept in from the outside. Signora Regina called it the White Room. She turned to leave but paused. "It was a clear moment, my decision to move to the country. They always are clear moments, after all." She bid me a good evening, and I found myself alone.

I had taken a series of buses before reaching my destination in the mountains north of Rome. Flustered by the nuances of public transportation, I failed to stow my enormous suitcase in the storage area below the bus. "*Scusa,*" I said to the passengers who hurdled over my suitcase when the bus reached their stop. "*Scusa,*" I said when my suitcase flopped to either side of the aisle and crashed into those unlucky enough to be seated near me as we went around a sharp curve. Weary from my travels, I lay down on the bed and stared up at the canopy of tulle, its airy billows like whipped white frosting. I could hear myself breathing, a sound I hadn't really ever listened to. It was slow and steady. I thought about deadlines and traffic and relationships. Then I dreamed of chocolate and watched the sunlight fall upon my hands.

The next morning I awoke to an aria playing on a record player in one of the other rooms. The recording was scratchy, but the high notes rang out as clear as bells. I flung off my blanket, got out of bed, and did something I could never imagine doing in my Los

Angeles apartment, which overlooked two gray Dumpsters. I threw open the shutters as they do in old movies and leaned out the window, my brown curls descending down the stone wall like ivy. Every so often, someone passed by on the dirt road alongside the house, children on bicycles and old women with loaves of bread purchased from the center of town. I listened to the tenor of their voices, rising and falling like waves tumbling ashore.

I latched the shutters and left my room. At the end of the hallway, I entered a quiet sitting room with a great panoramic view framed by balcony doors. I could make out dark green mountains, although they were phantomlike in the mist. I stepped outside and looked over the iron railing. There appeared to be nothing below, as though we were floating somewhere between heaven and earth. I came back inside and saw that a little Italian espresso maker was already on the stovetop in the kitchen. I lifted its lid and watched the dark liquid as it came up through the spout, bubbling and hissing. It was unlike the automatic drip coffeemaker back at the office. I looked through the cupboard for the standard assortment of coffee cups but found only white cups that looked as though they were meant for dolls. I poured some espresso into a miniature cup and reached for the jar of sugar. After pulling out some stray cat hairs, I decided to forgo the sugar. The coffee was rich and delicious. I poured another cup, then another. Suddenly, I heard a low male voice by the kitchen window. There was a man standing there, gesturing at me. I believe he was cursing in Italian.

"Um, *no parlo italiano,*" I said, struggling. "Are you looking for

Signora Regina?" He paused and looked at me. He was dark and had arresting blue eyes. I suspected his name would be something like Leonardo or Francesco, and that he was the man I was going to marry.

"*Americana?*" he asked, somewhat amused. I shook myself from the fantasy forming in my mind: Francesco (I was intent upon his name being so) embracing me in a field of barley. I nodded.

"There is . . . how you say?" he began. I waited expectantly, but he seemed to be searching for the right word. "There is *fuoco?*"

"*Fuoco?* I don't understand."

He attempted to pantomime something and said, "*Fuoco* . . . fire." I looked at him incredulously. He continued, "Surely there is fire. You drink the coffee so fast." He smiled charmingly. I felt strangely revealed as he stared at me. It was as though he were peeling away the layers of ordinariness and exposing things within me that were generally unnoticed. Realizing for the first time that I was in my pink bathrobe, I began to back away from the window.

"Well, it was a pleasure meeting you. I'll tell Signora Regina that you stopped by," I said as I hurried toward the bathroom.

"Signorina . . . " he called after me.

"Ciao!"

"Francesco, I am Francesco," he said, but I had already closed the bathroom door. I slipped out of my a-little-too-pink bathrobe and turned on the shower. Just as I began to step in, I stole a glance at my reflection in the mirror and saw the unthinkable: a light green face. A nighttime mint moisturizing mask, "so light you'll forget it's there," was plastered over my entire face. My lips and eyes popped out like a fish. I stepped into the shower, mortified by my propensity for such situations, and let out a small gasp. The water was freezing cold. I turned the knob all the way to the left and waited a few minutes, but it remained cold. Suddenly, there was a knock at the door. "Everything is okay?" Signora Regina asked nervously. I shut off the water, put on my bathrobe and opened the door a crack. "Actually, there doesn't seem to be any hot water," I explained.

"*O, per l'amore di Dio!*" She pushed open the door, went over to the water heater, and hit it a few times, which produced a tinny, echoing sound. "*Morto.* Dead," she pronounced. I looked like a melting fish—I had managed to get the mask wet. "Do you think we can have a plumber here by this afternoon?" I asked expectantly.

"Not this afternoon or the next. It is Ferragosto," she said, tossing her hands up in the air. I stared at her blankly. "Ferragosto is a big holiday in Italy. We won't be able to get the water heater fixed for many days," she continued. Normally, something like this would have thrown me into hysterics. I would have been on the phone with anyone holding the title Manager, but an unfamiliar feeling of calm swept over me, and I realized that I wasn't in a hotel, and that a hot water shortage wasn't life threatening. I tried to think of a solution. "I could boil a pot of water," I suggested, which seemed more favorable than immersing myself into a cold shower. Signora Regina looked surprised but said, "I have the perfect pot." She left for a few minutes and reappeared with a big black pot.

As I stood before the stove and waited for my water to boil, I thought about the shift that was occurring within me, the lightness that I felt within my body. Then I heard music. I looked out the kitchen window and saw Francesco next door, strumming a guitar, playing for no one in particular. So it seemed. Merrily, I grabbed the pot off the stove.

That evening, Signora Regina taught me how to make *sugo*. "The important ingredient is the *peperoncino*," she confided in me. "And I need a big handful of basil from the garden," she continued. "I'll get it," I volunteered. I took my glass of red wine and sat in the garden amid clay pots of fresh, fragrant herbs. I plucked the basil leaves and held them close. They smelled earthy, spicy, and sweet. "*Bella!*" I suddenly heard from the nearby hedge. I looked up and saw Francesco next door, smiling at me. As I walked toward the hedge, he disappeared like a rabbit down a hole. When I returned to the kitchen, I noticed Signora Regina walking back from the bathroom.

"It's the perfect pot," she explained, motioning toward a familiar black pot.

"Is that the pot you're going to cook the pasta in? Isn't that the pot I used for my sponge bath?" I asked warily.

"I'll wash it," she answered, shrugging her shoulders. It dawned on me that Americans are terribly obsessed with cleanliness. After all, it is the French who eat truffles dug up by pigs and the Italians who squash grapes with their bare feet, and there is something wonderful about it all, the body engaging in the world, unafraid of the earth's dirt. The kitchen soon filled with warmth and garlic and basil. I looked over at the computer and thought about checking my email, but the life I had back home seemed so far away, and the only important thing at that moment was the sauce, my very first sauce.

"Shall we have dinner out on the balcony?" Signora Regina asked when everything was done. We took our plates outside and sat at a small, round table. The air was still and cool. We sat there for hours, talking and laughing. I couldn't believe how much pasta I had eaten, not to mention the bruschetta, olives, and cheese. "*Peperoncino*," Signora Regina said knowingly, glancing at my empty plate. I began to get up, but she waved her hand in the air. "Sit down, I have a little something else," she said. I couldn't imagine eating anything else, but I remained seated. She entered the house and came back with a bottle and two glasses. "Amaretto," she said. The sky grew darker as I sipped the warm, sweet, velvety liquor. My gaze soon wandered next door to Francesco's house. "I met Francesco this morning," I told Signora Regina.

"Ah? And did he fall in love?"

"I suppose the art of flirting is very Italian?" I asked modestly.

"His wife would agree with that."

"His wife? I didn't realize that he was married. He looked at me in such a way that I thought . . ." I suddenly felt terribly presumptuous. Signora Regina leaned over and whispered, "He makes me feel beautiful." Her eyes almost twinkled. I smiled.

During the next week, I spent my days in the garden, writing letters while abnormally large ants, marching along the branches above my head, plopped onto the table like fat raindrops.

Sometimes I went into town, about twenty minutes by foot. Other than the stone houses scattered among the mountains, the town consisted of just one main street. There I found a church and a small market that sold very few items, mostly large bottles of olive oil. There was also an electrician who had a limited supply of gelato for sale in the front of his shop. *"La fanciulla vestita di bianco,"* he called me, "The young lady dressed in white." All along the main street, men looked at me the same way Francesco did. On my way back to the house, I liked to pick wild blackberries from the bushes lining the road. While I idled away the hours, Signora Regina worked tirelessly on the house, chipping away at old paint, often uncovering flawed but beautiful surfaces that had been hidden for years. She sang softly to the cats as she worked. They sang back to her, their string of *meows* forming a little melody.

My favorite times, however, were our dinners on the balcony. Signora Regina told me great stories, about grand opera houses and foreign countries. She had known all sorts of people: irate but brilliant directors, fussy costume designers, charismatic leading men, enthusiastic admirers. Our balcony conversations were generally vivacious, so I was surprised one night when Signora Regina fell silent. After a few moments, she said, "His name was Massimiliano."

"Massimiliano?"

"The man I met at La Scala. He was a wealthy industrialist from Milano. I met him after a performance of *Tosca*. I remember he came backstage for an autograph. After that, he came to almost every one of my performances."

"Were you in love with him?"

"I was."

"And yet you never married?"

"He asked me to marry him, but I was much younger and had my whole career before me. After things ended between us, he disappeared. Gone."

"That's terrible."

"It has been many years since I last saw him."

"Do you ever wonder where he is?"

"He is in Milano. Married."

"Do you think you'll ever fall in love again?"

"I'd like to believe it is possible. But you forget, I am no longer young. For now, these are my little loves," she said, motioning toward the cats, some balancing on the railing, some peering up at us from the garden, their eyes glowing in the dark.

"Do they all have names?" I asked.

"*Ma certo!* Of course! Tosca, Capriccio, La Contessa, Cio-Cio San, Mario, Radames, and . . . Cannoli."

We sat on the balcony for several more hours. I told Signora Regina about my pseudo boyfriend, the one who would introduce me as his "friend" when we were at holiday parties or backyard barbecues in the suburbs of Los Angeles, the one who ate two slices of buttered toast every morning because anything else would be "too different."

"And this man, why do you stay with him if he does not make you happy?" Signora Regina asked.

I thought for a moment. "Because I think it is easier than being alone." I couldn't believe that I had said it aloud. I must have thought it a hundred times, but I had never said it aloud. I was surprised at how candid I was with someone who was nearly a stranger, but such were our dinners on the balcony, and I treasured them.

On the morning of my last day, I awoke to *"Ebben? Ne andrò lontana"* from Catalani's opera *La Wally.* My suitcase was packed and I had my bus ticket, yet I sensed that I wasn't returning to anything. I went out on the balcony and stood before the railing, looking out. I was sure it would be the last time.

"The bus will be at the end of the road in a few minutes." I turned around and saw Signora Regina looking at me.

"I know."

"Did you know that the view looks different every morning?" She continued, "Every morning I see it as though I were seeing it for the first time."

"Sometimes it seems as though it's part of a different world," I said.

"You should see it when the first snow falls."

"I wish that I could."

"I'll save you a balcony seat," she promised.

As I pulled my suitcase down the dirt road, I caught a glimmer of the green bus, the same one I had arrived in only one week ago. I began to think about my coworkers, each starting their day with a cup of watered-down, burnt office coffee. I wondered how many times you could drink a cup of watered-down, burnt office coffee before deciding to run away to the Italian countryside where they had espresso, real espresso, served in little porcelain cups. I thought about the way Francesco looked at me—as though I were beautiful. I thought about the happiness I felt in Italy, not the fleeting kind, but the kind that remains with you always.

The bus stopped before me. *"Buon giorno, signorina,"* the driver said.

"Buon giorno," I responded, standing perfectly still. I held on tightly to my bus ticket. I had been going through the motions of life for so long that something inside me was breaking—not crumbling to pieces, but breaking free. I shook my head at the driver. He looked surprised but said warmly, *"Arrivederci, signorina."* I watched his door fold shut.

As I walked back up the dirt road, I realized that I had been caught up in a current, the kind most of us get caught in, the kind powered by office cubicles and daily commutes and to-do lists and on-and-off-again boyfriends and day-to-day mediocrity. And this was the place where I was able to break away, here, where canopies looked like white frosting and mountains like gods, where cats sang and all women were beautiful. With a handful of blackberries, I returned to the opera singer's house, uncertain whether I'd stay forever or just until the first snow fell.

Terez Rose

The Paradox
of the Rocks

The first time you catch a glimpse of I Sassi of Matera, in southeastern Italy's Basilicata region, you think you see rocky hillsides interspersed with a few houses and stone walls rising from a deep ravine. Upon closer inspection of the dusty, monochromatic scene, you realize the textures and shapes of the hillside are actually cavelike dwellings and houses built upon houses, numbering in the thousands. Some are partially hewn from rock, making it impossible to see where nature's architecture stops and man's continues. When your eyes adjust to this fresher perspective, an entire city—complete with churches, towers, palaces, and homes—emerges.

Sasso means stone, or rock. In 1993, UNESCO declared this community dug from the rocks a World Heritage Site, calling it "the most outstanding intact example of a troglodyte (cave-dwelling) settlement in the Mediterranean region." Large-scale tourism had not yet descended upon I Sassi at the time of my visit in 1995, particularly on a weekday in March, which helps explain why I found myself adjacent to one of the most spectacular sites in Europe but unable to find the entrance. From my hotel on the Via Ridola, I could find no signs, information kiosks, or souvenir stands; no busloads of chattering tourists to follow at a distance. Ten minutes later, however, a walk down a dusty medieval pathway yielded the prize. All around me stood the dwellings, deep in the heart of the city: rows and tiers of dusty houses crowding the space, stacked one upon the other like prehistoric condominiums. They funneled downward in varying shades of gray, tan, and ivory, punctuated by the occasional green or red shutters of occupied houses. Window and door frames marked the abandoned structures with black rectangles of darkness, like wide, mournful eyes and mouths. Further out, beyond the valley, cave-studded hills stretched out for miles, home to more than a hundred Byzantine rock churches.

I paused, transfixed by the ghostly world spread around and below me. The area, mostly uninhabited, was so quiet I could hear my heart beating. I tried to imagine the same scene crowded with thousands of residents, whose desperate poverty drew international attention only after centuries of social, economic, and political isolation.

The natural caves, inhabited seven thousand (some say as early as ten thousand) years ago, grew into I Sassi after seventh-century Benedictine and Basilian monks, fleeing persecution, began to dig deeper into the porous tufa rock, creating chapels and cells for themselves. Through the centuries, people came and went—Greeks, Romans, Cappadocians, Armenians, and Saracens. In the Middle Ages, a sizeable permanent community began to develop here. The dwellings increased in number, spreading out among the hills. Some continued to be carved out of the rock or were built using the rock as one wall; others were constructed on top of existing houses, the roof of one serving as a base or pathway for the other.

By the twentieth century, demand far exceeded resources. Some twenty thousand people crowded into the maze of narrow alleyways, houses, and grottoes. Sanitary conditions grew intolerable as the water supply dwindled, and poor families found space wherever they could, often in caves and abandoned structures, in the same room with their livestock—their most prized assets and a good source of winter heat.

Carlo Levi, a doctor, writer, and painter from northern Turin who was exiled to the region in the 1930s by Mussolini for his antifascist views, wrote about his experiences in 1945 in a book entitled *Christ Stopped at Eboli*. The book, published the following year, became one of Italy's greatest twentieth-century literary works, drawing attention to this neglected, poverty-stricken region of Italy. The title implies that this part of Italy had been forsaken even by Christ, who must have stopped north, at Eboli, instead of continuing down to this land of strife and despair. "Christ never came this far," Levi wrote, "nor did time, nor the individual soul, nor hope, nor the relation of cause to effect, nor reason nor history."

The Italian government, scandalized by the dwellings, called them "the shame of the nation," propelling Italy back into the Dark Ages. Over the course of several years, they herded the residents out of their ancestral homes and into state-built high-rise apartments constructed in new neighborhoods outside the city center. The crumbling dwellings were sealed up and stood abandoned for decades, a fading relic of the past.

Recent years, however, have shone a more positive light on I Sassi and the dwellings' historical value. Following a 1986 government ruling, property owners—those who hadn't been forced to sell to the government in exchange for new housing—were given permission to renovate and reconstruct. Anyone else who could show financial means and state-approved plans could acquire fixer-upper caves from the State as well. In 1993, I Sassi received its World Heritage Site status. The dwellings are now coming back to life, a mixture of affluence and decay, past and present, with the oldest structures and caves standing permanently empty.

Camera slung over my shoulder, I started on the crumbling path that twisted and wound downward. Occupants of the renovated homes stopped their tasks, their conversations, to stare at me, making me conscious of my blond hair and shorts. My hearty "Good morning"

and "*Che bella giornata*" (What a beautiful day) made them act less wary, but I could still feel their curiosity, their lingering glances. I continued my descent, a lone female and apparently the only tourist. It was a warm day, the sun already high in the sky—a welcome change from rainy London, where my husband and I lived as expatriates. The occasional breeze stirred up pale dust from the path, built wide enough to accommodate a donkey with an ample load. I felt like a time traveler delivered to a village in ancient Egypt or biblical Jerusalem.

As I wandered back up one of the dusty alleys after a few hours of exploration, an elderly man with a thatch of white hair greeted me. "Do you wish to see a church?" he asked in Italian. I nodded, curious, and followed him. He was smaller than I and stooped and deeply tanned. He opened the door, bowed, and swept his arm to invite me into the darkened room. I entered and he shut the door behind us. When my eyes adjusted to the dim light, I realized I was in his house, a snug, one-room structure with a low ceiling, carved-out walls, and an uneven floor. Alone with him. I swallowed my uneasiness and smiled brightly, devising escape routes in my head in the event he should turn amorous on me.

The man, however, only sank into a chair. He lit a cigarette and gestured to the room. "My home was a church a long time ago," he said. I nodded, then glanced around. His home was the size of a large bedroom with barely enough space for a galley-size kitchen, bed, table, and a few sitting chairs. "Sit, please," he urged.

Perching on the edge of a chair, I attempted conversation that would suit my rudimentary Italian. I nattered on in sentences befitting a child about how much I liked Matera and his home and the unexpected pleasures of the Mezzogiorno, Italy's south. He nodded, smiled, and remained silent.

I'm not the sitting-in-silence type. That, however, was what I sensed I needed to do in this Matera home where I was an impromptu guest. I may have been a restless American tourist, but even I wasn't crass enough to consider leaping up immediately, pumping his hand, and continuing my exploration. So we sat. I scrutinized the setting more closely. Photographs and religious icons covered the walls and tables. A stuffed, frayed teddy bear sat on the shelf above his bed. What memories were attached that compelled him to save it? Had his home looked like this before the dwellings were evacuated? What had life been like, here in I Sassi?

It is from Carlo Levi's sister, who stopped in Matera on her way to visit her exiled brother in 1935, that the world has gleaned so much of its information on I Sassi's past. A doctor herself, she claimed to have never seen in all her life such a picture of poverty. She told her brother about the children, either naked or dressed in rags, with "wizened faces of old men, their bodies reduced by starvation almost to skeletons, their heads crawling with lice and covered with scabs. Most of them had enormous, dilated stomachs and faces yellow and worn with malaria." She spoke of the despairing mothers "with dirty, undernourished babies hanging at their flaccid breasts,"

and how it was like being in a city stricken by the plague. Her presence drew crowds of children, who, instead of asking for candy, begged for quinine to provide relief from the malaria that plagued the region. Levi, moved by his sister's description of her painful impressions, detailed them in his book.

What sort of childhood, I wondered, had this elderly man before me experienced? I guessed his age to be around seventy, which would have made him a young man during the war years and the height of the poverty here. What had it been like for his family to leave their ancestral home? Had the forced relocation made life better or worse for them? And what was it like to live among a population now numbering in the hundreds instead of the tens of thousands?

"Is this . . . good here, now?" I ventured, waving my hands in the exaggerated international gesture of the linguistically challenged traveler, attempting to encompass fifty years of local history in my arms.

The man seemed to understand. He shrugged, his expression growing fixed. "It is different," was all he said. He paused and then his smile returned. Silence once again descended—the only thing we could equally share.

When it was time to go, I thanked the man and shook his hand. He smiled at my fumbling attempts to express my gratitude and declined the lire I tried to press into his hand. "It is good for you to know I Sassi," he said, waving away the money. After he bade me goodbye, standing at the doorway of his little chapel home, I started back up the path, pensive now, attuned to the sweet air, the crunch of the dirt beneath my shoes.

Lost in a reverie, I wandered up the passage another twenty meters and rounded a corner. To my surprise, I came upon the sprawling Piazza Vittorio Veneto in Matera's city center, complete with dignified churches, a fountain, throngs of people, and shops. Men in camel coats with hands clasped behind their backs congregated in groups of three and four. Babies squalled while their mothers gossiped and shopkeepers called out to each other. Goodbye, biblical Jerusalem; hello, modern Italy. I looked around, dodged a buzzing moped, and recoiled. I didn't want this world back so soon. Stepping into a shop, I bought a loaf of bread, salami, and water, and slipped right back into I Sassi.

I Sassi consists of two neighborhoods, side-by-side basins known as Sasso Barisano and the uninhabited Sasso Caveoso. Armed with lunch, I headed over to Sasso Caveoso. Here, the environment seemed more feral, windblown, and exposed to the elements, making my solitude feel more acute, more meditative. I found a shaded spot beside a crumbling stairway and ate my lunch there. Puffs of hot wind teased my hair, stirring the dust around me. Two cats approached, and I coaxed them closer with salami. They stayed for a while, grooming themselves while I ate. Afterward, they trotted off. One cocked its head back at me, as if to invite me along. I decided to follow.

By the time I'd packed up, the cats had disappeared into a rocky area. I stumbled around until I came upon a series of interconnected caves—the Convicinio di Sant'Antonio, a twelfth-century monastery and complex of churches. Creeping through a low archway of snowy white tufa, I prowled around the cool, low-ceilinged rooms. In one area I discovered frescoes, faded and worn but exquisite artwork nonetheless. One fresco was a crumbling portrait of a saint. The still-vivid colors of peacock blue, saffron, and crimson made the portrait spring to life. I paused and stared, hypnotized by the ancient work, by the thought of the centuries of people who had been here before me.

Fine art transports me. Ancient communities transport me. Standing there in the caves, studying these frescoes was like combining the Louvre and the Roman Forum, minus the tourists. No one else was around to break the spell. Just me, the cats, and a palpable spirit of the past. A feeling came over me, so intense, so reverent, it silenced my chattering thoughts.

Italy can do that to a person. But this wasn't a sentiment such as the Tuscan countryside or Rome and Venice might produce. The ravaged beauty of the frescoes, like that of I Sassi, was painful somehow—haunting and unforgettable. It jolted me, as if something had reached inside me, grabbed me by my comfortable life, and given it a great shake. The battered fresco in front of me became blurry as tears welled up and spilled down my face.

Why, I wondered, did looking at something beautiful make me feel so sad? And why, on the other hand, did the scene uplift me as well? It was, I decided, just one more paradox here in this land of contrasts. To find precious artwork in a place renowned for its poverty seemed as improbable as its one hundred fifty rock churches tucked into a community that had always clung to pagan mysticism, superstition, and sorcery.

Paradox, I decided, well described I Sassi. The area was both stunning and ominous, its otherworldly enchantment grounded only by its dark history. It had served as both a refuge and place of deep despair through the millennia. And here, deep in the caves, where prehistoric tribes once huddled, now stood a weeping, sneaker-clad, camera-wielding tourist who would hop on a plane and jet back to London in a few days, leaving this world behind. The searing images of the day, however, would be mine to keep.

The paradox of the rocks continues today. There are now two thousand I Sassi residents, and many of them live in troglodyte splendor, with enormous picture-glass windows and satellite dishes perched atop their opulent homes. Ten years' time has brought an increase in tourism and the venues that support it, such as the Sassi Hotel, a compound of caves that offers deluxe accommodations in the midst of Sasso Barisano. Trendy restaurant, *caffé*, and nightclub caves dot the Barisano neighborhood. When Mel Gibson filmed his blockbuster *The Passion of the Christ* here, following in the footsteps of Italian film director Pier Paolo Pasolini (*The Gospel According to St. Matthew*) and a host of others, he brought worldwide exposure to I

Sassi. Matera travel agencies now offer the increasingly popular Passion Tour package, which includes deals on the hotel where Mel stayed (the Albergo Italia, where I stayed as well) and guided tours of the filming locations, including the Crucifixion, the Last Supper, Jerusalem Gates, and the market. Christ, it would appear, has finally continued on to I Sassi—and brought with him the cash.

Although Matera's geographic distance from the mainstream tourist circuit will keep it from becoming overrun, I still wonder what might be lost in the inevitable commercialization process. Can the haunting beauty and the purity of I Sassi remain untouched? Has my I Sassi host started charging for visits to his home? As for myself, I imagine I'll go back in another ten years and attempt to recreate the experience I had. I'll seek out an isolated cave, fleeing the persecution of tourism, in search of that elusive moment of perfect silence, perfect understanding, again. The result is sure to be a paradox.

Kate Adamek

La Signora

The Italians have a saying, "God did not rest on the seventh day; He created Italy." After four years of living in Italy, I am a believer. Here is a country so beautiful, with a cuisine so perfectly palatable, it hurts not to be living there. Breathing the Italian air has the same intoxicating power as sampling her generous wine. Here live a people gifted with such a marrow-deep sense of the *bella figura* (keeping a good face) that even the display window of our small village *negozio* (grocery store) offered an ever-changing visual *festa*, with its bas-reliefs of seasonal fruits, artful arrangements of olive oils, and sculptures of squashes. Unless perversely determined, you are hard pressed to locate any ugliness that stretches more than a kilometer.

How could a population immersed daily in such luxury of

sensation do anything but reflect it back in spirits light with laughter, wide with kindness? Even the renowned Italian over-the-top emoting seems enacted largely for the entertainment of the audience. And even the Piemontese of the north, notorious for their penny-pinching ways, are only so in comparison to their southern countrymen. Up against the Swiss, for example, they brim with generosity.

Yes, there was all that, a place and a people to fall in love with. And then there was la Signora.

La Signora Ferraro was the *padrona* (owner) of our half of a large, renovated former farmhouse on a tiny back street of Revigliasco, a village tucked into the hills above Torino, in the Piemonte region. My husband, our young daughter, and I had moved to Italy, where he would take up the post of headmaster of an American school that served a small population of expatriate businessmen and their families.

La Signora—from early on I thought of her simply as that— owned the half of the house we lived in, as well as the house next door, where she and her husband resided. "Ferraro" was the name etched in brass above the mail slot in that house, but it was neither her husband's name nor officially hers anymore. But the Ferraro side was the propertied side of the marriage, and so, for la Signora, that name took pride of place.

It was only after several months that I learned that the Ferraro who lived in the other half of our house was actually la Signora's brother. As it turned out, the relationship between brother and sister was deeply and apparently permanently ruptured, though no one said why. It would not be long before I learned for myself how such acrimony could come about.

In late October, Northern Italy is filled with the amber rays of a sun slipping south for the winter, and the shops with a rainbow harvest of chrysanthemums. The colors of these flowers could challenge a Botticelli to reproduce the mauve of Mediterranean waters before a storm; the burnt red of Adriatic sunsets; the persimmons, pomegranates, and tangerines at autumn markets; the lavender and lilacs of summer fields; and the rich mahogany, rosewood, and ivory tones found in the furnishings of old villas. And talk about cheap! To buy fewer than a potful of mums for every room is a crime against bargain hunting.

One of those flower-filled mornings, I was going about my usual chores of cleaning up our first meal of the day and planning for the last, when from outside my door came a voice untouched by anything *bella*. "Signoooraaa!" The second call approached from inside the door. I came out of the kitchen to find la Signora standing in my living room, dressed more as peon than *padrona*. She was wearing a cardigan even moths would reject, a hem-challenged skirt and apron, galoshes, and something from a ragbag on her head. Though she wasn't more than average height—just a few inches taller than my own five-foot-two frame—her thick, utilitarian body and wide, large-boned face, with its traces of lost handsomeness, projected presence on a much grander scale.

"Signoooraaa," she smiled. *"Come stai? Ha tutto quello di cui ha bisogno?"*

I smiled back and assured her that we were *tutto bene.*

I was relieved that my beginner's Italian was enough for me to understand and respond to her own Piemontese-inflected speech, but my relief was short lived. After these first sentences, our command of each other's language hit the wall. In my memory, our conversations play back like dialogues between two kindergartners with ideas greater than their tongues express.

La Signora's words were perfectly nice and polite, but my suspicions were raised. This was the first time in the more than two months since we moved in that she had expressed the slightest interest in our well-being.

"*E lei, Signora, come stai?*" I continued the courtesies.

"*Bene, bene, grazie.*" Sure, her knees were giving her some pain. And we are not having enough rain, it's true. But . . . she raised her shoulders and hands in the classic what-to-do gesture.

"*Allora,* Signoooraaa," she added, "maybe you are fond of the fresh produce of the autumn?"

Cautiously I acknowledged I was fond of the fresh produce of the autumn.

"*Dunque!* You must come to where bends the road to Moncalieri. There my husband and I are selling the finest vegetables of the season fresh from our garden. Please, you come. I give you only the best."

Shame on me. Here she was, generously offering me home-grown produce—slaved over through the spring and summer, as I had watched her estranged brother do in the garden next door—and me full of cynical doubt. "Of course I will come," I told her. "Just this morning, I am going to Moncalieri to shop. I will stop on my way."

We were both smiling happily at the success of our communication when la Signora, glancing over my shoulder, dropped her jaw and looked back at me wide eyed.

"*Ma*, Signora! Signora, these flowers—"

"*Sì, sì,*" I said, turning to admire the large pot of mums on the piano. "They are truly beautiful, no? Absolutely *bella!* And so inexpensive! I got five big pots like this for less than twenty thousand lire!"

Her eyes widened even more. Obviously I had pulled off a Piemontese coup—such flowers and so many for so little money.

"*Ma*, no, Signora. That is to say, yes, they are beautiful. But I am afraid, Signora, you *cannot* have them in here!"

"Well, of course, after the blooms are finished I will plant them outside. But for now they look so wonderful inside. They bring the sun into every room," I bubbled along happily.

"No, Signora, no. You cannot put these flowers in the house. It is not, not . . ." here she used a word my Italian was not up to.

"*Non capisco*, Signora," I told her.

"*Ma*, Signora, you *must* understand. Everyone they understand this!"

But I didn't. And I could tell it was not a small matter here, for her face was growing red and her tone purple.

She tried again. "It is not . . . not, *ma* . . . how to explain—not *bella figura!*"

For something to be not *bella figura* may be the worst sin in the Italian cultural catechism. It is why public drunkenness is anathema, why women wear stiletto heels and furs to school plays, why the foyers of homes are often grander than anything beyond them. It is why Italy produced Verdi and Versace, Veronese and Venice. Why there are so many exquisite buildings per square kilometer that if Italy had the GNP of the United States, it couldn't maintain them all. In Italy the cover *is* the book.

"In America, Signora, we often bring potted plants into the house, just like cut flowers," I explained.

La Signora, though, was not interested in my reasons. Sharply for a woman her size and age, she stepped around me, picked up the offending plant from the piano, and stalked out the door with it. Returning inside, she ignored me and headed to the kitchen, sweeping up the mandarin orange blooms from the table, tossing them outside. Finally, spying the plant she suspected I harbored in the den, she marched in there, grabbed it too, and carried it toward the door. There was a moment I believed she was going to charge upstairs and deflower the bedrooms as well. But apparently even la Signora had limits as to how much *brutta figura* (ugly face) she would engage in to preserve *bella figura*.

It's an even call between my indignation and mystification. I follow la Signora out the door as she places the last pot firmly on the ground and turns to face me, arms folded fiercely across her bosom.

My indignation pulled ahead. "*Senti*, Signora. I know you own this house, and *scusi* if you do not like the flowering plants inside.

Ma, it pleases *me* to have them inside!" I fumed, reaching around her for the nearest one.

"Signoooraaa. You cannot . . . to put these flowers in *my* house," she said, as unassailable as the Pope. "It is very, very *male fortuna!* Very. And I do not permit the bad luck to come into my house!"

Now, if anything in Italy can surpass *brutta figura* as a high crime against humanity, it is *male fortuna*. Long before anyone had much time or energy to create the *bella*, fortuna ruled. It could make or break lives lived always a hair from the edge. The pursuit of the *buona* and avoidance of the *male* created whole catalogues of dos and don'ts, complex and mysterious as cave paintings or songs in lost languages.

"*Ma perchè*, Signora? Why are the planted flowers inside the house bad luck?" I may as well have asked why we need air. Surely even in the United States, they "grave" (I think she meant "bury") dead flowers. "But, *ma*, naturally, Signora," I reassured her. "When they are dead, then I will take them outside and put them into the ground."

This was not the correct response. It unleashed a string of agitated Piemontese dialect. I heard the word "*novembre*" mentioned, but this was only "*ottobre*." What was the problem? Now utterly lost on the subject of potted mums and *male fortuna*, I conceded. "*D'accordo*, okay. I will not bring the flowers inside of her house."

"And you will to grave them?" she insisted.

Fine, I thought, fine. I will to grave them, bury them, burn them at the stake. Do anything at this point to get la Signora out of my hair, my house, my sunny morning.

I did not stop at their stand later that morning for any fresh produce of the autumn, as I did not go to Moncalieri to shop. Instead I drove to the American school in the next village, where my husband was headmaster, and sought the source of all esoteric Italian lore, Bianca, his administrative assistant. I told her my story, asked what happened.

"*O, Dio mio!*" Bianca cried in disgust. Bianca was a woman probably close to la Signora's age herself. But while Piemontese-born, she was a city girl, modern, sophisticated. "This is so much old nonsense, silly, middle-aged [she meant "medieval"] superstition!" No one but these hopelessly behind-the-times peasant peoples believe anymore that because on the Day of the Dead, *secondo di novembre*, we bring these flowers, these chrysanthemums, to the graves of our beloved dead, it is *male fortuna* to bring them into the house. Naturally, perhaps you don't want to carry them as a hostess gift when you are invited to dinner. But it is perfectly fine to bring them into your house. Maybe not the bedroom, of course. But the living room, kitchen, study—sure, why not? This Signora Ferraro, she is . . ." She shrugged and raised her eyebrows.

Home once again, I carried the flowers with the caution of a cat burglar one by one back into the house, placing them once more onto the piano, the kitchen table, the study desk. To be safe, I did move the ones from the bedrooms to the upstairs living room. I loved the last splash of summer they brought into the chilling air. I had, after all, no dead in Italy on whose graves to lay them.

This established the tenor of my relationship with la Signora for the remainder of the four years we lived in her half of the family house. When we complained of a stopped toilet, she claimed I flushed tampons down it. Our upstairs water heater didn't work for nearly two weeks before she called in a relative so incompetent that a few months later he electrocuted himself on a similar job in another house. She challenged my use of the postage stamp–sized plot of dirt bordering our patio to grow a kitchen garden, although it previously sat fallow. And she glared at me with dark suspicion over the few missing plums produced by the tired tree growing there.

Her habit of marching uninvited into the house, with her twangy "Signoooraaa!" became entrenched and was always a harbinger of my own *male fortuna*. She didn't trust the cleaning woman I had hired; she fished for information about her brother and his family while darkly warning me of their iniquities. "*Senti*, Signoooraaa. Do you know those people over there?" pointing to her brother's garden. "That son-in-law of theirs is from Napoli!" she said, as if reporting he was a serial killer. Or "That woman over there"—her sister-in-law—"does not wait for the full moon to make her *salsa pomodoro! Madonna!*"

Furthermore, she claimed Cesare and Mariuscia at the local shop would cheat me, and the butcher was a thief. We must not put on our tire chains until we get out of the drive (which, as our street was the width of one compact car, was impossible without causing a major bottleneck). And the one time I did finally stop for the fresh autumn produce she had offered, she charged me more than I paid at the Cesare and Mariuscia's shop, where it was of far better quality.

You might ask why we remained in a house with such an imposing drawback. You need to know the rental property market in the desirable suburbs of Torino—think Upper East Side, New York, or Malibu or Marin County, California. Besides, when not in the long shadow of la Signora, it was a truly lovely little house, full of light and air, with a long view of cypress-ridged countryside and distant Monte Viso from the upstairs balcony.

Underpinning all my encounters with la Signora, to say nothing of our lives in general, was the ceaseless barking of Sulta, the slave dog. Sulta was a giant schnauzer with a life of such unremitting misery that if it were not for his endless voicing of it, I would have felt deeply sorry for him. Pinned into the train-compartment space that was la Signora's backyard, Sulta went for long sieges possibly without food or drink, certainly without companionship of any kind. La Signora and her husband, a man of near invisibility, spent days on end staying down in the city with their only child, a priest. And while normally Sulta barked nearly as much as he breathed, during their absence he barked even more—especially in the night, perfectly timed to coincide with the deepest part of my sleep cycle. And no force on earth or in heaven, other than la Signora, could quiet him.

In the last months of our Italian sojourn, la Signora's absences stretched to whole weeks at a time. After a mild stroke, her husband had been put into a public nursing home, which, to hear it told, was nothing short of a prison with nurses' aides. (And it was told often in Revigliasco, the inhabitants shaking sad heads over the scandal of the Ferraro millions of lire being withheld from his care.) Adding to my own displeasure with la Signora was her decision to sell our home out from under us, prompting a return to the United States and my departure from a place that I loved as I had none other in my life. Now when Sulta broke my night's rest, I heard the trumpet of la Signora's victory in his bark.

One night, weeks from our departure, at 3:00 AM, as Sulta's unrelenting barking broke my sleep, and my husband slept undisturbed beside me, I crept out of the bedroom and downstairs to the phone. Looking up the priest-son's number left in case of emergency, I dialed. When, after long ringing, he answered, I told him in a panic-edged voice that I must speak to la Signora. He asked what it was about. I told him one lie: "A burglar is breaking into your parents' house, I believe. I've seen a light, there was noise," and one truth: "And Sulta will not stop barking."

With lightning speed, la Signora was on the line. "Signooraaa?" she asked worriedly. "*Che succede?*"

"*Scusi,* Signora. I am sorry to disturb you so late. I believe there is a thief in your house!"

"A thief?! *O Dio mio! Nella mia casa?!* But why you are believing a thief is in my house?"

"*Perchè,* Signora, because all night . . . *tutta la notte* . . . the dog has been barking. All the night long!"

"*Ma*, Signora, he is always barking tutta la notte. Are you not always telling me so?"

"*Sì*, Signora, *è vero*, it is true. But tonight I believe it is different. He is barking more loudly. And with more, *come si dice* . . . more *ansiosa*, anxiety. And now, I believe, perhaps I am seeing a light *nella casa*. And maybe a sound, too—from inside!"

"*Una luce*, Signora? *Una suona* from inside? *Dio mio*—are you certain?"

"*Sì, ci credo*—I believe it. *Ho paura*, Signora, very afraid! *Per favore*, send someone to look. *Per favore! Ho paura!*"

"*Senti*, Signora! Listen, do not to have fear. Wait, wait for a moment. I talk to my son."

I waited all right, a glow of retribution filling my petty heart even as my feet chilled on the tiles.

"Signoooraaa?"

"*Sì?*"

"*Senti*, Signora. We are coming up right away, *subito!* Don't to have fear! We come soon!"

"*Grazie*, Signora! *Grazie tanto!* I only hope you aren't too late!"

But my lone triumph, my little payback scheme guaranteed to wreck the night's rest of an old woman and a priest, was later thwarted by la Signora. Less than a week after the "break-in," la Signora was once again breaking and entering my home.

"Signoooraaa!"

"Ah, Signora," I said politely. "*Come stai?*" And then, because I had heard that her long-suffering husband had passed quietly away in the state-owned nursing home, I added, "*Mi dispiace,* Signora, to hear of your husband's passing. My sincerest sympathy." I had already sent a card and flowers—chrysanthemums, of course.

"*Sì, sì,* Signora. Grazie. It was a peaceful death, *grazie a Dio.*" She stood before me, the bereaved widow, shaking her rag-scarfed head. "In fact, that is the reason I am coming to you now. You remember, surely, the night you thought the thieves break into the house? You said Sulta was barking, barking more loud than usual?"

I kept a perfectly straight face. "*Sì, signora. Ci ricordo bene.*"

"We never find anyone, you know. No lock broken. Nothing missing. Nothing. But, Signoooraaa," she nodded at me sagely, "now we know what it is making the *cane* to bark so much. And what is making the light you are seeing!"

This was news indeed.

"*Sì,* Signora, *sì. Senti,*" she dropped her voice to share the secrets of the ages. "*Senti.* That was the very night my *caro* husband was taken into heaven. I am sure Sulta was knowing this. Of course *i cani* are always knowing when someone dies. So, naturally, he is barking in grief and sorrow. And to say *arrivederci* to his *caro* master! And what's more . . . " she paused for full dramatic effect, "I am positive that the light you are seeing was the spirit of *il mio carissimo marito,* my dearest husband, stopping once more at our home to say farewell. Fifty-three years we were married, Signora. Imagine, fifty-three years! *Grazie a Dio,* Signora, you called so we could be together one last time!"

During my sojourn there, la Signora was the *scuro* that outlines the *chiaro*, the *brutta* that by contrast magnifies the *bella* of Italy—the Italy of Machiavelli as well as of Michelangelo. Without her I might have appreciated less Cesare from the *negozio* bringing a perfectly ripened cantaloupe to the door for my lunch one day. I might have begun to take for granted the greater hearts than hers that mostly surrounded us: Gabriella, who taught me to make fresh pasta and gave me a machine for doing it one Christmas; the Baduinis, who invited us every summer to their ancient country villa so we could sit in the late warm afternoon sipping *spumante* and watching the sun slip behind the cherry trees; the friends who brought us a lace tablecloth when invited for Thanksgiving dinner. Those who welcomed us into the sanctity of their families to share hours of talk and laughter over endless courses of food; who rode with us to the hospital when our daughter broke her arm; who fixed our rental car for nothing when it broke down in the seedy section of a city; who day after day struggled endlessly and patiently to comprehend my broken *italiano* without the merest smirk. All those whose grand and small kindnesses made me fall hopelessly in love with a country and her people. Without her shadow, the light of Italy might not have shone quite so brightly for me. For this, I am forever in her debt.

Ronna Welsh

Sweet on Sicily

I've been up since five o'clock, having flown from
Rome to Catania, an industrial city on Sicily's eastern
edge that has long been harassed by volatile Mt. Etna. I'm riding a
near-empty bus through Siracusa, once a prosperous outpost of
ancient Greece, now a university center whose well-preserved
archaeological sites attract tourists. My destination is Noto, a small
town at the island's southeastern tip, known for its countless
Baroque churches and the gelato at Caffè Sicilia, in the center of
town. Corrado Assenza owns this *caffè*, and I am here to be his
apprentice.

I left New York months ago under the pretense of furthering
my culinary career with a string of international apprenticeships—
no small matter. After years of toil in the New York chef trade, I had

begun to lose any sense of my work's reward. In the last few years, I had grown tired of proving my worth with burn marks, flattened arches, and spider veins that map years of strain to my legs. I had watched my passion for cooking get smothered by poor work conditions and get overtaken by my cynicism for celebrity. So I had come to Sicily and, upon the casual recommendation of a well-traveled colleague, to this modest pastry shop in this tiny town. I was looking for an escape from the pressures of work and the accompanying pressures that work put on the rest of my life. In Sicily, no one had great expectations of me.

From the bus, rocky hills, appearing deceptively lush from afar, come into clear view as we wind down narrow roads on the well-traveled route southward. I squint to discern a pattern in the landscape among the small white stones, taupe blankets of dirt, and wiry shrubbery; I squint to make sense of this land, wondering how I might adjust here. But with the growth so random and the land so expansive, I find little visual coherence. Around another bend, canyons and valleys come into immediate view, through which cut a meandering parade of goats. Lacking other meaningful cues, my eyes follow their lead, drifting, aimless.

The heat outside leaks through a rattling window and presses upon my heart, smothering any residual anxieties about having left home. In moments I am far from the noise of thundering subway cars and steel pans slamming stovetops. I am detached from the pressures of a young but uncertain marriage that has suffered at the hands of my career. Looking out the window, I am caught up in a dream of Sicily, a place that paints a romantic picture of desolation, whose reputed problems of poverty and prejudice loom so large that they promise to dwarf my own. Sicily—a place cast so much in the traditions of the past that it beckons escape from the present. "Sicily is magnificent," I'll write to Matthew once I get to my hotel, and then attempt to undo this understatement. "It is affecting, too." How so, however, I won't be able to explain to him for some time. Given my restlessness in our marriage over the past year, this will cause him no end of concern.

My hotel in Noto is tucked behind a cluster of two-story houses facing a courtyard decorated with plants and laundry. Wet socks that dangle on a line between windows provide accidental shade from Sicily's relentless sun. This morning, I take my place at a small outside table and watch two rotund Italian women chat between balconies through a divider of drying sheets.

The manager brings me breakfast, timed with my meek emergence from my rented room. I take coffee bitter—*forte*—served on a tiny plastic tray with a sorry selection of overprocessed, shrink-wrapped baked goods. Sharing a bench in the tiny lobby, we rehearse an impenetrable exchange of words—artful compositions of misinformation fueled by goodwill, sustained by smiles. The precise meaning of our conversation is elusive to me, but the emotive element is obvious. After a lengthy break in banter, I take leave for the pastry shop.

Corrado's English is impeccable. He learns quickly that my Italian is not, his shiny, black lacquer eyes forgiving under coarse brows. His charcoal and silver beard stretches with a courteous smile, a graceful sign that will become the hallmark of my visit. Nives, his wife, speaks little English, as does everyone else I meet in Sicily. Her greeting consists of a nod, as if she's sensitive enough to her own language limitations to not draw attention to mine. She feeds me a golden brioche crowned with coarse sugar. I wash it down with oily espresso and sweet almond milk. Corrado's desserts are strangely light, even gelato, even four scoops of it, at 11:00 AM. Chocolate gelato with cinnamon and lemon and orange peel is as smooth and dense as fine lipstick. It is direct, obvious, and committed. It requires no translation.

That afternoon, still on my first day, we visit a friend of the Assenza family. His farm is deservedly famous for citrus fruit, the stuff of marmalades, gelato, sorbet, granita, and cake decor. Under the dense canopy of lemon trees, I help Corrado gather buckets of fruit, relieving him of the bundles cradled in his stretched t-shirt. There are summer lemons that look like large limes, with rinds the color of light fresh peas. We find ourselves keeping company with a trio of lice-dotted stray dogs and a gargantuan pig dressed in shit and hay. The farmer, a man of sixty-some years, is in similarly wretched condition. Droppings of rotted fruit dot the small patch of land.

In the car, I arrange on the dashboard a still life of carefully procured lemons I rescued from inevitable decay. To my display Corrado adds three small oranges, which he pulls from his own shirt pocket, a gesture of a shared sentimentality that overwhelms me.

Down the road, we park by an almond tree to pick pods like fat earthworms dangling from swaying limbs. We grab some and pull at their jackets, exposing the soft seeds inside. A pass by budding olive and fig trees lets me add to my coffer of countryside samples, which I shall take back to the hotel and arrange at the foot of my bed.

A few yards farther in, I stoop beside a patch of wild fennel and begin to saw away at the bramble of three-foot-high stems. They are as wide as drinking straws, tough as bamboo. My thrift-store pocketknife inelegantly rips the stalk in two; the ends look stringy, crude. I chew one. It tastes of celery and bitter licorice, at once minty and medicinal. Corrado sucks the plant's extracts, relishing its juices as if for the first time. Following his lead, I grab several stems to chomp on and scurry up the rocky incline, chasing the sun over the dusty hillside.

With our fennel collected in crates, we pack up the hatchback and continue our drive up the steep, narrow passes above Noto before Corrado grinds the car to an abrupt stop. The seventeenth- and eighteenth-century buildings appear etched from a single canvas of sandstone; they are cherry in the shade, oaken in sun. We're too far up to see the faded sketches on the asphalt of Via Nicolaci, chalk drawings of flowers once filled in with colorful fresh petals from the previous month's spring festival. But I notice the Church of San Nicolo, which rolls out its steps like a tongue onto Corso Vittorio Emanuele. The sun catches a sharp edge of the modest cross atop the cathedral's pediment. Otherwise, the city's glow is tender. The streets of town are framed by the occasional swatch of green, but it's the general continuity of mellow, sculpted stone that renders it beautiful.

We drive toward Noto Antica, Noto's original town, which was leveled in the area's infamous 1693 earthquake; it's now a large plot of ruins. These include crumbled archways, chiseled away by sun and wind, and the remains of modest houses, neglected by all but opportunistic weeds and the occasional tasty plant. I steal some as Corrado laments the government's neglect of the archeological artifacts that surround us. I am emphatic with sympathy, if only to mask a somewhat guilty elation at traipsing between courtyards not partitioned by museum bureaucrats.

The surrounding harsh terrain is marked by hand-laid drystone walls, standing about four or five feet high and two feet across. They separate grazing space from that used for cultivation and serve to redirect water in case of a sudden flood. They are visually striking, too. Like strings of tooth-shaped pearls, they cut through scruffy, khaki land, tying Sicily visually to its more affluent neighbors along the northern Mediterranean shores. Under close inspection, I notice the walls are full of pock marks, deep recesses, and dusty coats, which, coupled with my knowledge of the island's tumultuous history of often debilitating colonial rule, remind me that Sicily is still the region's stepchild.

There are two main takes on Sicily. One view is of the island as a poverty-stricken, mafioso-run, isolated backwater lacking resources and ways of comfort. The other likens Sicily to a cauldron of unbounded infatuation, passion, a place for the sublime and the sanctimonious. In either case, it is difficult to detach feelings from the island. I do resist reducing Sicilian culture to the caricature of fabled excess, but I am nevertheless astonished by its striking beauty and willful spirit. Knowing little Italian, I am clumsy to express my enchantment with the land. Paying close attention is the only way I know how to come close to showing the respect I feel.

Shrouded in tree shade, sage plants dot the landscape like fluffy nests, defying the limitations of a scorching sun and dusty soil. I look about and see them at once, everywhere. Corrado and I grab enough in four square feet of ground to fill all the crates left in his car. Their leaves are familiarly soft but hardier than I've ever seen. Dried branches, skeletons from last season's sunburn, rattle in the hot breeze, making music and dispersing seeds to ensure the herbs' continued residence here. I take a picture of our crated aromatics, a testament to the plants' heritage and our day's work.

On our drive back to town, I am restless to see Caffè Sicilia's kitchen, but I don't show it. Before I am primed to cook, however, I must meet Corrado's children on the way home from school, sit with his mother while he changes his work shirt, and accompany a favorite customer on a walk about town. I will study the Assenza family tree, tracing the *caffè* back through generations, following Corrado's career as a young kitchen apprentice, then as a doctoral student in agriculture, through to his return to Noto to relieve an ailing uncle—his mentor—of the business's responsibilities. Cooking, I come to understand, is less about knowing how to do things than about understanding why one would.

In fact, by the time I get to visit the kitchen, Corrado has little time to put me to hard work. Instead, I taste in rotation layer cakes and gelati. I watch him round over a hefty bowl filled with lightly starched hazelnut cream, bringing a taste to his tongue before setting a whisk in motion to aerate it. Once at full volume—the cream seeming to rise by its own volition—he pours it into bittersweet chocolate domes resembling mammoth truffles. I taste the cream's remains from the bowl, a habit Corrado seems amused, if not flattered, by. It is not the season for making enormous blocks of nougat, so Corrado mimics the process for me, conducting a pastry scraper across the casket-size marble table, which, at Christmastime, would be blanketed all day in boiling sweet syrup. Corrado and I share feelings of mutual good fortune and slip easily into our respective roles of teacher and student. He asks nothing from me, because I have already cast him my rapt attention sustained by an unyielding curiosity, which he accepts graciously. This apprenticeship, unlike some others, requires no typical "in the trenches" time.

Hours later, I eat alone at a trattoria within shouting distance of my hotel. In front of me is a plate of homemade sausage. Just beyond that, a family of eight eats their own antipasto and pours their second bottle of wine. My gaze lingers over one sleeping boy's head. He belongs to someone at the table, though to whom is unclear. Out of the kitchen comes the chef, a fortyish woman with meaty breasts that strain an otherwise billowy apron. She spoons the boy to her arms, as if preparing to devour him for her own meal, and then turns to me with a knowing smile, sensing the envy in my stare. She has shown me what I want before I even know it myself: work that sustains commitments to family, the land, and the community even through inevitable shifts in personal tastes and cultural styles. This wine-induced epiphany I keep to myself, not even sharing it with Matthew that evening on the phone. I need to make sure it gels in the clarity of morning.

The next afternoon, back from another foray into the hills, Corrado and I return to the pastry shop, still cluttered with herbs left behind the day before. Francesco greets us at the back door. He is a deliciously pudgy eleven-year-old on whom I have an instant crush. His short black rug of hair and caterpillar brows suggest his father; Corrado's own hair, graying now, still stands thick on his head. Francesco has his mother's eyes, eyes of the north, brighter and smaller than Corrado's, but of a deep mahogany owed to the Sicilian in his genes. He has inherited his father's charm, despite the bashfulness of youth. I discover later at dinner that Francesco is old enough to be served wine, although the goblet is a little shaky in his clutch. And he eats even the small heads of shellfish and fish with tiny bones, with the gusto of an uninhibited teenager, which Corrado admits, and not without resignation, he is soon to become.

In the main prep room, Corrado and I pass a young man rolling out disks of cannoli dough with the ease of ironing a shirt and with the speed of a champion oarsman. He places a fried shell in my hand. I eat it and ask for another. Corrado smiles, then nods in the direction of a treasure chest into which I stick my head. Sniffing at a week's worth of freshly fried shells, I raise a curious brow. I feel a tug at my arm, and Corrado wrests me from my investigation and leads me to dry storage. Here rest several cardboard boxes of considerable heft. I peer inside. Solid pork fat. My God, I think. They're fried in lard!

With ascending curiosity, I steal indiscriminate tastes from a line of knee-high plastic barrels brimming with an infusion of leaves and flowers. I taste catmint, sage, and thyme foraged on past countryside excursions, possibly with apprentices who had come before me. Some of this nectar makes it into the gift packages that Corrado will slip into my suitcase for my trip home, along with a knobby rectangle of pistachio nougat, honey in another form. Both will remain unopened on my New York kitchen shelf for a while, memories of sweet times well sealed.

It's been two hours since my last dessert, which means that there's now room for another. I eat a *cassatina*. This I can take in only small bites—its layers of royal icing, candied fruit, and pistachio marzipan a triptych of sweet excess—and then only with concentrated coffee. I indulge, later, in plenty of fruit-shaped pieces of marzipan, despite their teeth-chilling sweetness. Oh, and I drink and eat my fill: of almond milk, made from the extraction of oil-flushed nuts; of gelato, of course; and of granita, its fruit base so expertly aerated that the sweet ice falls into a fountain glass like shaving foam.

The lemon granita balances between solid and liquid on my tongue. Like a softly starched shirt, it has body but little stiffness. It is slightly tart and fragrantly sweet, a pale chamomile yellow. The granita becomes a blank canvas onto which I paint images of my days in Noto: the brilliant countryside sun recharging the roots of unprofitable citrus trees, Corrado stooped to collect fallen lemons at risk of rotting, kids and neighbors unloading a car of crates, handsome cooks paring fruit to parts. The citrus juice went to the freezer for granita and then straight into my mouth. It is a privilege to taste so deeply of effort and care, of community strength and personal commitment. Surely, I think, it is a slight to taste any other way.

New York, five months later. I take a break from my shift in the kitchen, where I lead a motley crew of talented cooks. We share diverse backgrounds and have distinct professional priorities. In this kitchen, we host local contingents of students, art dealers, elderly ladies, romantics, and neighbors with their dogs. Restaurant critics hardly find their way here, because our menu does not push the bounds of trends, and the decor welcomes only those who find shabbiness attractive. I am told it is not the place for "serious" cooks, which is exactly why I prefer it here. At work, friends can visit to chat across the counter of our open kitchen. Matthew will sit for dinner next to a table of regulars we have each befriended. Here, personal growth counts as job training, so I still try to take two months off each summer to travel and write. Corrado has taught me to simplify things in work as in life, making room to fit the two together.

Reflecting on all of this, I sit down at the reservation desk to write Francesco a birthday note. I can't remember the exact date, but Corrado promises he'll translate my good wishes at the appropriate time and also forward me his son's anticipated reply. Inside an accompanying package, which includes Pokémon cards, I tuck a copy of a recent photo I found stuck to the pages of my address book. There's Corrado, pointed white cap, starched apron, and creased eyes. Beside him is a *cassata* that I also had tried to frame. I had insisted that Corrado pose beside it; it was gorgeous, and he had assembled the cake for my benefit moments before. His gaze, I now recall, had locked onto something off camera. It was a customer, of course, a cousin, I think, whom Corrado then beckoned to join him and who, in subsequent pictures, with bold gesticulation, obscures the cake from view. I had made more attempts to photograph Corrado with his work later that day, but then cute Francesco, his smile painted with ricotta filling, had interrupted each composition, striking poses for my lens. I never did capture the shot I wanted, but I at least have the one that means the most: the one of Corrado's family and work, evenly rendered.

Amanda Castleman

Roman Traffic Alfresco

All roads do lead to Rome, specifically to Piazza Venezia. Buses blast around the rotary as tiny Fiats dart across the undefined lanes. It's a swirling, sucking whirlpool of metal. And I'm riding the wave bareback on a beat-up moped. This is Italian traffic, alfresco.

Everyone's pumping their horns, so I inch my thumb over and press the red lever. *Parpppp.* My powder-blue Honda Sky emits a sheepish bleat, lost in the great din. But it gives me courage.

I muscle aside a Topolino and shoot off past the Capitoline Hill. Michelangelo designed the spectacular piazza, the Campidoglio, crowning the god Jupiter's crag. A statue broods there on the *caput mundi*, the head of the world. Eleanor Clark described it best: "Marcus Aurelius on his famous plump-bellied bronze horse, whose forelock was going to sing to announce the end of the world and may still," she wrote in the superb and shiftless 1950s travelogue *Rome and a Villa*.

I salute the true philosopher king and veer southwest, sweeping past the apartments cannibalizing the Theater of Marcellus; the queue of Japanese tourists at the world's most inscrutable sewer drain, the Mouth of Truth (the *Bocca della Verità* at Santa Maria in Cosmedin); then across the muddy, neglected Tiber River, often blond, now emerald, sometimes sultry, ever sluggish.

Caesar Augustus found a landscape of bricks and left it marble. Ever since, the Romans have been cheerfully draping it in wet laundry, football flags, and graffiti. Buildings stack haphazardly, Renaissance consuming medieval, ancient frescoes flaking in basements. They quarried the Forum, pastured cows there, then reverently excavated it as a national treasure. Everything—and nothing—is sacred.

A priest hurries past, sucking on a Coca-Cola, his Ray-Bans perched atop a balding pate. Snatches of opera overlay raw street slang, the market hawkers' chants: "Not stolen, not stolen. Beautiful things, not stolen!" Citrus scents snake past thimbles of espresso and hot slabs of pizza with frayed charcoal fringes from the traditional *forno a legno*, wood oven. Grease-sheer, super-size McDonald's bags pile outside the Pantheon, but fresh-potted violets guard the grave of English poet John Keats.

A thigh-high miniature pony clops in a six-foot-square, flagstoned front garden. An anarchist disco hums and humps under

Monte Testaccio, the textured hill of amphorae shards, the dockyard discards of ancient Roman wheeler-dealers, who shipped olive oil in these vast terra-cotta jars from the Empire's far-flung provinces. A first-century folly, a pyramid, the trendy tomb of nonentity Gaius Cestius, preens a block from the central Piazza San Silvestro post office, a piece of fascist sleekness showcasing steel beams and glass. Puppets and Prada vie in the park promenades.

Soft, ox-eyed icons of the Virgin peer out from almost every corner; streetwalkers stalk below, girdling the city like sirens. These foreign prostitutes are unmistakable in their crude makeup and gaudy scraps of clothes. Little subtlety is employed: Women pose among the dry grass and roadside litter, flashing pneumatic tits and pubic topiary at oncoming traffic.

Ben Hur's cinematic chariot rumbled here. Anita Ekberg's little black dress absorbed the waters of the Trevi Fountain. Federico Fellini defined paparazzi, made *la dolce vita* legendary. Neorealistic film rose and fell like the Empire itself, forever imprinting Western culture. *Mamma mia:* This town pretty much invented Western culture, with a few gifts from the wily Greeks and a sporting late-game assist from the British Empire, which reignited admiration for classical art, literature, and philosophy.

Sunset stains the buildings, already deep hues of ochre and umber, the garnet glow of chianti. Scarlet poppies wash over the ruins. Trees overhang the quiet road as it switchbacks above Trastevere. I pass two military policemen, stiff as cypress columns, the guardian trees of graveyards. The young *carabinieri*—clad in designer uniforms, navy with natty red piping—uncoil. These beautiful boys wave their machine guns, laughing in the summer air. "*Ciao, bella,*" they carol. Was a pat greeting ever so gorgeous? But I gun my mighty 49cc engine, too intent for juvenile flirtations.

I hear the chuckle of splashing water and squeeze the hand brakes, coasting to a stop. The Fontanone, the great fountain of Gianicolo Hill, towers over me, all solemn marble and turquoise waves. I wheel my moped to the overlook, a stone balustrade trailing ivy onto an embassy. And there is Rome, flushed rosy at dusk.

The whole city stretches out below—the crooked, sooty alleys, the prenatal bump of the Pantheon, the gaudy Vittorio Emanuele monument. Honeyed light pours down, coaxing buttery tones from the pale tufa, crisping the umbrella pines, deepening the peacock sky. The mess, the defiant thrum, the glamorous grannies in stilettos on cobbled hillsides: *tutto è perfetto*. The Eternal City is glorious beyond compare.

Henry Wadsworth Longfellow perhaps summarized it best when he wrote:

> . . . *'Tis the centre*
> *To which all gravitates. One finds no rest*
> *Elsewhere than here. There may be other cities*
> *That please us for a while, but Rome alone*
> *Completely satisfies. It becomes to all*
> *A second native land by predilection,*
> *And not by accident of birth alone.*

Puffing tourists crest the hill, gasp in admiration, and race to the edge. These brave pilgrims have seized the day. Carpe diem. They have blazed off the guidebook path, struggled up the steep slope. *Veni, vidi, vici.* This epic view is their reward, a scene not found on lurid postcards, a glimpse of glory that will forever define *la bella Roma* for them. And in the eighty-degree heat, they truly have earned it.

I, on the other hand, drove. I am cool, even refreshed by the breezes stirred by the moped. Sweat stains may foul their t-shirts, but I am ready to swan into the finest restaurant wearing a summer frock, flowing scarf, and absurd high heels (no one said going native would be easy). In fact, an elegant open-air *caffè* lounges right here in the road. The season being summer, Romans colonize the streets, improvising theaters, bars, and outdoor cinemas with Felliniesque fervor.

Il mio motorino lets me dart down to the Colosseum at whim, effortlessly zip over to the Baths of Caracalla for an opera performance (which once starred an elephant until archaeologists nixed this weighty interpretation of *Aida* due to wear and tear on the 1,800-year-old ruins). I coax a friend onto the back and speed off for rich gelato, followed by cappuccino, the foamy *crema* crusted with chocolate powder.

We nip over to see Pasquino, the talking statue under the Palazzo Braschi walls, near the Piazza Navona. A fifteenth-century curmudgeon gave his name to the now armless, eroded sculpture: Romans have been lampooning politicians by this proxy since, girdling his marble flanks in poetic placards. A June 2004 *New*

Yorker snippet captured Pasquino's tirade against Prime Minister Berlusconi's sycophantic role in the Second Gulf War: "Faithful vassal of the Emperor, Silvio, in the U.S.A. yesterday, has returned, and, after licking Bush's ass, recited in Parliament the part he had learned perfectly, entitled: 'His Master's Voice.'"

On a dull afternoon, I touch base with Romulus and Remus, the founding twins, still suckling a bronze she-wolf on the Capitoline. I sip fresh orange juice and Campari—that cloudy ruby cocktail—in a cloister designed by Donato Bramante, currently a *caffè* and exhibition space. Bouncing along the backstreets of Trastevere, I smell leather dye, lemon-laced biscotti, and horse manure from the police stables.

The *motorino* chugs out to architect Renzo Piano's turtle-backed Parco della Musica and circles Richard Meier's fresh casing for the Ara Pacis, the Altar of Peace built by Augustus in 9 BC. I stride the see-through floors of the slick Crypta Balbi Museum, then defy ringworm by petting cats in the nearby Largo Argentina animal sanctuary, where abandoned pets twine through temple ruins. Famished, I cough down ticklish *carciofi alla giudia*—Jewish-style, batter-fried whole artichokes—in the old ghetto. I swoop down to the Vatican and check on St. Peter's. Because I can. This is how to experience Rome, not slogging along in a baseball hat and sneakers, amid locals' sneering and snickering.

Freedom and adventure, as always, exact a price. Driving in the Eternal City is scary; some might say terrifying. The traffic is infamous for its exuberance—and lawlessness. And we're not talking quaint little mishaps, à la Audrey Hepburn in *Roman Holiday*. These drivers do whatever they please, all the time.

The attitude is nothing short of Machiavellian. Any opportunity is grasped, consequences be damned. Everyone—from the crucifix-clasping, black-swathed widows down to the urchin pickpockets—is looking out for numero uno. The Italians even have a special word for this ruthless self-gratification: *menefreghismo*, the state of not caring. It's all done with great verve, however, as Eleanor Clark explained:

> *What makes these streets Roman, and not those of any old European city, is the demonic energy that goes into everything, and the divine disregard for any other form of life . . . also an element of miracle in the way the motorcycles and other traffic get through, shooting straight from hell, without anyone's changing his expression or pace or direction at all.*

Absolute disregard for authority fuels the chaos. "Rules are just serving suggestions in this country," an expatriate friend once mused. Writer Folco Zanobini agreed:

> *The Italian conception of legality is, on the whole, more elastic than rigid. A prohibition, a misdemeanour, an illegal action can all be circumscribed and rescaled by many exceptions.*

Indeed, vehicles hurtle through pedestrian zones, blast up and down one-way alleys, and quadruple-park, blocking entire squares and streets. Mopeds speed on the sidewalks or sputter under the weight of entire families. It's not uncommon to see scooters on the school run, small children wedged between their parents' legs, sans helmets.

Religion, it seems, contributes to the Mediterranean mayhem. Many devout Catholics place themselves in the hands of a loving God, then floor the gas. If it's time to die, the Lord's will be done. If not, they'll live to drive another day.

"They simply fail to realize the dangerous nature of the scooter, the fragility of the vehicle," Giovanni Catanzaro, a municipal police chief, told *Wanted in Rome* magazine. "Their behaviour is superficial, excessively offhand. They're careless. They think themselves immortal. They don't respect pedestrians, they overtake on the left and right, the highway code doesn't exist."

Even the most basic road signs are open to debate. Urban legend claims the mayor of Naples was asked to explain a traffic light. "Green obviously means go," he replied. "Red means slow down and proceed if it looks safe." He stopped with a self-satisfied air.

"And the other bulb?" a journalist prompted. The mayor shot right back: "Yellow? The yellow, my friend, is there for gaiety."

Many drivers share this cavalier attitude; others are just plain ignorant. No special training is required for the less powerful mopeds. In fact, no license at all is required for a 49cc model, like my crusty hand-me-down Honda. It's quite humiliating, really, being cut off by pimply fourteen-year-olds on new Vespas. I resign myself: These *bambini* were born on the mean streets, I'm a day-tripper.

But I've got the bug. Driving in Rome is dangerous, but it's also sublime. The locals are aggressive speed freaks, but they are all the more alert and honed for it. And traffic engineers are even aping the Italian experience now. "Chaos = cooperation," cried a December 2004 *Wired* article entitled "Roads Gone Wild: No street signs. No crosswalks. No accidents. Surprise: making driving seem more dangerous could make it safer."

È vero, absolute control is needed to navigate the absolute confusion. All my senses spring alive as I float through the traffic, flashing by the aqueducts, shattered columns, and Baroque domes. My worries melt away. My heart swells.

That old tart, the Trevi Fountain, with its splayed nymphs, accepts bribes, according to Jean Negulesco's 1954 film *Tre Soldi nella Fontana* (*Three Coins in a Fountain*). Tradition claims one coin—cast backward over the left shoulder—ensures a return to Rome; two bring love; and three, a wedding in the Eternal City.

My motivation won't be the art, the ruins, the fine wines and food, however precious. No, my euro is for another shot at Zen and the art of moped mayhem.

Marguerite Rigoglioso

The Rape
of the Lake

There is a lake, of waters clear and deep,
Not far from the walls of Enna, called Pergo.
Even Cayster never heard
Such singing of swans, so many have nested here;
With dark branches, a wood gives shade,
Encircling the lake as though to defend it:
Here flowers always bloom, winter never falls,
Here eternal spring smiles . . .
    —Ovid, *The Metamorphoses*

Writing in the first century AD, Ovid immortalized Lake Pergusa, a body of water that can still be found in the very center of Sicily today. Once the jewel of this Italian island, Pergusa's waters are neither clear nor deep; its swans are few in number; its forests have receded; and its flowers have been replaced by an auto racetrack that encircles its entire three-mile perimeter like an asphalt noose. Lake Pergusa, which Italian scholar Enrico Sinicropi as recently as 1958 called "an enchanted place where dream is easily confused with reality," is slowly dying, the victim of man's assault and neglect.

It is May 1997. For the second time, I have come to Lake Pergusa, drawn by a vague but persistent calling. I have learned that this lake is the very spot where the Greek Goddess Persephone was separated from her mother, the grain Goddess Demeter, and was abducted into the underworld by her lecherous uncle, Hades. It was here that the earth opened up as the maiden picked flowers, swallowing her in a stunning instant, her arms flailing, her mouth gaping in a silent scream like some figure from Picasso's *Guérnica*. It was here that the grief-tears of Demeter fell in such profusion that they gathered to form an eternal pool of water.

Persephone and I are intimately acquainted. Her story took up permanent residence in my psyche when I was ten years old, the moment my grandmother told me my mother was gone, dead of a heart attack brought on by her deterioration from lupus. Like Persephone's, my hell descent began with one sudden blow of mother loss.

Recently, I have discovered that Persephone and I are linked in another way as well. Sicily was given to the maiden goddess as a gift from her father, Zeus. Sicily was "given" to me by my father, too. Both of my paternal grandparents came from the old town of Corleone, making me a genetic daughter of this ancient land.

The first time I came to Sicily, last year, I was on a pilgrimage of sorts. I was investigating the remnants of worship of Demeter and Persephone that was once widespread in the land of my ancestors, beginning with the arrival of the Greek colonizers in the eighth century BC. I crept about the island, seeking out the Goddesses' twin, circular stone altars, their ancient temples, their clay busts in museums. I was searching for proof of a truth that had been slowly emerging inside me: that Demeter was much more than just a fictional character.

It was then that I met Yvonne Kohler, a writer and artist who had left her native Wales twenty-five years ago and had been living in Sicily ever since. Her most recent project was running a small bed-and-breakfast on an organic farm with her Sicilian husband. A practicing Buddhist and an eminently sensible and intelligent woman, Yvonne told me she believed Demeter was a living consciousness. Given Sicily's strong connection with grain growing (it's called the "bread basket of Italy"), she considered Demeter to be the most powerful "landowner" spirit of the entire island. One year during a brutal drought, she and a Tibetan lama had fashioned an image of Demeter to help call upon and focus protective energies as part of a rain ceremony they conducted, and the skies had finally opened. I tingled as I listened to Yvonne; it felt as though she were giving me the final "permission" I needed to embrace Demeter as a living presence in my life.

I am back in Sicily with the sense there is something more I must uncover, a message of critical importance to understand. On this particular day, the bus leaves me on the main road that runs through the little town of Pergusa all the way up to the mountaintop town of Enna, where the high overhang called La Rocca Cerrere, Demeter's Rock, still holds the remains of a temple to the grain deity. It is from this rock that Demeter looked out to Lake Pergusa and, no longer seeing Persephone playing by the banks, began her agonized search for her beloved daughter, turning the fields barren until at last she persuaded Zeus to bring the maiden back. Demeter's rock offers panoramic views of almost the entire island: rolling hills, green and amber waves of grain, slate-blue sky, and snowcapped Mt. Etna to the far east, its volcanic plume arching into the sky.

Demeter's Rock looms in the far distance as a young woman directs me toward Lake Pergusa, which I am visiting for the first time. The approach is startling: a wasteland of corrugated steel walls, a paved roadway some one hundred feet wide, and an empty grandstand. This is Pergusa's autodrome, the racetrack that is used for high-level Formula 3000 races. The shrill peals of motors make the birds nesting in the lake's thick reeds scatter in flight. I find a small opening in the racetrack wall and see the banks of the lake. But it is not a lake anymore. It is more like a swamp.

I walk and walk along the racetrack, looking for a better point of entry, a place to perch, meditate, sit with nature, but none appears. It is hot under the Sicilian sun. The asphalt broils beneath my feet and stretches before me like an endless highway. I realize that I cannot sit by the lake, simply because one can't anymore. Its banks have been closed off to admirers by the mechanical tangle of the autodrome; the lake's glassy surface is visible only from the hillsides above.

Yvonne has told me that the building of the autodrome in the late 1950s and early 1960s violated national and regional laws prohibiting construction close to a public body of water. Money from the races has always gone into the pockets of a very few, and despite the efforts of a handful of enlightened citizens to peel off the steel and concrete, the moneyed interests have continued to prevail. As I contemplate the environmental violation before me, I realize that Lake Pergusa is a place where the Feminine is still being raped. Money-hungry businessmen and corrupt officials have seized this delicate piece of nature and ravaged her, just as Hades did Persephone. I wonder what has made people unconsciously reenact the drama.

I take a bus back to Yvonne's farm. She tells me about Maria Cimino, another practicing Buddhist who is tirelessly working to save Lake Pergusa through her efforts with the World Wildlife Fund. "She really believes the lake is a sacred place," Yvonne says. As she speaks, I feel a strange pressure on the top of my head, as though a hand has been placed on my crown and is bearing down.

I know I must meet Maria. Plans that would have taken me out of town suddenly fall through, and I find I am available to attend Yvonne's Buddhist gathering two days later. Finishing up my shower that morning at Yvonne's, I hear someone burst in and plop down on the toilet. We introduce ourselves with the curtain between us; it is Maria. We are soon talking with ease. When I ask about the lake, she launches into a passionate and well-informed discourse. I stand there in the stall, dripping wet but mesmerized by her words.

The only large natural lake in the center of Sicily is Pergusa, says Maria. The lake was formed thousands of years ago, most likely by a sudden sinking of the rock layers that left a huge basin in the earth. It may well be this event, she conjectures, that later became transmitted through folklore as the story of hell swallowing up the maiden. Rainwater and tricklings from the rock strata filled the cavity and remain the lake's only sources of water. The lake's geochemical properties, including its saline water, make it a microcosm of the ocean and therefore a fascinating place for scientific study. Renowned even up until the last century for its incredible diversity of flora and fauna, the lake remains an important bird nesting spot and a key point along the European migratory routes of many species of waterbirds. Perhaps most remarkable of all, Lake Pergusa periodically turns a deep red color. For this reason Italian professor A. Forti, who studied the phenomenon in 1933, named Pergusa "the lake of blood."

Maria tells me about the dance between microorganisms and sulfur that at unpredictable intervals results in this natural cleansing process, which goes back as far as any of the local people can remember. Standing naked in the shower, I am trembling not with cold but with excitement. I have a deep sense that this cyclical reddening of the lake is very old. It is probably no coincidence that Ovid named Lake Pergusa in association with the Goddess. He must have been expressing a cultural memory of the original, pre-Greek goddess religion that centered around the lake. Yes, I think, this lake has been turning red for millennia. The ancient peoples of Sicily held the life-giving processes of the woman's body as sacred, saw any manifestation of red in nature as symbolic of the menstrual blood of the Goddess, and must have seen this periodic reddening of Lake Pergusa as a powerful blood mystery.

I am filled with an inexplicable sensation of recognition, as though my deep memories of a past I cannot quite recall are jumping inside me like sparks. I understand. Lake Pergusa, hallowed place of my ancestors, is one of the most potent nodes of Goddess energy in the world, and She is crying for help.

I finally step out of the stall with a towel draped about me and meet Maria face to face. I have met a Priestess of the Lake, though I am not sure she's fully conscious of her role. Maria continues her impassioned speech, describing the ecological deterioration that has taken place in only the past thirty-five years. The concrete of the racetrack prevents the lake from being able to expand naturally, she says, while the intensive building of homes and their accompanying wells and sewers are draining the basin of its water. As a result the lake, which was fourteen meters deep in 1860, is now less than two meters deep. Pollution has disturbed its chemical equilibrium, leading to the extinction of most of the fish species that once populated its waters. The shrinking of the lake, poaching, and other kinds of shooting sports have led to dramatic reductions in the bird populations. Any legal victories on the side of environmental allies have been suspiciously skewed or overturned in favor of the moneyed lords of the racetrack. Maria tells me that she herself has received anonymous death threats because of her work to save the lake.

"Maria," I say, "would you take me there to conduct a little ceremony, a prayer to help save the lake?" By the next morning, our spiritual task force has grown to include Yvonne and two American friends of ours who are also staying at the farm. We drive to Maria's house in Pergusa, a half hour away. Traveling along an access road that runs parallel to the lake's racetrack, a snake passes in front of the car. In two trips to this island, I have never seen a snake. I take its appearance now as a sign: The serpent, an ancient symbol of the underworld, is intimately linked with Persephone. The Latin form of her name, Proserpina, means "first serpent."

We arrive at Maria's house, which is separated from the lake by a hillside. She has converted much of her yard into kennel space that houses thirty-five stray dogs she has found roaming the countryside. Inside her house is another dog, a cat, and a dove that lives peaceably in her bathroom. Maria emerges from the bathroom with the bird perched whimsically on her head. I recall a vase painting I've seen from seventh-century Greece of a goddess surrounded by earth's creatures: dogs, birds, snakes, fish. Yes, I think, in Sicily you can still find people who carry the old religion in their bones.

Maria has suggested we conduct our ritual at an abandoned church nearby. The church, four or five hundred years old, was built next to the entrance of a cave she believes was once an important cult site to Demeter and Persephone, and perhaps even a place of worship to the original pre-Greek goddesses. Old pagan practices, she says, were carried into Christian times in the form of celebrations like the feast of the Christ of the Lake, which had taken place every year at this church until 1935, when the festival migrated to a local village constructed under Mussolini's auspices. The church was deconsecrated and left to ruin.

Maria climbs into the car with her accoutrements for our ritual, including a photo collage of her Tibetan lama and Buddhist deities. Just before we get out, another snake slips in front of the car and quickly disappears into the brush. No one notices but me. I smile. Maria directs us two hundred meters down a dirt road to a makeshift fence made of wood and barbed wire. From the fence we can see the remains of the old church, flanked by a tall, wide tree. To reach the church we trudge through tall grass filled with burrs. As we approach we can see that the old building is now nothing more than four roofless walls of crumbling yellowish stone and mortar. Stepping through what was once the doorway, we enter an interior that looks like a miniature forest: trees everywhere, plants clinging to the walls, and bushes covering the ground. We make our way to what was once the altar, passing through brambles that reach out to leave stinging welts on our arms and legs. Clearing out a place on the ground, Yvonne and Maria assemble a Buddhist altar of brass water bowls on a yellow cloth. In a special pot to the side, they light a small fire, breaking up the burning wood into coals. The rest of us place personal objects, symbols, and pieces of jewelry on the altar.

Yvonne hands out sheets of paper with a special chant for a

Surngo ceremony, a Tibetan Buddhist offering ritual to honor the local spirits. She and Maria begin the prayer, the rest of us stumbling as we follow the phonetic pronunciation. When we've finished the chant, Maria speaks. "The person who cuts his roots is destined to die, like a tree," she says somberly. "We're in a society that is denying, nullifying, and forgetting the past. We are in great danger. Lake Pergusa is a place of tremendous historic, religious, and cultural importance. We ask the Spirit of the Lake to help restore serenity, silence, peace, and prayer to this place. We ask that the racetrack be peaceably removed so that the lake can flourish as it did in the time of Ovid."

"Amen," we all say.

Yvonne and Maria throw a flour-and-butter mixture onto the fire as an offering. "The deities like things that smell nice," Yvonne explains. "There are spirits that actually live on smoke and smells." We watch in silence as the mixture sizzles and turns black, throwing fragrant gray billows of smoke into the air. When the smoke dies down, the ritual is completed.

I think of Demeter, hoping She will be pleased.

Epilogue

The battle to save Lake Pergusa continues today, even as local government and private supporters of the racetrack oppose our efforts. Faced with the lake's lagging restoration, Maria Cimino has assembled a committee of scientists to offer their expertise, and I've collected 122 international signatures on an appeal letter to send to various government officials in Italy and Brussels.

It is difficult to watch this ancient and sacred lake shrink. Perhaps divine intervention will yet save it: When I launched a website on Lake Pergusa (www.lakepergusa.org), the first support sounded from Italian Americans who practice *stregoneria*—or Italian witchcraft—which, many say, survives from Italy's pre-Christian religions dedicated to Demeter, Persephone, and other Greco-Roman deities.

Fran Davis

Stonework

Waking in a stone house in Umbria, I listened to the mutter of wind, the click of rain on wooden shutters. Against the stone walls, the rain was almost soundless—so different from a wooden house, with its creaks and moans. I sank deeper under the quilt, burrowing in like a nested bear. Inside, the house was soothing solidity, a shelter in the earth's bones. The falling rain was a long sigh, streaming in darkness along the tiles, nearly silent, only the roused sleeper listening.

I am still listening to inner sounds, still divining, trying to get a hold on Italy. Instead, the hold—part poem, part dream, all enigma—is on me. Every night the same dream visits me: I circle, stepping over ancient stones, loose cobbles. Vines cascading over walls block my way, forcing me to backtrack in search of another path. There are no people, no sounds, only rock and vines, and the earth that I know is Italy. It's a dream of frustration and dead ends. The blocked path of the dream mirrors my experience in Pierle, a tiny town at the edge of the Niccone Valley. A ruined castle loomed over the town, its broken parapets and gaping windows begging for exploration. But all the entrances were sealed. I stood at the castle's base, gripping the rusted steel of a barred door, and peered through at tumbled stone and walls curtained with ivy. Just as my entrance to the castle was barred, I know that in some essential way I've failed to penetrate the mystery that is Italy.

You can linger a few weeks in the Italian countryside, live in a stone house on a farm, drink cappuccino under chestnut trees while the nuts fall around you, eat the lovely crescent-shaped pasta of Gubbio, but they are only teasing glimpses, like a series of stills, hinting at life lived in a different mode, on different terms. Always there will remain something unknowable about Italy, something very old and very alive.

In Siena, where I lodged in a medieval building, I lay in bed every morning and gazed up at the ceiling. The crossbeams high above were eighteen inches square, ending at the wall in carved corbels, nicked and scarred from several hundred years of remodeling. I tried to envision the pulleys used to lift such enormous beams, the straining men, the hands of the workmen who carved the wood, but the weight of my imaginings—all the work and masonry and wood—came crashing down around me. I was just a woman lying in a bed, staring at a ceiling, insignificant as a fly. Italy's past, its long history, can do that, flatten you like an insect, especially if you're from a new place, a country in which the oldest things standing are not buildings but trees.

Tuscany left me dazzled and enthralled. I was constantly catching my breath at the first sight of a fortress town in the slow, glittering light of autumn, or a Romanesque abbey that was already occupied and aging well when Columbus left home with a gleam in his eye and the urge to travel. Tuscan roads followed the spines of the hills, as if balanced there. On either side, plowed fields of golden soil plunged away in sensuous curves. Surveying those fields, I wondered about the men who worked the plows. As they ripped open the golden soil, did their thoughts run toward restitution, the curves they would inscribe on the hillsides? Did they dream of the seeds they would sow, the wheat, sinuous and whispering under a crackling sun, the warm loaves they would eat?

What Italy invites the traveler to do is guess. And guess again. But guesses are like a fist of wheat grains thrown into the wind. Whether any of them fall to earth, take hold, and bear the fruit of revelation is a matter of chance.

Oak-forested and slumberous, the province of Umbria was a respite from vivid Tuscany to the northwest. Rivers flowed slow and easy through fields of corn, tobacco, and peppers. Ranks of dried sunflowers stood by the road, their tilted faces like rusted clocks. We settled into a rented converted barn—my husband and I and two old friends. We fell into the rhythm of days, woke to look down on the bowl of mist that was the Niccone Valley, and watched it dissolve in the sunlight. We made morning runs to the village of Mercatale for fresh bread and *cornetti*, little horn-shaped breakfast pastries. We ate grapes from the vineyard outside the gate and bought salami and olives, tomatoes and pears at the coop in Umbertide. The farmer who owned the barn sold us wine and olive oil and, when the weather grew chilly and the rains came, firewood.

We spent our days exploring, filling an endless need to suck up as much of Italy as we could. We drove miles to see towns, churches, views, castles, ruins. When we found the portable stalls and awnings of a weekly market, we shopped with the locals, observing the things they bought—clothing, curtains, cookware, vegetables, and cheese. My friend Joan and I imagined staying forever, learning Italian, buying clothes in the markets—knits in plum purple and shoes with lethally pointed toes. In the evenings we drove home to our kitchen, our beds, windows shuttered against the rain, a fire in the fireplace. It was a haven, an island in a sea of sights and sensations. I felt lulled but never settled. There were constant reminders that I was a stranger: I couldn't understand—or comply with—the landlord's admonition not to feed the starving farm cats who cried at our door each morning. The hot water heaters in our flat seemed to turn off and on at will. The superfluity of keys perplexed me, every door and cabinet and chest with its own particular key. There were scorpions hiding under chairs and luminous, flying beetles that bumbled into my hair. And there was gunfire in the woods.

Autumn is wild boar hunting season. We saw hunters gathering along the roads—a dozen or more cars parked in a clump, dogs in cages, camouflaged men with bandoleers warming their hands around a morning bonfire. We watched their preparations. The hunt for wild boar—*cinghiale*—is an elaborately staged event. Men with bright orange vests pulled over camouflage shirts took positions every fifty yards or so along the road. Most were unarmed, serving as spotters or beaters to drive the fleeing boar back toward the shooters.

I grew up in a family of hunters in rural California. My father went out alone, or with my brother or an uncle. Witnessing a group hunt, Italian-style, was a novelty. Judging by the number of gunshots echoing from the wooded slopes, the method was grimly effective. Our landlord assured us that boars were plentiful. Their mounted heads decorated the walls of meat markets and delis, staring out with beady eyes at the prosciutti hanging from ceiling hooks. *Cinghiale* in stews and sauces appeared on most restaurant menus. And, for a parting taste of Italy, the Florence airport shop sold wild boar salami.

We learned why it took a small army to bag a boar. Male boars can weigh 145 to 400 pounds. Black-bristled and strong-necked, with a head like a wedge, they're easily riled, and their tusks can be deadly.

I never saw the boar in the woods, so I imagined him. Nocturnal, solitary, he rests in thicket so dense the air is dusky even in daytime. At the sound of barking, he raises his heavy snout. He's on his feet by the time the dogs arrive. In the distance, the men, graceless, noisy, crash though brush. The baying dogs thrash their way to the boar's lair and harry him through the undergrowth, leaping and dodging away, snapping at his hocks. Taller, stronger, he whirls and fights, pivoting on his light hindquarters; perhaps he rakes a dog with a tusk, draws blood. Eventually the dogs drive him from protective cover. He runs from the darkness, where he has always been safe, toward the light, where the men are. He's a black streak, high on his feet and fast. But men are everywhere among the trees, surrounding him, shouting, waving branches. Wherever he turns, the way is blocked.

If hunting wasn't of necessity a group effort, Italians would probably do it en masse anyway. They obviously enjoy doing things together, especially celebratory things, like festivals and competitions. In Siena we just missed *Il Palio*, a ferociously competitive horserace around the main piazza, but the signs of ongoing celebration were everywhere. All of the seventeen competing districts, the *contrade*, were festooned with lanterns, insignias, and shields emblazoned with their emblems: goose, rabbit, panther, drum. In the *contrada* of the ostrich, we came upon a church square awash in confetti and paper, tables and chairs, flying horse figures, shopping carts draped in checkered plastic, huge silver bowls, and clusters of enormous grapes. It was like discovering an elaborately prepared set for a play that had just finished its run. Along the narrow streets of the *contrada* of the turtle—this year's winner—men were bringing in trees and constructing arches and ornate stages, columns, and pavilions for a weeklong victory celebration.

I'm not sure that attending the celebration, merging with the crowd, tasting the food, drinking the wine, would have brought me any enlightenment. The roots of *Il Palio*, and the ancient rivalries it feeds, run too deep, more than eight hundred years deep. I try to imagine what it would be like to be a twentieth-generation Rams fan, for example, and the layers of trappings and rituals, superstitions, and strong convictions that would accumulate over so much time. Perhaps it would be something like *Il Palio*—a competition of ancient origin staged so often, so long, and so passionately that it became an institution, one that defines the people who participate, who keep it alive year after year through pageantry and celebration.

The lesson I drew from *Il Palio* was to look backward to try and understand the present. So I did my American best. I tried to penetrate the mystery locked in stone that surrounds everyday life like an aura, one that Italians wear as easily as skin.

In the fortress city of Perugia, home to an annual chocolate festival, I paid a euro to visit the Etruscan well. Entering a stone vault, I followed a winding flight of steps down to the well shaft, where I stood on a dripping catwalk and looked into echoing, moss-rimmed darkness. High above lay the street where Peruginos were setting up booths for the chocolate festival. The well is as old as its city: three thousand years.

Nearer the city walls, dark caverns contain the remnants of another city and its churches, streets, and buildings. Escalator shafts snake through sections of this ruined city, carrying people back and forth from the parking lots and the new town below. Peruginos barely glance at the ghost city as they pass. It is briefly noted, merely a staging area between escalators.

I breathed the chill air of ancient caverns and passageways in

Siena, Assisi, and Orvieto, where an Etruscan city of the dead is scraped into the porous tufa. All of the old mountain towns, the fortress cities, have their undersides, tunnels and suites of rooms, chapels, and grottoes carved out over the millennia. Beneath the cathedral of St. Francis in Assisi, where the Giotto frescoes hold spellbinding sway, is another church, and deep below that, where ventilators rumble like the breath of some gigantic beast, lies the tomb of the saint himself.

Walking the hill towns, I began to regard the earth under my feet as skin draped over ancient bones. I studied maps of cities and imagined a dark efflorescence beneath the gridded lines—the shadow cities below. They were the hidden roots, a town's covert underside, the yin to newer yang. Mystery caverns, repositories of funeral urns and carved marble caskets, hollows where old secrets settle like dust: Sibylline and ancient, hidden yet enduring, they were the feminine counterpart to the hard masonry of the architecture above. Visiting the underworld places, I felt the pull of time beneath my feet like gravity.

How do Italians cope? I wondered. How do they maintain a sense of time and perspective, living with all these layers? I managed to ask an Italian about that fine balance. What was it like to walk every day on the roofs of history? His shrug was unreadable. "It's just there," he said. "Like you and I."

In America, this new world, we're excited by excavations into our brief history. We have Underground Atlanta and Underground Seattle. Old signs and gaslights, broken crockery and inscribed bricks give us a spooky thrill. Italians don't visit their past, they coexist with it; they walk with ghosts, reuse their stones, copy their earthenware.

Italians seem secure with the stewardship of their ghosts. Their streets are old and sure, the paths well marked. Living among stones cut and set in place by generations of ancestors confers a sense of continuity and strength, permission and perspective. Their culture is founded on rock. That rock may be washed by tides, by the blood of armies, but it is always there, along with the path and the people.

To travel in Italy—to drive the roads, eat the food, settle in one place—is to occupy a comfortable room where you are a temporary guest. I left with little understanding of what makes the Italian heart tick, what passions drive the feuding *contrade* in Siena, what archaic voice calls the hunter to the hunt, what thoughts flit through the heads of the young women carrying the statue of the Virgin on a feast day. I left without understanding, but I left altered. It was as if I had tried to probe time, plunged into darkness only to be driven back by light. I may have failed to read the passion inscribed in the stone and earth of Italy, but I live with its vibration.

Beth Schommer

Largo Colle Aperto

For a living, I organize the complicated logistical aspects of Italian scientific research missions into Asia's Himalayan and Karakoram Mountains. I use Italian with government ministries and alpine guides. I use English, my native language, to make arrangements with people whose mother tongues are Burushaski, Urdu, Sherpa, Nepali. A darted mountain goat just died? A Polish trekker has acute mountain sickness and needs a helicopter rescue? Just leave it to me; I'll take care of everything, threading back and forth from English to Italian, weaving a solution to nearly any problem. At work, not just my nationality but my pragmatism and proactive thinking have earned me the title *l'Americana*.

Yet there I sat in my car in the middle of Largo Colle Aperto, a sort of square on top of an open hill in between Bergamo's urban lower town, Città Bassa, and its medieval-walled upper town, Città Alta. There in the heart of this Dantesque purgatory, neither *bassa* nor *alta*, I sat, stalled. Stuck. As *tharn* as a *Watership Down* bunny frozen by oncoming headlights. Unable to get out of the car and walk into crowded La Marianna, the oldest and best *gelateria* in Bergamo. Unable to stop one of the proud Bergamaschi, strolling like tourists into and out of the walls of their Città Alta. Unable to walk up to the man at the newsstand waiting to pay for his pink *Gazzetta dello Sport*. Unable to say I need help: *"Ho bisogno d'aiuto."*

I'd been on my way to run a series of carefully orchestrated errands lined up on a mental map to optimize travel time between locations scattered across a town split in two. It was already past 5:00 PM by the time I left home, navigating the hairpin turns that led from my green, semihilly neighborhood, Fontana, just beyond lower Bergamo's typical European radial city spread, up the northwest flank of Città Alta. I entered the outer bulwark of the old town (upper Bergamo was once the farthest outreach of the Venetian Empire and today is home to some of the most sought-after real estate in Northern Italy) through Porta Sant'Alessandro, an arching stone gate watched over by a bas-relief St. Mark's Lion bearing an open book in its paws, supposedly a sign of peace. There were still two and a half hours before the storefronts would be sealed with that final Saturday clang, that ringing threat of no more errands in this country—a country that has yet to stoop to 24/7 anything. I had already successfully completed point number one on the itinerary: Stop at the newsstand in front of La Marianna, the only place besides the train station (definitely out of my way) to get an *International Herald Tribune* weekend edition, which contained my Sunday treat, its crossword puzzle.

There sat the paper next to me on the passenger seat. I'd parked at the bus stop, hopped out of the car with hazard lights blinking, handed over my two euros, and dove back into the driver's seat, all in less than a minute. Next on the list was a drive down the hill and out of town, through Bergamo's creeping industrial sprawl to the cheap wholesaler where my Italian boyfriend and I had ordered our light fixtures more than a month ago. I buckled up, reached for the steering column, and turned the key. *RRR-rrr.* I turned the key again and pumped the gas (which I know damn well you don't do with automatic fuel injection). My lovely white Renault Clio had played this trick on me before: The engine would sometimes just mysteriously resist turning over. I only . . . needed to . . . keep . . . trying . . . *RRR-rrr!*

Rap-rap-rap! An old man in an outdated gray suit and hat stood at my window; his cronies watched from the nearby bench. I rolled down the passenger window. *"Basta!"* he shouted. "You're going to flood her!"

My best answer came out an exasperated "I know, but I don't know what else to do." Then a younger man, waiting at the bus stop, took advantage of my window being down to launch a heavily sarcastic, *"Ma la BENZINA, c'è??"* My next great answer: *"Certo!"* Of course there was gas in the car! I rolled up the window, and both men turned away, their thoughts nearly tangible, identical: Woman Driver. I shuddered and turned the key again.

I was becoming the subject of a humbling and at times terrifying Italian pastime: staring. Worse, I was on the brink of making a *figura* of myself. Few anxieties are more paralyzing here than the threat of public humiliation. It became clear that I was a borderline spectacle: Buses were pulling up behind me, and I was having to wave them past. The passersby were watching hungrily at each of my failed attempts to get the engine to turn over. I heard kids from a high school–age scooter gang laughing boisterously. At me?

Why hadn't my car stalled in a more innocuous locale, like in the parking lot of an Esselunga supermarket downtown, or in front of the calm, helpful, organic co-op that followed the light fixtures on my list? No, I was stalled in the middle of an illusion recreated by the locals weekend after weekend: This was Città Alta, and I was interrupting their subconscious fantasies of other times and nobler destinies. The growl of my engine was breaking up the orchestral, *bella figura* hum of emperors, crinolines, monks, and cannons that the old town's villas and walls exuded, in which the Bergamaschi swam like happy fish. "Poof! Welcome back to the real world!" my engine seemed to say.

Their stares burned into the nape of my neck, not just because this was a country of watchers, but also because I was disrupting their privileged pseudoexistence in this well-preserved monument town. Later they would drive back up their mountain valleys or down into their agricultural plains to humble suburban villages. But these people had come to Città Alta and certainly didn't want some foreigner sitting in the middle of one of the best vista points with a car that wouldn't start. As I tried to ignore the staring, I too began to feel some clung-to illusion fading, eluding my grasp, a mist beginning to dissipate, and fear rising in my gut.

In between attempts, I tried not to watch the time seeping away on the dashboard clock. At 18:00, I thought, *I'll still make it.* By 18:20, I knew I'd be giving up on the stop at the organic co-op that followed the light fixtures on my list. The thought of no fresh goat cheese or whole grain bread to go with the spinach frittata I'd planned to make for dinner left me feeling even more unaccomplished. Defeated and nearly desperate, I began mentally scanning the freezer for frozen pizza, my palms hinting cold and sweaty. I concentrated on my breathing, practicing nonattachment to the groceries and, finally, also to the light fixtures. By 18:40, it was "Will I be going *anywhere*?" I tried to remember the futility of time and remain calm. "Come on, you've been in worse situations." *RRR-rrr.* "You've studied yoga for a third of your life." *RRR-rrr.* "You spend a quarter of your life traveling internationally for work. You've trekked through the Himalayas, for God's sake!" I was getting upset. I would not get upset. So what if my car was stalled? Things like this are perfectly normal—they can even be funny. I tried to laugh, and a weak smile came out, then passed. The words of Sogyal Rinpoche, Eckhart Tolle, Guru Buddha, my yoga teachers, were floating through my mind, as ineffective as eggs that wouldn't attach to the uterine walls. What was going on?

I considered calling my boyfriend, who had gone sailing for the afternoon. We had finally decided to move in together, had identified common goals and shared values, and had found a near-perfect rebuilt farmhouse in the fields that lovers swooned above from Città Alta. Yet I resisted that unexpected, weak-sounding inner voice suddenly urging me on: *This is his turf, let him fix this car problem, you've got someone to rely on now, go ahead, surrender.* Digging in the glove compartment, I found my expired ACI membership (the Italian version of AAA), then the number of the Renault dealership mechanic. After several rings, a man picked up the phone. "Sorry, can't help you. We are closed on Saturdays."

I gave in and, renaming my voice of weakness the sage voice of pragmatism, dialed my boyfriend's number, only to get that mechanical female voice: *"Messaggio gratuito, il telefono della persona chiamata . . . "* His cell phone was switched off.

While trying calmly to consider my options—and coming up blank—I found myself dialing his parents' home. I hated the thought, but hadn't his mother just phoned me the week before "because your own *mamma* is too far away to check in on you properly"? I know, I know, what was I thinking baring vulnerabilities like that, especially to an Italian *mamma* who has entrusted her son to me? But unlike my own folks five thousand miles away, my boyfriend's family was conveniently located right down the hill in Bergamo *bassa*. His dad, Gigi, was an efficient little handyman who I was sure would be happy to come to rescue his son's foreign girlfriend, look under the hood, and know what to do—or at least he would take me away from Largo Colle Aperto, that place of limbo between the upper town and the lower, that last wide-open junction where the protective city walls meet the (dangerous?) freedom lying beyond.

There was no answer.

I got out of the car, searched the faces of the people walking by. Not a glance in my direction, no offer of help, not a question. I got back in, leaving my door open like an invitation. It's not that I was too shy to walk up to someone, to open my mouth and speak in Italian. Although I still have an accent, my Italian is even laden with the marked singsong cadence of the Bergamo dialect. By now, I'm actually (almost) used to the worst that can happen when speaking to a total stranger: that complacent smile, that *"Non sei italiana?"* That look of curiosity, animosity, that moment of indecision. Sometimes a reward: "You can barely hear her accent!" or a fleeting condemnation, *"Ah, si sente!"* that, for a split second, strips you naked . . . *non sei italiana*. Ah, yes, I can hear—you're not Italian.

Maybe I had flooded it and should wait. I tried to let five minutes pass. I scanned the headlines of the *IHT*, opened to the funnies, flipped to the crossword, then closed the paper. After ninety seconds, I turned the key again. Nothing. A whole part of who I was seemed to have vanished—that me who could trek to Everest alone, that me who studied eastern philosophy in my free time, that me who could take care of myself. That me who two years before had traded in her public transport pass and red one-speed Holland bike for an Italian driving course and a stick shift car. That me who'd recognized in this Northern Italian town a comforting balance between the earnest work ethic of my earthen Dairyland background and the *va bene così* Italian culture I'd grown to love, that divine ability to say "it's just fine the way it is" to almost anything.

I began to redial my boyfriend's number, over and over, obsessively, until I finally got through. "Just ask someone to help you push it into a parking space, go for a walk there in Città Alta. I'll come pick you up in about half an hour. We can get a mechanic to look at it on Monday." It was then that I unraveled, started to cry. I tried to keep the tears out of my voice, but he either didn't notice or pretended not to, just reassured me he was on his way: *"Stai serena, arrivo."*

For eleven years I've done it on my own. Sure, there've been other boyfriends, boyfriends' families, roommates, friends, people I could say "I need a favor" to. But I had spent eleven years in this foreign country, moving every year or two, changing perspectives, changing jobs, changing towns, changing hobbies, "ain't gonna pin me down." And now I couldn't think to ask for help to push the car off the road? What was happening?

Recently I'd begun longing for roots, you see. Permanence. Stability. Family. I blissfully ignored any implications that might have on my independence. My boyfriend and I, both successful grownups, had simply run out of patience shuttling back and forth between two separate homes (his in Città Bassa, mine in Città Alta) and agreed to make just one for the both of us. We'd begun to talk of family, even to consider ourselves one. Why not go back home to the United States, where I already had a family (parents, a brother, a nephew)? What? After all these years? Go crawling back? No, instead I'd begun to look around me, at the ones who'd stayed, fifteen years, twenty years, twenty-nine years, thirty-five . . . women born in one place who'd be buried in another, who called two distinct countries "home." Who'd willingly divided themselves in two, generally for love, spreading their homes across the continents in honor of an ideal meant to unite. I observed these women, by now comfortable in their foreignness, even if their accents might still be thick, merrily cackling when they got together once a month, their sacred meetings seemingly enough, a place to unleash their own language as if casting magic. Women able to don their otherness with the same relish as a dog rolling on a cool summer lawn, scratching that itch they couldn't otherwise reach.

I was on the verge of becoming part of that group. My boyfriend, we . . . no I . . . I was deciding to stay.

Would that entail my becoming enmeshed in the social fabric of this walled town? As I sat in my car, stalled in between two places, still outside the walls of Città Alta but too high to be in Città Bassa, I saw myself standing just outside the decision to consider myself here permanently, yet certainly no longer here temporarily. I was at the threshold of commitment to a person, to a place, that would entail, eventually, relying on others from time to time. I saw myself addicted to the control that went with self-reliance and felt my fist starting to let go. Would I be able to walk into those stone walls looming above me and relax in their protective embrace, giving up the freedoms without for the security within? Would the people here want to let me into those walls, designed to protect from outside invaders? Would the often walled-minded Bergamaschi—the hard-working conservatives who reluctantly accepted foreign tourists or laboring immigrants only to the point at which they wouldn't over-run their jewel of a town—welcome an outsider as one of their own? The lack of response from the engine to my key in the ignition became my own silence in answer to the question: Where do I belong? And in my solutionless frustration came a resounding: What am I doing here, anyway, wanting to put down roots in this foreign place, yet tripping over them as if settling down would entail relearning to walk? The answers felt as obvious, yet as elusive, as say-ing: Push the car to the curb.

The older man of the three I had asked to push me was super-ficially nice, trying unsuccessfully to be patient. By that point, I was slamming on the clutch instead of the brake, pulling the hand brake to a halt in a panic, and I couldn't get the steering wheel to turn. I looked like all the things I had cultivated my persona to avoid: flus-tered, foreign, *incapace* (incapable). *"Mi scusi, sono un po' scombussolata da tutto questo,"* I spoke to the man who avoided the tears welling again in my eyes, telling him I was disoriented, dis-combobulated. My accent was a caricature (was I exaggerating to get pity?), but he didn't comment. Wonderful word, that *scombussolata*. It feels like: *My compass is all messed up, the needle spinning like a planet out of control, a planet rotating through space—coming apart, or being formed?*

Then I was finally out of the car (it had been pushed into a Colle Aperto parking space, miraculously empty and rarer than gold on that breezy hill) and was walking alone now inside the walls, through the crowded narrow streets of Città Alta. The age of the cobblestones themselves was comforting as I rode the tide of window-shoppers, mostly locals, with a smattering of foreign tourists: a blond German family, guidebook in hand, and a fist of loud American college students with enormous backpacks borne like turtle-style shields. Although the obvious outsiders were stared at and observed, the impeccably dressed locals were ignoring me as if I were one of their own. Wandering compassless in a river of people then, I became free to be nowhere, identify with no one. The anonymity I'd sought since I first left Big River, Wisconsin, was unleashed in the crowd, and meeting no one's eyes, I was free to be neither here nor there, unlabeled, unbranded. I was curled into myself, like when I used to travel by train, nose buried in a book, ears plugged with music from my Walkman, ignoring the indignant complaints of the Italians for every minor flaw in the train's running. The train might stop in the middle of nowhere, as Italian trains were apt to, but I would turn to the window, stare out into the black, and remain oblivious, caring only to hide that my book was in English, to avoid the inevitable *"Sei straniera?"* (Are you a foreigner?) The same way I would avoid being pigeonholed by whoever was sitting next to me on my frequent intercontinental plane trips: "Oooh! You live in Italy! How exciting! George, did you hear that, she lives in Italy!"

Walking past the windows lined with focaccia, I could erase my links to any recognizable social fabric. I could be anyone, needed no one. A mystery. Free.

The downside? I stopped where the crowd thinned out in Piazza Vecchia, at the heart of the walled town, and walked to the now-familiar central fountain. Still dazed, I watched the children crawling on and off the fountain's decorative lion heads and heard the pigeons flapping as they swooped among the outdoor *caffé* tables for crumbs. How could a flooded engine have drowned my independence? Or had I been flooded with waters released to cleanse a heart opening to love, a heart that was splitting, like a seed that needed to split in order to put down its threadlike root and send its first green shoot skyward? It's true, no place I now called "home" would really fit perfectly right again, like the favorite jeans you rarely wear because they pinch at the waist and rub at the crotch if you sit for too long. Choosing to settle down would not take away that otherness I cultivated as much as I preciously hid it. But why did it hurt to ask for help, to be torn between baring and hiding my foreignness? Why was it so hard to admit I hadn't been able to think of the answer on my own, to admit that safety nets were made of love and place and social fabric? Did those other foreign women, the ones who'd stayed, ever stall and drift?

With only my newspaper to show for the afternoon, I waited for my boyfriend there, on Largo Colle Aperto, where the roads from Città Bassa and Città Alta endlessly flow into and out of one another. We walked to the car, he opened the hood, jiggled a couple of wires—just, you know, to see. Of course, it started on the second try: *RRR-rrr-RRRRRRR* . . . I felt raw, skinned alive, tender flesh exposed, too much so to laugh when he smiled.

Ann Lindsay

Italy of the Poets

Open my heart and you will see,
Graved inside it, Italy.
　　—Robert Browning

The fuel consumption needle indicated that we were at the end of the reserve tank as we cruised up to the Italian border. With only a few more yards of France to cross, we were loath to cash another traveler's check into francs, in those days before widespread use of credit cards at gasoline stations. As we sat in the long lineup of cars waiting to cross the border, a hitchhiker we had passed a few miles back drifted up to the passenger window.

"Your rear tire is flat, lady." He almost seemed pleased. Of course it was pouring again, so I held the umbrella over David while he changed the tire. Our first stop in Italy was a gas station, an appropriate enough introduction to a country that has a love affair with anything on wheels. In these dispiriting circumstances, I took stock of the past six months. We had jumped from the security of teaching positions and health insurance benefits in Canada into the creative chaos of a year's worth of camping in Europe. *The Oxford Book of English Verse* had been our guide on a literary pilgrimage from John o'Groats to Land's End. But once across the Bay of Biscay, the land of wine, olives, and sunshine had closed the books. St. Tropez and the French Riviera just didn't seem like the place to be reading Milton. Our bodies had begun to separate from our minds. We were on a Gap Year from our careers.

That first night in Italy, we slept in an empty parking lot on a hill overlooking the Ligurian Sea. In spite of this prosaic entrance to the Italian Riviera, we found ourselves turning back to the poetry books. It couldn't be helped. Italia had been the home of Byron, Keats, Shelley, and the Brownings for many years. Like a mother, it had nourished them with the inspiration for some of their greatest poetry and then had wrapped them in death. I understand the attraction. Coming into Italy always feels like returning home. Not because Western civilization originated in the forums of the caesars, but because the people seem so comfortable in their skins. Whether it's a bent signora scrubbing down a sidewalk or a golden goddess with silk-draped legs flung over the side of a motorbike, they are at ease with themselves, in the moment, the place where poetry happens. They seem to be everything we were not; although we were more or less awash in verse that spring of 1969, our lives lacked poetic intensity. As we stared through the rain-streaked window of the van, we decided to let the poets lead us across the top of Italy to the Adriatic coast.

Genoa, the birthplace of Christopher Columbus, admired by Charles Dickens, later designated the European Capital of Culture for 2004, probably merited a stop. But since every one of the campsites nearby was closed, all we remember of Genoa is an industrial seaport under glowering skies and blurred by the swish of windshield wipers. The next stretch of road could not be driven on a rainy night. The Bracco Pass is a tedious two-lane highway with steep gradients. In desperation, we pulled in past a *CHIUSO* sign swinging from the gate of an empty campground. A workman was hosing down the washrooms. "The weather is no cooler here than it was in Spain or France. Why are there not more campsites open?" We encountered our first Italian shrug, accompanied by hand movements slightly different from those accompanying French shrugs. Then he waved us over to a spot under a tree with a view of the sea and our own newly cleaned private washroom and bade us *buon giorno*.

The next day's drive brought us to the outskirts of La Spezia, where the poet Percy Bysshe Shelley had spent the last few months of his life. The only campsite was on the outskirts of town, a muddy field with some chickens and a large black dog. It was as though this shoreline had been infected by a blight, causing patches of decay that spread down to Livorno. Beaches were either dull, commercial, or vulgar, with peeling pink changing huts emblazoned with grand names—Florida, Eden, Roma—alongside Coca-Cola signs.

David viewed this sad landscape as a personal insult to his favorite poet. "Poor Shelley would drown himself again willingly if he could see how squalid parts of this coast have become." From a castle at Lerici on this section of the coast, in July of 1822, Shelley had set sail in his small boat, the *Ariel*, to visit friends at Leghorn. In his pocket was a copy of verses from *Adonais*, the elegy he had penned on hearing of Keats's death in Rome. It contained the lines:

From the contagion of the world's slow stain

He is secure.

At this point, we did not feel secure from the world's stains.

The *Ariel* was caught in a Mediterranean storm, which washed Shelley's body ashore a week later. The authorities buried the body immediately in quicklime and sand, afraid it would "pollute" the beach. Lord Byron and Leigh Hunt burned it some time later to quell fears of plague. Shelley's hopes for a world made beautiful by the enlightened rule of imaginative legislators lie buried with his ashes near Keats in the Protestant Cemetery in Rome.

The Italian Riviera has improved its image in the past forty years, but I'm not sure that even now it's what the Romantic poets had in mind. The stretch of beach north of Leghorn, near Marina di Masa, where we pitched camp for another disgruntled night, was particularly seedy. Garbage and cheap restaurants littered the bay from one end to the other. We had refused to stay in two other places, virtual mudholes that were asking more per night than the havens on the Costa del Sol. It was time to abandon the coast, turn inland, and take the autostrada directly to Florence. We entered Florence from the west end of the city, but our guidebook indicated that the municipal campsite was on the eastern side. Even the most hardened philistine could not have remained unaffected by the barrage of art we encountered in that drive across Florence. Because art has been fused to the commercial life of the city since the days of the Renaissance artist/craftsmen, it impacts on every level, from museums to market stalls. It permeates small craft shops down dusky alleys, infiltrates trattorias and bars, shines from the goldsmiths' windows on the Ponte Vecchio, soars above the city in the red-tiled dome of the great Duomo. So I should not have been surprised that the municipal campground was actually beautiful. After a succession of dismal overnights, it was indeed a treat. High on a hill within the city limits of Florence, we parked amidst cyprus and spring wild flowers. The pathway down to the hot (!) showers was very romantic; ivy curled over the edges of old slabs of stones, and the way was dotted with pieces of ancient chipped statuary, fragments of columns. A fountain niched into an old stone wall dripped with greenery. The grocery store sold grappa.

Comfortably settled at last, I set us a rigorous sightseeing schedule for the first day—a tour of the vast Palazzo Pitti in the morning, followed by a visit to the fifteenth-century Palazzo Guidi, where Elizabeth Barrett had found shelter with Robert Browning after fleeing from her tyrannical English father. "Best not to wear those new shoes." David was referring to the beautiful soft brown leather pumps (with matching bag) that I had bought in an attempt to appear Italian. Three hours later, having ignored his advice and tramped the miles of marble in the Pitti, I hobbled up to the massive doors of the Palazzo Guidi, clutching the brown bag and my injured pride. Elizabeth christened their suite of rooms within the palazzo Casa Guidi, to add a coziness to the only home they would ever share. I tried to imagine these rooms behind the elegant arch of gray stone where she had written her *Sonnets from the Portuguese;* bore their son, Pen; and died, content with the new life she had found in Italy. The quote at the opening of this essay is engraved on the walls of their son's palazzo on the Grand Canal, where Robert returned to die.

I pulled open the massive doors, eager to enter their love story. Inside Casa Guidi were several apartments, with a sign indicating that the historic one was up a flight of stone steps. On the Brownings' door, another sign informed the visitor that the opening hour was 4:00 PM. Since it was only 2:00 PM and my feet were throbbing, I had to be satisfied with a photographic memento. David took a picture of me inside the archway, brown shoes neatly together, brown purse fondly cradled. We weren't meant to dress like visiting academics and gaze at these poets' manuscripts behind doors in Italy. Robert Browning's love of the Italian landscape had sent him out into its streets and countryside, where he found the dramatis personae for his monologues. His characters spoke forcefully in the idiom of the time, leaping from the pages like the young scamp in front of us, kicking his soccer ball against the walls of Casa Guidi as our shutter snapped.

I changed the fashionable footwear for a pair of comfortable sneakers and headed down the dim backstreets of Florence where Browning had found the furnishings for their apartment. In a warren of small workshops, craftsmen still forged iron chandeliers, chipped inlaid designs for marble tables, and decorated wooden chests. The open squares were lined with stalls offering high-quality gilded wooden trays and mirrors, hand-dyed marbleized writing papers, and decoupaged boxes. Even though these vendors were basically operating souvenir stalls, their merchandise had been arranged with the same care given to diamonds in a Cartier case. Smaller items were neatly piled in rectangular wicker baskets and arranged by color or textural compatibility, as structured as a verse in *terza rima*. Browsers left with a respect for the merchandise even if they had not made a purchase.

In one of the crumbling corner buildings, a tortoiseshell cat sat on a pile of books in the dusty window of an English bookshop. As I approached to stroke her, the proprietor spoke from behind a pile of used books, "We call her Molly because she prefers to settle on that pile of James Joyce's work." Under the cat's curled body were Joyce's epic tales of wandering and introspection. In the sort of odd illuminating flash that he favored, I realized that he had strung together routine daily occurrences and small domestic scenes to forge a new sense of self in what have come to be recognized as the greatest works of twentieth-century literature. There was a chance that Italy could become our Dublin if we celebrated the poetry of the everyday.

Florentines were instinctive masters at yoking the mundane with the sublime. Piazza della Signoria, with Michelangelo's marble *David* and Cellini's bronze *Perseus*, might pass for an outdoor gallery if it weren't for the fact that soccer games, political riots, and celebrations of municipal life regularly take place here. A scene in E. M. Forster's novel *A Room with a View* dramatizes this juxtaposition of the abstract with the concrete: A culturally inquisitive English heroine sets out for a day of sculpture-gazing with her Baedeker guidebook in hand, only to find herself involved in a brutal local squabble on this very public open space.

This connection between the world of art and the life of the street was also evident inside the Uffizi Gallery. When I think of our visit there, I cannot separate the collection from the setting. Botticelli's *Primavera* would be no less a work of genius were it hanging in an airport, but viewing it suspended between a painted beamed ceiling and a marble floor seemed to catch its spirit. From the windows lining the long galleries, Florence under blue skies was more beautiful than the paintings. At the end of a sunlit gallery, an elegant marble lady reclines, with all the time in the world to gaze on the Arno at her feet. It was a hauntingly beautiful interaction between static sculpture and living city.

Just beyond her, out of the window, I could see a corridor linking the art of the Uffizi to the commercial world on the shop-lined

Ponte Vecchio. I coveted a black silk dress splashed with vivid long-stemmed red tulips and brilliant yellow daffodils in the window of a tony boutique on this bridge. It was in my nature to feel guilty about admiring an object too much. My profession dealt with concepts. But it seemed fitting that a corridor should link the Renaissance masters to the black silk dress on the Ponte Vecchio. They would have enjoyed painting a courtesan dressed in it. Italy was helping to melt the distinction in my mind between thoughts and things.

On our last day in Florence, we stood under an open arch of the covered Ponte Vecchio, looking up the Arno toward a range of snow-covered mountains. David gasped, "We have to drive through those brutes tomorrow on our way to San Marino." It was our intention to camp at the top of this hill fortress before plunging down to Rimini to dip our toes into the Adriatic Sea.

The short run north along the coast from Rimini to Ravenna reminded us of those first few sad days when we had just arrived in Italy. As we drove through an area bleared by countless funnels belching sulfur fumes, petroleum factories, and oil tanks, I bleated, "Don't tell me we're camping here tonight."

"No, the guidebook says that there is a campsite near Lido di Dante. We're going through his hell right now. Brace yourself for the purgatory of the suburbs."

These allusions to Dante's *Divine Comedy* reminded me that the primo Italian poet finished off this epic in Ravenna before dying there in 1321. The campground at Marina di Ravenna was *paradiso*—a fragrant pine woods near the sea. David suggested that we go up toward the Basilica di San Francesco in search of Dante's tomb. His intensity of emotion, his dreams of a united Europe and the enlightenment of its peoples, had brought many of our English poets to Italy centuries after his death. When we found the tomb near a secluded garden off a lovely square, we opened a bottle of trebbiano di romagna, wine from the region where he rested. Like Browning, Dante had been another man of the street, writing in the vernacular of his fellow citizens, fusing lofty visions with the minutiae of daily life. Stretched out in the tall grass, we drank to the message in his *Paradiso*: Ultimate paradise comes from inner peace.

The British Automobile Association guidebook calls the road to Padua a flat, monotonous road skirting the Euganean Hills. We broke the monotony with an excursion into these volcanic hills. After a climb up a narrow gorge through vineyards and woods, we were delighted to find ourselves in the small village of Arquà Petrarca, where there are two signs in the plaza. One directs you to the house of fourteenth-century Poet Laureate Petrarch, and the other to his tomb. In exile from Florence, Petrarch traveled across France, wrote sonnets to Laura that influenced Shakespeare, and went on to climb Mont Ventoux. An early humanist, diplomat, and scholar, he set the parameters for the Renaissance man and earned his resting place here among the Euganean Hills. Near his pink marble sarcophagus, we lunched on a mortadella panini and looked out on the same scene that had prompted Shelley to pen the poem *Lines Written among the Euganean Hills.*

Where we saw only a benign spring day, with the warm Italian sun swelling the buds on this ancient hillside, Shelley had seen a future of tyranny under Austrian rulers and ruin for the cities spread below on the plain of Lombardy. His prophesies for the two cities where we were headed, Padua and Venice, were of special interest:

> *In thine halls the lamp of learning,*
>
> *Padua, now no more is burning;*

David set a challenge for the trip into Padua. "Let's see if the lamps of learning are still burning in Europe's second-oldest university."

Statues of scholars, poets, scientists, and philosophers bordering the canal in the heart of Padua would normally have set the tone for this city of learning had they not been upstaged by the huge striped circus tent sharing the square with them. We squeezed around an outdoor table with a group of circus clowns who recommended the local spritz—equal parts prosecco, soda, and Campari. The crowd pouring out of the big top led us into a central quadrangle, dominated by the highly decorative Palazzo della Ragione, originally a hall of justice and now the center of a lively market area. Its surplus of balconies, fluted columns, arches, and filigree made it seem more like a palace than a food market. On either side spread the fittingly named Piazza della Frutta and Piazza delle Erbe, six rows of parchment- and oyster-colored canvas tenting, under which carts sold vegetables, shoes, and crockery.

In a shop window under the pale ochre stone colonnade, rows of freshly made pasta lay like skeins of yarn on steel trays. Behind the counter, a woman was bent over a marble slab, kneading egg, flour, and water to make a ball of dough. Using an elongated, tapered wooden pin, she began to roll the lump into increasingly thin layers until it was almost translucent. This was cut into tagliatelle and fettuccine noodles. An assistant lovingly shaped tortellini and wide slices for lasagna. We bought some ravioli stuffed with pumpkin and a container of their famous *ragù*, known to the rest of the world as bolognese sauce. Under the shadows of the statues of scholars around the canal, we set the pasta to boil and heated the sauce on the camping stove.

"Oops. We forgot to check on the lamp of learning."

"That's all right," replied my mate through a mouth full of pasta. "We can report to the poets that the streets are bright with life." The Italians were teaching us how to treat public spaces as our living room and poets as very human companions.

A quick map check that night confirmed that we could reach Venice the next day. We opened the poetry book again to see what Shelley had to say about this Queen of the Sea:

Sun girt City, thou has been

Ocean's child, and then his queen;

Now is come a darker day,

And thou soon must be his prey.

Since those prophetic lines were written in 1818, the sea has been steadily claiming more of Venice. Our campsite was on the mainland near Mestre, so we had plenty of opportunities on our daily runs into Venice to check the accuracy of the poet's prophesy. The narrow causeway connects the polluting twentieth-century factories of the mainland to the eleventh-century treasures of the Venetian Republic. Byron's lines that refer to a palace and a prison on either side of the Bridge of Sighs could apply to these two larger landscapes. As we crossed the finger of land connecting the golden Byzantine domes of *la Serenissima* to the prison of industrial waste opposite, we sighed all the way.

Byron had boasted of swimming the canals, climbing onto the terraces of *contesse,* riding horseback on the sands of the Lido. We opted to board a vaporetto for a ride across to the Armenian monastery of San Lazzaro, where the poet had studied with the monks twice a week. In a cloistered garden setting, a library, small museum, and study rooms are home to treasures, including books and manuscripts used by Byron. The visit offers the reflective side of a poet we usually consider a Don Juan, plus the bonus of a dramatic view of Venice and its domes from the lagoon as he would have seen it in his quieter moments.

The market under the arcades near the historic Rialto Bridge is serviced by canal barges that unload produce onto floating docks. In a quick half-hour's shopping trip, we picked up *vitello de la mare* (a variation on tuna), ropes of garlic and red chili, yellow tulips and mimosa, spinach-stuffed ravioli, and a hunk of parmesan. The intensity of this market drew us back every morning. Vendors sang to each other and arranged Cézanne still lifes while dealing with customers in a friendly banter. "That red lettuce and those broad beans are grown on the island of Erbosa, just out in the lagoon. You can't get fresher than picked this morning before sunrise." I loaded my basket with the ingredients for a pot of minestrone. The butcher shaved off beautiful slices of veal scaloppini, then suggested we stop in at the tiny bar next door for a *cicchetti e ombra* (snack and white wine). In this town, the snacks could be stuffed squid or a toasted *crostini* with *baccalà* (a creamy spread of salt cod and garlic). My epiphanic moment came as I reached out to stroke the sardines spiraled against each other in a circular wooden box at a fish stall facing the *caffé*. Ezra Pound's *The Study in Aesthetics* had materialized right there in front of me. In this poem, a young street urchin named Dante hears his friends call out when a woman passes, *"Ch'è be'a"* (That's beautiful). He makes the same exclamation when he sees the sardines rowed up in their boxes. Beauty, harmony, is recognizable in fish as in women. Ezra Pound died a recluse in Venice but a champion of modern aestheticism. Our challenge would be to integrate this sensibility into the way we made our living.

The month that we had allotted to see Italy in this year of travel was drawing to a close. April was to find us heading north to Austria. We hugged the coastal route that ran toward Yugoslavia, a more attractive stretch of coast at that time than the Riviera. Dark green pine trees bordered cliffs that plunged toward the teal blue Adriatic. There was a well-equipped campsite a few miles before Trieste, at the small village of Sistiana. Caravans fringed the rocky shore and sheets flapped in the breeze, which meant that hot water would be available. We soon had our laundry line strung up with the others, and the van, our clothes, and ourselves soaped down for the upcoming northern adventures. David set off to explore the large caves honeycombed with gun emplacements and returned with some surprising news. "At the camp store I picked up a map of a walking trail along the cliffs that leads to the site of Duino Castle, where the poet Rilke wrote while visiting the owner." I knew nothing of Rilke or his writings. Since *The Oxford Book of English Verse* was no help with a German poet, we went into town in search of a bookstore.

Trieste stands at the crossroads of two empires on the border with Slovenia—not fully Italian, still clinging to memories of its importance as an Austro-Hungarian port. We spent hours ambling along streets lined with elegant Austrian belle epoque buildings. The art nouveau warehouse on the wharf that holds an aquarium and a fish market almost made us forget our mission. The owner of a small bookstall explained to us that this most cosmopolitan of Italian cities, where European cultures mixed, was the perfect milieu for Rilke. We carried a book of his poems to a *caffé* on the canal. He clinched our Italian experiences in his "object poems," crystal-clear descriptions of things from small wildflowers to large cities, which could only be appreciated, he maintained, once you had run the gamut of experience. Perfect. In between smelling the roses and admiring the architecture, we had been filling the van with collectible pieces of old kitchenware, intrigued by their honesty of design and their usefulness. Italy's poetry for us sprang from the sensual, the concrete. Rilke completed our transition from romantics to retailers. When we returned to Canada, we opened a kitchenware business that specialized in objects that were "noble, nude, and antique," a bit of inventory advice from the poet Swinburne. This may not have been the interpretation Rilke had in mind, but it kept us happy for the next thirty years.

Perhaps it was because we had found our métier that Trieste appealed to us. We sat for a few sunny days by the sea, eating pastries and drinking valpolicella. Or maybe it was because this city had attracted modern exiles, the most renowned being James Joyce. In a series of rented flats here in the first decade of the twentieth century, he wrote *Portrait of the Artist as a Young Man*, a definitive comment on the interior journey in search of the self. My journal records that we felt at home here. The poets had steered us into a comfortable niche.

Susan M. Tiberghien

Emilia's Petition

I met Emilia one September afternoon when I was waiting at the village corner for the schoolbus. We were living
in Comerio, near the lakes north of Milano.

Our youngest child was toppling out of his stroller, and Katie,
soon to be three, was pulling on my hand. Emilia joined our trio as
if she belonged.

"Do you wait here every day?" she asked me in English.

"No. I take turns with my neighbor." I wondered where she
came from, dressed up like a parrot, a red felt hat plopped on her
head, a plaid bathrobe worn as a wraparound coat. She stood close
and looked up at me firmly.

"What days are your turn?" she asked.

"Mondays and Wednesdays."

"Good. I'll come and wait with you," she said in French, switching from one language to the other without a blink and tapping me on the arm to show it was decided.

So each Monday and Wednesday Emilia would come and wait with us at the bottom of our lane for the school bus to bring home our two oldest children. Our village was halfway between the European school in Varese and the European research center at Ispra, on Lago Maggiore, where Pierre worked.

"Signora, you are American?" she asked.

"Yes."

"And *il Signore Ingegnere* is French?" Her head bobbed up and down with each question.

"Yes."

"And you have four children?"

"Yes."

"And you speak both English and French?"

"Yes."

She seemed to know all about us.

"*Bene*. Everybody else in the village speaks Italian. Now I'll be able to speak some English and some French."

One afternoon when the school bus was late and we had waited together for a long time, I invited Emilia up the hill for a cup of tea. As we walked up the lane, her red hat bounced with each step. I looked closely. An elastic band tight under her chin held it fast. The older children had asked me if I thought she had any hair underneath it. She turned and winked at me as if reading my thoughts.

"Emilia," I said, changing the subject, "where did you learn your French and English?"

"At school in Milano, a long time ago." She nodded her head in agreement with herself. "It was during the war. The first war."

We arrived at the big white house on the hillside high above Lago Maggiore and climbed the stairs to our apartment. Emilia kept on her hat and bathrobe and entered the living room, stopping in front of the bookshelves and squinting at the titles. She took her time, sometimes nodding in approval, other times shaking her head.

"Emilia, do you read English?"

"Yes."

"And French?"

"Yes. And Chinese and Japanese." She gazed out the window to the village and the old church, the red roofs clustering around its steeple, and the cemetery not far away.

"Where did you learn Chinese and Japanese?"

"In China, during the second war."

Emilia told me she had left Italy when she was forty, just before World War II, to go marry someone whom she had never met—an Italian living halfway around the world in China. She was working in Milan for Kodak, and he was working in Port Arthur for Kodak.

"He liked the way I wrote business letters."

"And so?"

"And so he wrote and asked me to come marry him."

"And you took off alone for China without ever having seen him?"

"Yes. It was my last chance. I was almost forty. I arrived early one Saturday morning with my small traveling bag. I came back some ten years later with the same bag." She blinked both eyes. "He met me at the boat and had a missionary priest waiting to marry us. On Monday morning, I was typing business letters in China instead of in Italy."

"Did you fall in love?"

"Heavens no! We stayed together through the war, and that was enough. When we came back to Italy, he wanted to go to an old folks' home." She shook her head. "I said no. I thought it would kill us both. But he insisted and, sure enough, it killed him. I was alone at his burial, alone with the priest from the old folks' home."

She stopped talking. She had run out of words, like a dizzy top no longer spinning. Even her red hat sat still, slanting a bit to one side.

One Sunday, when I invited her to our midday meal, she arrived carrying a large manila envelope under her arm.

"This is my petition. I want you and *il Signore Ingegnere* to sign it."

I asked her what it was about.

"It's about letting dead folk be cremated," she said, looking at me intently. "Italy is too chockfull of old bones." She spread out her petition on the Sunday table. It was written in Latin. There were two pages of signatures.

"But Emilia," I said, "why is it in Latin?"

"It looks better. Everyone in the village thinks it's Catholic if it's in Latin. And then they sign it without reading it."

Emilia explained that every year she sent her petition to the Italian government in Rome. And every year she collected about one hundred signatures, most of them the same as the year before.

"I won't give up," she said with a chuckle, "until they've changed the law."

Our children asked her one day to take off her parrot's hat. She obliged and pulled off the hat and the tight elastic. On the top of her head crouched a disheveled gray bun with more hairpins than hair.

"I used to have long, thick, black hair," she told them. "When I was living in China, I wore it pulled back in a fat pigtail. I must have pulled it too tight, for it started to fall out. It came out by the handful."

Our children listened in dismay.

"But never you mind," she said, upset to see their distress. "Look here, while I was there, I learned how to slant my eyes."

We all looked. It was true. Emilia knew how to slant her eyes. Just like we could shut our eyes, she could slant them, making the corners go up on their own.

"How do you do it?" asked Peter, our oldest child, all of eight years and not believing what he saw.

"First you must go to China," she said, slanting her eyes at him.

And she plopped her red hat back on her head, becoming once again the Emilia we knew.

It was my husband who persuaded her one Sunday afternoon to take off the plaid bathrobe she always wore on top of her dress.

"Emilia," he said, "I want to see you with your dress, without the bathrobe."

"Ah, you Frenchmen!" She smiled to herself and took off her bathrobe, showing us a plain gray woolen dress.

"It becomes you, Emilia," Pierre said. "It's the color of your hair."

She took off her hat and tried to pat her hair in place. Pierre was right. I could even imagine how she perhaps looked when she first arrived in China after traveling halfway around the world, hopeful for adventure and perhaps love.

"You know," she confided, "I do wish it had been the French correspondent in Port Arthur who'd asked me to marry him instead of the Italian." She opened wide her black eyes and smiled still again.

We listened.

"He was ever so attractive. We lent one another books. We learned Chinese calligraphy. We studied Japanese together in the evening." She looked away, far out the window, beyond the village, beyond the lake. Something had stopped her, there in the middle of her story, a memory in the midst of all the years of war and turmoil she had suffered.

"And then?" we asked.

She was quiet.

We waited.

"And then he was called back to Paris at the end of the war. I never heard from him again." She shook her head and closed her eyes.

Little by little we got to know Emilia. We invited her for midday dinner each Sunday. She would arrive at our front door with a tin of English tea biscuits. The cookies lasted most of the week. The tins lasted much longer. We kept them for marbles, Legos, and buttons. One of the tins stayed with us for a long time. When we opened it, we smelled not only the tea biscuits but also Emilia, her lavender perfume that I did not notice until we were gone.

The children continued to prefer her with her plaid bathrobe and red felt hat. The straggly bun of hairpins made them uneasy. She would slant her eyes for them while she wore her hat, and then, to really please them, she'd chatter away in Chinese. They said that was how they liked her best.

One time, instead of the round tin of English tea biscuits, she brought a large, rectangular, gift-wrapped box.

"Something special just for the children."

It was Monopoly in Italian. From then on after the noonday dinner, she'd sit down on our balcony overlooking the village and lake and play Monopoly with our oldest children.

If ever Pierre or I would watch, she'd send us away. "It's time you two had a moment alone. Now off with you, but no nonsense, no fooling around, mind you; you have more than enough children as it is."

Then she'd say she was only teasing.

One Sunday when she was leaving, a rainstorm broke, and we drove her down the hill to the village. She didn't want us to come to her door and asked us to leave her at the corner. Then the following Sunday, she told me I could come if I wanted, but alone. "There's barely place for me."

We walked down the lane. Emilia was quiet. I could hear the little brook to our right rippling over the stones and fallen branches. Emilia kept stealing sideways glances at me, as if making sure she wanted me there. I was the only American in the village, and she was inviting me to her house. We crossed the street and went into the village, down past the butcher shop, the bakery where I went with the children every morning for fresh *panini,* and past the old stone church.

Her house was back from the narrow road, on a little alley and up a few wooden steps. She opened her door and let me in. There was indeed only one small room. In the far corner stood a washstand and a table with an electric plate; that was her kitchen. Half under the sink was an old-fashioned bathtub. She heated the water in the kettle. The toilet was outside in the back.

In the near corner was her bed, piled high with blankets and a bright embroidered silk spread on top. The spread, she said, was the only souvenir she brought back from China—red and blue-winged birds against gold-threaded sunlight. Against the walls, shelves were stacked high with books—old books, some with leather bindings, and paperbacks piled still higher on top. I wished later that I had looked at the titles, remembering the way she had looked at ours.

We signed Emilia's petition four years in a row. But the Italian government wasn't ready to budge. They wanted everyone buried and accounted for. Emilia shook her head and said it was the fault of the Church. Her petition might well be in Latin, but she was far from kowtowing to the Catholic hierarchy.

"John XXIII, there was a good pope," she said. "But look at what they did to Galileo."

She knew we were regular churchgoers. When we didn't go to the church in French in Ispra, we'd take our place in the church in Comerio. We'd sit near the back, behind the women on the left and the men on the right, there where we could sit together as a family. The Italian sounded very close to the Latin that it had recently replaced. And we never saw Emilia.

She would meet us afterward, bright and cheerful, her faith and goodness coming from its own source.

Come spring of our fourth year, it was time for us to move on. Our new baby was a few months old, and Pierre was leaving his work in Italy.

Emilia came for one last Sunday dinner. We walked up the hill together after church. Her hat was askew, and we couldn't get one word out of her.

Once inside, we tried to cheer her up. We kidded about not listening to her and having still another baby. She smiled and nodded. Pierre asked her what she was reading. She shook her head. When finally she answered, she said she wasn't reading much. Her eyes weren't so good anymore.

The older children asked her to play Monopoly. They got out the game, the cards in Italian, and opened it on the table outside. But Emilia's heart was no longer in it. She said it was best she be on her way.

We hugged her and promised we'd come back. She seemed to know it would be otherwise.

"We'll come back and sign your petition," we said.

"And one day," she said, "you'll see, they'll give in."

And off she went, without turning around, down the lane to the village, her red hat disappearing out of sight.

Our first letter came back unopened. The envelope was dirty and torn. The word *"deceduta"* was scribbled over her name.

A year later, when we returned, we learned that the village had buried her in their cemetery. We found her gravestone and stood there for a long moment, crying hard and trying to say goodbye.

Years later, when the Italian government finally changed its cremation law, I thought of Emilia. In fact, I thought I heard her groan.

Or did she chuckle?

Nora Pierce

Grappa

It is July and the air conditioning is broken on the
Trenitalia. I've peeled away my cardigan and sprawled
across the seats with the windows pulled down and my belongings
in a puddle at my feet. I'm sleeping the sleep of one who has
recently been in a long-haul economy-class seat. And so it truly star-
tles me when I stretch into drowsy sitting and notice a man staring
at me from the seat across the aisle. His right hand moves furiously
inside his fashionable Burberry pants. I look away emphatically. I
consider standing, finding the conductor, but the aisles are empty
for as far as I can see.

There's a rattle inside the train, something threatening to fall
off of the luggage rack. An Air France luggage tag dangles in the
air above the man. He must be French. I settle into this thought

deliberately, because I like Italy so much I don't want it to be spoiled by some random pervert. A slender strip of mirror attached to the ceiling clearly reflects my voyeur, now entirely out of his pants and displaying a milky yellow penis smoothed by circumcision. I do something now that strangely makes me think of my mother: I stare directly at him. In New York I would deflect the professional panhandlers this way. I'd ask them if they could spare some change just as they approached to solicit the same. "Spare a dime?" I'd say, and they'd look surprised, even sometimes apologize for their lack of generosity, and then wander off politely. But it does not work here. It seems to make him think I am participating. I decide, in a jovial leap, to blame this on my mother. My mother, the superwoman who raised me in such a fog and whirlwind of grrrl power and feminism that I am completely oblivious to my own limitations—especially any notion that there is danger or consequence to simply being a girl in the world. And so I've been traipsing around the planet, eating out alone in Reykjavík and Managua and sleeping in low-rent hostels with doors falling off their hinges. It's just me and one fabulous antique suitcase. Like Huck Finn, I'm lighting out in search of that uniquely American ideal of self-reliance and freedom.

But I keep running into this kind of thing, these nasty little roadblocks that insist it's not as easy to be a woman traveling alone as I stubbornly want it to be. I shout for the conductor, whose approaching footsteps alarm the man enough to zip up his pants. It is not easy to explain the incident to the conductor, a distinguished-looking Italian gentleman wearing a fatherly expression of concern.

When I resort to sign language, he gets the idea and ushers off the perv at the next stop.

The train grinds loudly into the lonely station, and a young man lifts my bags down from the luggage rack and deposits them politely on the platform before retrieving his own.

"*Grazie,*" I offer.

"*Prego, bella!*" he protests, as if it is ridiculous even to thank him for such a basic act. This happens everywhere in Italy, and I suppose this is why the women can get away with such impractical shoes on the impossible cobblestone and always appear to have freshly emerged from some misty, scented boudoir.

From the sleeping huddle of old men beside a row of cars, I solicit a taxi and head for Assisi. It is a labored climb—and a winding one, around roads in the shape of a Slinky, slowly wrapping around the rising hill. A sprawl of pink and white bricks appears with sloped Mediterranean roofs, a madness of steeples and windows. It seems as if Assisi's settlers decided simply to build themselves into the hills, digging into them with shovels and holding back the earth with stones.

From the taxi, I can see packed buses arriving. They unload long lines of tourists who snake up the hill like worker ants, pausing periodically to unfold maps or flip through guidebooks. The Slinky road takes us past boutiques of kitsch and religious ephemera, past the basilica's magnificent rows of restored arches.

I am arriving at the beautiful hour of early evening, when the swallows have given up their whining and the view is so pervasive and stunning that on first sight, and for a long while afterward, it is impossible not to hold my breath. I take in views as if they were birthday presents or desserts. I have to distract myself from them in some arbitrary way so that I can savor the beauty in a slower, fuller way. So I order a drink on the hotel terrace and set myself to detangling my anklet chain. And there it is—slowly fading to darkness, a flat expanse of earth that makes me feel as if I might find what I'm looking for after all.

"*Scusi, signorina . . .*"

Interrupting my dreamy view is a man with a comb-over, of whom I take a quick and unkind inventory. Obviously American: the Texan accent, the new hiking boots and REI shorts—probably bought for this adventure (a tour no doubt), which requires neither hiking boots nor shorts since it probably consists of air-conditioned buses and cool museums.

He sits down at my table and tells me I'm lovely.

I am neither attracted to him nor interested in his company, and I am in fact annoyed to be taken from my quiet moment with the flattened expanse of glittering towns beneath me. But I say thank you.

I nod sympathetically as he goes on about his dog at home, the blisters that have developed on his feet, and his inability to ignore a "beautiful flower" such as myself when he sees one. As he talks, I eavesdrop on a man and a woman nearby. The woman looks about fifty, with hennaed hair and strings of quartz crystal and Buddhist symbols tied around her neck. She wears a green sheath of a vaguely

Roman sort that drapes around her like the folds on an ancient statue. "My name is Silk," she says to the man as she holds her hand out dramatically and explains how a guru she studied under in India gave her the fluid name.

"Bruno," the man says to her, "You teach-a me English. I show you Assisi."

Assisi is meant for the pious. For centuries, it has been a symbol of peace and a destination for those devoted to the ideals exemplified in the life of St. Francis. But judging by the practiced flirting of the town's men, I have to wonder how often the pilgrims are thwarted here.

I've turned my attention to the cities below, and the possibility of beautiful olive-skinned men whose boring stories I wouldn't mind listening to, when I suddenly remember not to put up with him, and I get up abruptly. "I've forgotten to return a book," I say, "so excuse me, please."

"You'll come back?" he asks. As I turn to go, I bump into a slender man in aviator sunglasses and tight jeans straight out of the 1980s.

"This is our tour leader, Antonio," Comb-Over says.

"Call me Tony," says Antonio, in a ridiculous attempt at an American accent that falls somewhere between Tony Danza and Gilligan. He holds out his hand for me, and I am forced both to take it and to endure a sloppy kiss on the knuckles before scooting my way past to the receptionist for my key.

Antonio follows me to the front desk, leans in way too close behind me, and whispers, "His voice is so annoyink, no?" referring to poor Comb-Over, left sitting alone on the veranda. "Would you like to come for a drink in my room?"

What is this place, I think, *Rikers Island?* I recoil so obviously that I can't believe he doesn't notice.

"No, no, no," I protest. Why am I smiling?

"You vacation," he says, "You relax."

"No, no, no." I search for an excuse, but all I've got is "I'm exhausted." The truth is, I'm not tired at all, am not interested in retiring to my room, and why do I *need* an excuse?

"You are beauteeeful," he says, "You have drink after sleep." Again, I decide to blame this on my mother, who I suddenly miss terribly. Other girls seem to have been taught how to deal with men like this, yet I am possessed of this compensating diplomatic manner toward them. What do I do now, Mom?

"No, no," I smile, adopting his stilted way of speaking. "Way too tired, no? But thank you. Sorry."

"When you rest, you come. I make you wonderful drink. Grappa. You have grappa? Very Italian."

I have grappa, I think, *plenty of grappa. Enough to pickle my liver and yours, you hateful man.* Why do men always judge me as the shrinking violet? Is it not possible that I could have lived in the world for all these years and tasted the grown-up drinks? The offer for grappa was made as if it were an offer of candy to some poor unsuspecting little girl. *I've got your number, mister.*

"Yes," I say to him, "I'll have to try it. Maybe some other time."

"I'm leaving tomorrow," he calls out to my back.

"No, no, no."

"What a dick," I exhale, finding as I round the corner that I have said it to an elderly woman, tiny under a canvas backpack and wearing binoculars around her neck like a nomadic birdwatcher.

"Oh, excuse me," I say, "I'm so sorry."

"What?"

"SORRY," I say.

"Oh no, dear, I don't hear so well anymore."

She reaches out to me kindly, taking both of my hands into her own and leaning in to hear, as if for a whispered confidence.

"I'm Nora," I say.

"Oh yes," the woman smiles, "Leah Murphy. Isn't it beautiful? I have always wanted to come."

"YES," I shout, "VERY BEAUTIFUL."

Her enormous backpack disappears down the hall, and I find myself envying her lack of hearing.

I have to sneak out of the hotel for dinner for fear that I may run into the insistent Antonio, so I find an obscure stairway, a back door, and steal, relieved, into the night. I tell the taxi driver I'm looking for a good place to eat. I'm disappointed when he drops me off at what looks like a misplaced Club Med. There are beach umbrellas propped up outside, tiki lights, and a disco ball. All the furniture is arranged around a pool table on which people are playing a game I don't recognize, involving great big balls and tiny little pegs like golf tees. There is a trio of young women at the bar trying to order drinks in Italian. They crack each other up over whose language skills are the worst. When I pass by and say "excuse me" in English, I find myself invited to their table, and, before long, taken into the circle like an initiate in a girls' school clique.

"We're going dancing," the Australian says. Her name is Lucy. She is tall and sturdy looking, with perfectly gathered and knotted braids and chocolate-colored arms in a fuchsia silk tunic.

I pull my chair out a bit to show my cat burglar get-up, the simple skirt and baggy sweater I wore to sneak out of my hotel. "I'm underdressed."

"Oh, but I have the perfect shoes," Lucy says, and goes to her room, returning with a scandalous pair of spiky red heels. There's a vaguely bondage look to them and straps that snake around the ankle. "Borrow them, girl. You *must*."

I agree, partly because it is a welcome change from months of sensible sandals and ragged jeans. In their hotel room, I let them dress me up. They straighten my hair and rim my eyes in kohl. I feel a strange sense of power in the shoes, like Dorothy in her ruby slippers. I try clicking the heels and lose my balance slightly, the last glass of wine sinking in slowly.

Out in the darkened streets, we search for the bar Lucy knows. The shoes have given me height and transmitted something intangible, so that I move with greater sway in my torso and chin up, as if I have suddenly taken off a great overcoat and stopped struggling head down against the wind. Why was there never a superhero with stiletto powers?

I notice a man beneath a tree as we pass a deserted park. Just as we walk by, he flicks his cigarette out, and I have to duck quickly to miss his arm. "Oh, I'm so sorry," I say, though I have the uncomfortable feeling that he put his arm out to stop me. I fight an urge to turn around, feeling as if his gaze is still on us. Then, just as we pass a telephone pole, he comes up from behind and tries to wrestle Lucy's bag from her. She's still attached to him, tethered to him by the purse she clutches like a buoy, yet strangely, none of us move. Lucy turns to him, screaming "Fuck!," and aims the little spray can on her keychain, which I had assumed was an asthma inhaler, directly at his face.

The mace makes a gentle arc, and the air seems to still itself for the rainfall. We all stand motionless and quiet, as if trapped in Jell-O.

"Now we run," Lucy says suddenly, startling us all out of our quiet fear and leading the way as we run down the cobblestone hill. I find that I have run through the mace, and my eyes have begun to ache in a slow, numbing burn. But what runs through my mind, and in fact what I say out loud, repeating it over and over like a mantra, is, "I can't run in these shoes." As if this were some awesome epiphany, the shoes crippling me in this particular situation. I call out to the others and then again to myself, "I can't run in these shoes."

But in fact, I navigate the cobblestone deftly, the spike in my heel planting itself in the weeds poking out of the seams in the way a climber with spikes might rappel up the road. And then we're in a bar. A smoky bar, with men drinking Peroni and old women with tall glasses of dessert wine, and Lucy is speaking in broken Italian with pieces of French and English, explaining and breathing and explaining, and then there is a phone call made, and I find myself seated with the two girls at a table, warm gray cups of cappuccino swimming in front of us. Later, judging by the fine welts and bruises that surface on Lucy's arm, we decide he must have had something sharp.

On the way back to the hotel, we sit in silence in the back of a tiny taxi. Next to me, Lucy is absurdly reapplying lipstick. The taxi drops me off at my own hotel, and as I step into the soft light, I see a woman alone on the couch. The woman lifts her eyebrows and dips her head forward. "Ciao!" she says, almost shouting. It's Sparkle, from the couple on the terrace. Or is it Silver, or Silk?

She is spread out alone on the tattered hotel couch. Between her legs on the floor, a half-full glass of wine has spilled little puddles all around, like pools of blood from a haywire nosebleed. A former bartender, I instinctively take the wine glass and place it on the bar. When I return with a napkin for the spilled wine, two great globes of tears have formed beneath the woman's eyes and are inching their way slowly down her cheek.

"I've been a vegetarian for thirty years, and for what?" she says. "I give up, thatsssit!"

Her great big plastic earrings shimmy pea green in the wake of her emphatic gestures. She saws the air in the exaggerated emphasis of drunkenness. "They wouldn't let me in," she says, "St. Francis would not have closed the church to me. St. Francis would have let me light a fucking candle."

I nod sympathetically.

"I just wanted to light a candle to St. Francis, and they were closed for money. Had to be for money."

She says the word "money" as if it were filthy, and I look at the constellation of diamonds on her left hand and the casually perfect Ferragamo ballet slides cradling her slender feet.

"And they think I'm a terrorist! I know they do. They think I'm going to blow the place up. They called security." Here she takes a great gulp of air. "Security," she imitates their condescending coaching tones. "It's okay now. Let's move on. It's all right. St. Francis will hear you anywhere." She coos in baby tones, "St. Francis will hear you anywhere. Can you believe it? I've prayed, I've fasted, I've been to India, to Japan, to Mexico. I've meditated and prayed for peace. I even had that fucking detestable colonic. All day I walked the streets and prayed for peace, and nothing! Nothing!"

I survey the scene—the dozing bartender, the discarded bottles of wine, the door propped open for the cool night air, the empty lobby—and consider what to do. I would never leave a girlfriend alone in this state, and though I don't know this woman, my conscience won't let me leave her here like this. But how to get her upstairs? I'm sure she'll insist that she's fine, but it's clear, nonetheless, that standing will cause her to pass out.

"Sounds like it's time to call it a night." I mime an elaborate yawn.

"No," the woman says. "I'm fine." She reaches for her wine glass on the floor, searches for a moment when she cannot find it, and then is struck by another thought.

"And then Bruno! Bruno!" She reaches both her arms out in a big circle, and balloons her cheeks out, "Great big fat Bruno, and he grabs me and hugs me, and the next thing I know, he's licking my face. Bruno."

"Why don't we go up together?" I say.

"No, no, I'm fiiine."

So I sit for a moment next to her on the couch and picture great big fat Bruno licking the swollen pink of this laser-resurfaced face.

"I want to be enlightened, goddamnit; I want to be saved." She leans in, and I find myself taking the little head in my hand as the warm tears fall down her shoulders. *Me too*, I think, *me too*.

In a few minutes, the woman is asleep, breathing with soft regularity, heaving a great abandoned weight onto my shoulder. The night is still outside, and soft lights wink through the opened doorway. And now I can take it in, the marvelous view. The basilica is a beacon in the distance, lit from beneath in gauzy pink light.

We climb the stairs together slowly. I coach her through every step. "Just a few more," I say. "You can do it." She looks up as I'm closing the door to her room. "I'm going home tomorrow," she says. She sniffles weakly then, burying her face in the pillow. "I'm going home."

I place the stilettos, which I've forgotten to return, outside on the small terrace and climb into my bed fully clothed. I pull the covers up to my eyes, pull my knees into my chest, and look out through the open door, where the shoes sit muted and red in the moonlight. I'm afraid to have them in the same room. The pillow on my cheek makes me feel grateful, and I say a quick prayer that I'll be free tomorrow. At 2:00 AM, the phone breaks my dreamless sleep. "Hello, my love," the voice coos deeply. "Are you rested and ready for a drink?"

Anita Olachea

Season of Fires

The town of Vinci, Leonardo's birthplace, sits on a low
rise at the edge of the Arno River Valley, about halfway
between Florence and Pisa. Its museum is packed with reconstruc-
tions of his inventions, and the bare farmhouse of his early years
stands in a field up the road. Across the valley, the Apennines are
stacked in profile one against the other like a stage backdrop, but
close to town, the ground lifts slowly; slopes are dense with vegetation or cut by neat rows of young trees and vines.

If I were asked to name the one sound most associated with
those hills above Vinci, it would be the wind. More than the next-
door rooster's nerve-wracking *cock-a-doodle*s in the early dawn (one
every twelve seconds, which leads us to speculate on ways to do
him in), more than the penetrating drone of buzz saws and power

mowers in the pruning season, or the world war–level explosion of gunfire all around when hunting season opens in September.

Almost year round, the wind here does things that one would connect more with mountain peaks and northern wastelands than with the gilded Tuscan landscape. In winter it howls and roves around hurling snow or blasts of icy rain at the windows and doors. In the mid-seasons it moves small twisters across the hills, bending the trees to the ground and tearing away branches and part of the olive crop. In summer there are no storms without a moaning wind to drive the rain down the chimney and under roof tiles, to snap the electric power so that we stumble around blindly, trying to position buckets in the hearth and spread newspaper around the wood stove to stave off flooding and its consequential mopping up. The wind— delicious to burrow into bed at night and hear it rattle, impotent at the roof and shutters. The wind—you can bet on it . . . except in August. August brings stillness and heat; it is the unrelenting apoth-eosis of summer in middle Italy, and you must cower in the house with the shutters drawn, not letting so much as a toe cross the door-sill into the overheated outer regions. Windless August, the season of yellowing grass, sweltering noondays, and green olives; the sea-son of fires.

Perhaps three miles north of Vinci along the tightly winding state road lies the community of Tigliano. The little stone house there has been ours for more than thirty years; it sits low in the hills at the base of loaf-shaped Monte Albano, and our view is solid olive trees interspersed by vineyards and an occasional herd of sheep. This area of olive groves and pine and oak woods, between Florence and the sea, burns famously in the dry months. *Ferragosto*, the traditional vacation period in the first half of August when all of Italy grinds to a halt, is always tinged with apprehension: Will it happen again this year? And when? You awake one morning and know it's begun. The valley is full of smoke; the helicopters dragging sacks of water pass over and over; spirals of smoke rise from the far side of the ridge above our house. Everyone's uneasy. We know a line of fire can run down a dry hillside in a matter of seconds. Television gives us a bird's-eye view of the day's damage, the pockets of still-smoldering vegetation trailing up the mountainside.

By evening the air is heavy with the smell of burning—the sunset is veiled, gray-violet and blue through the haze. We wet down the grass around the house and debate going to bed dressed for an emergency. Neighbors passing on their way home try to be reassuring: "Bah!" someone says, "looks like the worst is over." But his voice is doubtful, and he can't take his eyes off the curlicues of smoke drifting through the sky. There are horror stories of whole groves going up near Lucca, but much closer too—here at the crest of the road, just right of where it meets the highway. And indeed, the next day, driving into town, we round a curve and find a slope of blackened derelicts with truncated limbs in strange, contorted positions, painful as the aftermath of any violence; a landscape from hell.

One year, things took an even uglier turn: A pyromaniac, a self-declared firebug, was roaming the area and setting the blazes. His modus operandi was to call the police, naming his next target, set the fire, and then disappear. For the local people, this was no longer a natural phenomenon but a personal aggression. One is ever on the lookout for that here—a neighbor inching his confines into yours, someone else's net set too far into your land, or wastewater channeled downhill onto the roots of your vines. Each centimeter of property is staked out and defended. But these fires, for ill will and intentional harm, went far beyond the ordinary offenses and magnified the feeling of resentment.

This tiny community, a pinhead even on the Touring Club's expanded map, is an amazing microcosm: Alliances bond and break and reform in new ways. A neighbor's every word and gesture is weighed and examined, interpreted this way and that, then stored along with all his others, like sums in an account book.

This was a revelation to me, an American East-Coaster, who, if I'd thought at all of rural Italians, had done so in stereotypes: jovial and open-hearted cultivators of vines and olives, living their modest lives close to the earth, speaking the very language they would have used seven hundred years ago, the dialect later diffused as standard Italian. Primitive, in my unenlightened view, free from the petty bickering of more advanced communities. Our first timid contacts with the real thing supported the illusion: Primitive they did seem to be, all those years ago, carting bundles of firewood on their heads, curing physical complaints with magic gestures and chants, spying newcomers from behind the trees. That generation has vanished now; nothing of the kind survives today, except for an ingrained sense of wariness, well dissimulated, and a certain scrappy sensitivity.

But a tendency to diffidence and suspicion gives a little in the face of a certain threat; fire and firebug are instead elements of cohesion, bonding us all closer in an uncommon cause. The farmers, up and out before dawn, shoot guarded looks in all directions. They work on their terraced fields, clearing the ground around olives and vines so that there's no grass for fire to feed on. Nervousness accentuates the cadence of their Tuscan voices, and aspirated *c*'s fall thick and fast:

"*Se lo enhontro . . .*" (*Se lo incontro:* If I meet up with him.)

"*E hosa farai?*" (*E cosa farai:* And what'll you do?)

"*Lo concio.*" (I'll tan his hide.)

Our closest friend, Remo, wears a perpetual scowl. "*Diobono!*" he says, stopping by the house; "*Diobono,* everybody knows these fires don't set themselves!"

In the evening we venture out after dinner, up the road in the dark without a moon to help us see where to put our feet. No one else is about, though this would normally be the time for strolling and socializing, catching the stray wisp of breeze after the heat of the day. Vast cones of light from police cars out on the highway play down over the fields and up the mountain, searching through the trees, an eerie substitute for moonlight. People have shuttered themselves in, as if afraid the madman might come skulking around, peering through their windows. We pass beneath the darkened terrace where a granny shop used to supply life's basics, including the town's only public phone, a service no one needs nowadays. Guard dogs are out, nervous on their chains and baying at our footsteps;

chickens and pigeons flap in their nests, adding an undertone of coos and clucks to the general restlessness. Every creature is on edge, and there's something unpleasant, a sort of collective breath-holding, to the atmosphere.

One night, as we start to turn back toward the house, we see two trees ignite on a hillside across the valley, first one flare, then a second. *Poof!* Just like that, two dervishlike licks of flame against the sky, almost joyous. We're fascinated and spooked—the more so as sirens start to clamor out on the main road, filling the dark with dissonance and panic. Did *he* call them, beating a fast retreat then, perhaps on a scooter, into some nearly hidden path through the woods? This is a far cry from the sort of crime that inhabited my distant, urban youth. Our fear, as we head for home, is unreasoning—we've become primitives ourselves.

For a few days more, the firebug led the police on a merry chase. Every hour brought new rumors: He'd been sighted; he was blond and foreign; he was dark and local; the police had tracked him down; no they hadn't; he'd left the territory. . . . The men took to huddling together in the bar in town and moving in groups; the women hardly dared to hang out the wash. Running out into the insistent heat to perform a rapid chore, I did a lot of looking over my shoulder. He was everywhere; he was nowhere. Tension swelled like a bubble, straining against its own skin.

And then it burst. They had him. This time it was true—word came that he'd been caught. Remo was triumphant: "Did you hear? They got him! Over by Lucca! The people wanted to lynch him, string him up on the spot. Ha!" He told this with relish, as if something about the scene as he imagined it satisfied his sense of justice. The news at noon confirmed it all, how the man, canny enough to elude round-the-clock patrols for almost two weeks, and to so invade the collective psyche, had—purposely?—left a trail of telltale clues, rags and empty gasoline cans, in his shack. A crowd clamored around as the *carabinieri* led him out, a jacket covering his head. "Who is it? Who is it?" Arms reached for him through the protective cordon, trying to snatch the jacket away, but he was hustled through the mob and into the waiting car, which sped off. Poor, angry, itinerant, and in the end anonymous, he was cheated of any notoriety he might have hoped for as he disappeared from sight.

The pyromaniac has taken his place in local folklore. Every August, when smoke drops its gray curtain and helicopters bumble around overhead, the story is shaken out and retold, and people nod, serious, considering once more this manifestation of human folly, in all its mystery. As the season changes and the heat breaks under a downpour, the wind blows up again and comes to claim its rightful place. It moves over the short grass, digging out the remnants of summer, the last traces of ash and scorched twigs, and whisks everything away. We watch the trees bend, the silver olive leaves flicker against the gusts, and feel that now it's safe to leave. In a few months the olives will be ready to harvest, and another cycle will commence, always different, always the same.

Wallis Wilde-Menozzi

Le Donne
di Servizio

When my family and I lived in California, the idea of
having a *donna di servizio* (cleaning lady) was as far from
my mind as was the thought of living in Italy. I whisked my Hoover
around once every week; I patently resisted acquiring an iron.
Clothes in Palo Alto sported a natural wrinkle; with the sun as a
dryer, they often lightened to a desert white. When we left for the
university or the office, our outfits looked like most of our neighbors': faded and relaxed. We were mimetic. The house, with plenty
of sunlight and green plants and piles of books and toys, never
looked in or out of order. "Lived in" was the laudatory phrase for
describing the style's essence. We feminists of the 1970s put our kids
in co-ops. Our husbands learned to load dishwashers and whip up
overly meaty meals.

But then I moved to Italy, where the institution of the *donna di servizio*—with its complexness and quite often double standards—caught me up. Like so much else that happens when a person searches for ways to stay on her feet in another culture, I developed ideas that had previously seemed futile to me. Suddenly the clothes I wore were inadequate without the hiss of an iron's passage. ("Is something wrong? Have you fallen down?") Grime that licked the windows was enough to cast a room into a deep depression. Milanese relatives slyly wrote the date of their visit in our bookshelves' dust. A gnawing sensation that I needed a *donna di servizio* for my own image in Parma, the Northern Italian city I lived in, persisted. I found myself in a more exigent, domestic world.

In Italy, the *donna di servizio* has a conservative social role to play. She is a fixture, one way or another, in so many middle-class homes. Her polishing is needed for marble floors; her organizational skills are mandatory to maintain the rhythms and expectations of an Italian house; her way of starching impossible curtains is required every six months. She's an iconic part of the seasons.

Four hours of paid cleaning became a face-saving solution for me and was all the domestic intervention I could abide—after my mother-in-law became my de facto cleaning woman. My mother-in-law arranged the furniture, ironed our underwear, and aired out our sheets in a well-meant attempt to save me from social judgments. In spite of my protests, she continued to inspect our laundry. She reordered the entire library on the basis of book size. In intense three-day sessions (while I was gone) she would haul up heavy ladders and brooms from the basement and wash every ceiling and light fixture until she nearly collapsed from exhaustion. However, my mother-in-law didn't want to be replaced. Hearing of my plan to hire someone, she upped her services, often arriving with four-course meals in bulging plastic bags.

In her way, my mother-in-law was a classic *donna di servizio*: A splendid cook, an excellent knitter, a ruthless scrubber—she insisted on a house so washed and ordered, it could have been featured in a magazine. She was also fiercely loyal to the family. Yet having my house criticized and reordered was not going to work. When I finally put my foot down and found someone, a high stone wall of incomprehension and hurt appeared: Who could be so stupid as to refuse having the house put in order by a loved one who asked for nothing for her time?

My first *donna*, Rina, worked in houses to prop up her other business, a dry-cleaning store that had debts. To some people with an economic sense, this might have seemed the wrong place to put her energy. But Rina didn't want to give up her business. She wanted a life better than the one she had had in Naples. This is a theme for *donne di servizio* who are Italian, and for the *extracommunitari*, the immigrants who are not. Many *donne* are volcanoes of ambitious plans.

Rina brought her adolescent son along while she cleaned. She did everything for him—wiped his mouth after he had tea, got down on her knees to tie his shoes. She asked me if I could tutor the boy while she washed my floors. She couldn't help him study; she had to clean. Unfortunately, he had no intention of studying. I must admit, I balked at the idea that I should spend those hours doing his fractions. But Rina remained hopeful. She noticed my long feet were the same size as his. Adolfo was unable to participate in the school trip without walking gear. Wouldn't mine do, in spite of his strong objections that no kids wore purple walking shoes? "Let him just try them on," she pleaded. "They are perfect!" Soon she was pointing out that my tablecloth was not elegant enough, and that she had no time to press my clothes, but I could send them to her laundry and she would bring them back the following week. The relationship became a real one—where, like many women in Parma, she had a viewpoint that was slightly aggressive.

Rina was not a bad initiation into this queendom of *donne di servizio*. She was enterprising and ran my household with an eye for making more money and improving herself.

"You see," my husband said when I mentioned that Adolfo got mud all over my purple shoes, "cleaning women are more trouble than they are worth. They begin to run you the way they want. And no one can scrub a floor like my mother."

The next *donna di servizio*, Bruna, bawled. I took her on when Rina found a factory job in order to pay her laundry business debts. Bruna had lost her husband and needed, I decided after six months of listening to her tears, to be adopted. She was as traumatized and as alone as an abandoned pup. Besides needing comfort, she often asked to lie down on the couch after a chest-racking sob. Once she had our confidence, she would request to turn on the TV. Three o'clock was the hour for her favorite soap opera. Her workday with us, unless she watched her program, created a gap in the plots.

Bruna mostly craved company. She wanted to be one of us. To have lunch. To sit down for tea. To receive a fax. "Oh, signora, how can that writing come through the phone? Oh, send me one, send me one." Bruna wanted and was given one of my daughter's dolls to sleep with at night. Her chubby sadness filled our house to a near standstill on Tuesdays. Only chocolates and hugs consoled. When I finally told her that I couldn't keep her, she asked again for a fax. Certainly that day Bruna's weariness, her resistance, melted as the watery paper unscrolled from the machine. Her wide smile grew more and more hushed. Her voice rose to its highest pitch. "Signora, someone wrote 'Tanti, tanti baci. Many, many kisses.'" Bruna giggled madly. Beaming, she pressed the fax to her breast. "Signora, it's to me." I hope, somehow, that its desired mystery has continued to burn in her life.

I met Maria, a slight, olive-skinned woman, in the park. As two obvious foreigners, we often gravitated toward each other. Her two children, she told me, had remained in Manila.

"You can't imagine, signora, what I feel," she would say while bending down to wipe off the face of a curly-headed child with shining eyes. Down she would bend again to tie the child's little brother's shoes. "My two girls live with my sister. I haven't seen them for eight years."

"Maria," the children would shout. "Maria, push us. We want to go on the swing."

The young Filipina saw her own daughters only in photos. I followed their progress as they lost their front teeth and, much later, began to develop figures. Maria faithfully hoped it would all work out because her savings from cleaning would finally bloom into an apartment.

Two more years. Then one.

"Signora, I will be going back in September."

I saw her two days before she left. Her thoughtful smile revealed complex feelings as joy pushed out the doubts and stoicism. "Good-bye, signora. I will never forget Parma or the two Parma children. But you are the only one I can tell that my tears are not about leaving them or the city. I am so glad to be going home."

My goddaughter, who advises abused women, told me about another young *donna di servizio*, Lola, from Tobago, who was desperate to get her sister, Florita, into Italy. The best she could find was a family who offered illegal conditions. "No permits. We don't want to pay her pension taxes."

"Where will she sleep?" Lola's heart shrank when she saw the windowless room down in their cellar, where a dangerous furnace took up most of the space. The head of the household said, "She can work seven days a week. Because without a permit, it will be much safer never to go outside."

"An offer like the furnace room can lead to blackmail, and from there, terrible things," my goddaughter told her. Lola didn't want to listen. Anything was preferable to leaving Florita in Tobago.

The police held Florita back when she tried to slip into Italy as a tourist. For two days, black-haired Florita and red-haired Lola communicated through the customs barrier at Fiumicino, where she was kept in check. As this was Italy, pity and compassion held sway, with a concerted effort to ease the rules. The police brought sandwiches with lettuce and cheese, while encouraging Lola to find a proper sponsor. By Florita's third day of sleeping in the airport, my goddaughter had found an honest employer for her. The custom doors opened, with many officials cheering Florita, who clutched a handful of papers protecting her. Lola's arduous mission from Tobago to Italy moved a notch. Her doggedness, with help from people who believe in helping, had obtained her sister's legal entry in Florence.

Lola and Florita: May their futures as *donne di servizio* be as bright as their names! As dreamers, they have come to a land where many will be open to giving them a hand. I too will soon be looking to hire someone like them. My present *donna di servizio*, Giulia, an Italian from Parma, wants to retire. Our lives have traversed many central events in the eleven years during which she has spent four hours a week in our house. When her husband died of cancer, she stopped coming for a year. When she broke her arm in our house, I taught her the exercises to rehabilitate it. When her son married, we looked at the fabric for his suit together. When my daughter married, she brought flowers. When my husband had a stroke, she worked extra hours. Giulia has told me how she was beaten by her father, that her stepmother was cruel, and that it all taught her how she wanted to be kind.

Once upon a time, a cleaning woman represented a class relationship in a society where class had mind-numbing consequences. Now I know there is a complex and special relationship that forms between women working in the same house. Giulia has allowed me to teach her things that are outside the strict canon of Parma households. She has learned to make pancakes. She is amazed that I don't shout when I want her to improve a task. She has even gotten used to washing my front windows that, in spite of the neighbors' comments, still have no curtains after twenty-three years. "Transparent," she says. "Not hiding. *Bello*," she says, musing on its meaning for her own life.

Mandy Catron

Nor Ever Chaste

Divorce me, untie or break that knot again,

Take me to you, imprison me, for I,

Except you enthrall me, never shall be free,

Nor ever chaste, except you ravish me.

—John Donne, *"Holy Sonnet XIV"*

Except for an undercurrent of murmur and shuffling feet, the church was silent. The air felt cool and light in my lungs and smelled distinctly of damp stones. This was maybe the eighth in a succession of imposing, buttressed structures I'd visited in the past month. Without fail, I felt quiet and reverent in the presence of gothic arches and stained glass. I'd grown accustomed to seeking solace from the baking sidewalks in places of worship, but I entered Chiesa di San Domenico with a very specific objective: to view the six-hundred-year-old head of Ste. Catherine.

I was hung over, saturated in chianti and gelato and the hedonistic revelry of life on a hill in Tuscany. Siena was where my best friend, Erin, spent five months sleeping days and drinking nights. It turned out that people really did sit for hours in the piazza playing spades, and just after dusk, guitars and bongos really did materialize. Always someone was awake and sprawled on the bricks of the campo, blowing smoke at the black air. And a bottle of wine—good wine—was really only four euros. Siena was a town right out of a Shakespearean comedy, with curving stone streets and laundry strung from one window to the next. I believed in Rome, and Florence, and Pisa, Michelangelo, the Medicis, and *Pietà*, but not Siena; it was pre-Renaissance reverie, rising out of vineyards like an island of stone. Could someone really live here? I wondered.

Erin and I milled in the coolness with the rest of the tourists, occasionally floating into groups of fanny packs shuffling behind a colorful handkerchief tied to a stick. The *chiesa* topped Erin's list of things to show me in Siena—no, not the *chiesa*, the head of Ste. Catherine. After three months of studying dark-haired men and cigarettes and where to squat in the streets to pee after midnight, she'd decided I'd be her excuse for seeing some landmarks. It was my last stop before boarding a train to Pisa, a plane to London, and another, larger plane to Virginia. After five months in London, I wasn't ready to face the end of my junior year of college and my pretend life in Europe. I went into the church with two pieces of knowledge about Ste. Catherine:

1. This was the final resting place of her head and right thumb.

2. In her mystic ecstasy, she had a vision of becoming spiritually espoused to the infant Jesus.

In middle school I was my art teacher's favorite student. And when I got to high school, I expected that would continue. After all, I could draw still-life apples better than anyone in my class. I could faithfully reproduce the sloping curves and the reflection of fluorescent classroom lights on the waxy red skins. I saw every blemish and irregularity of color and carefully recreated it in oil pastel.

Our first assignment in Art I was a pencil drawing of one of our hands. This was my chance to show Mrs. McElroy what she could expect from me for the next four years, to make a mark as a capable artist at Abingdon High School. The drawings would be posted in the hall outside of the classroom, and I felt sure everyone would do as I would: evaluate each hand, choosing the best, most accurately rendered pieces, and make a mental confirmation of those individuals as "talented." As a teenager, I felt it was important to have something I could do better than any of my peers. Because I wasn't exceptionally pretty or outstandingly funny, and because I may have been the most tuneless alto in my chorus class, I had decided art was where I would stand out. At fourteen, making a mark somewhere felt like a particularly important step in establishing my identity.

I chose a pencil with soft, dark led and captured the stretch of skin over each tendon and vein, the angle of each metacarpal, the rise of knuckles like a mountain range, the small, ridged fingernails. If something was slightly disproportionate, I erased and redrew until I'd gotten as close to perfection as possible. I stared at the paper, and then my hand. The fingers looked too long and seemed to dominate the palm, but that was accurate. My pediatrician had called them piano-playing fingers and was disappointed each year when I admitted I still hadn't started lessons. I examined my arm where it opened into hand. On my wrists I have large, protruding bones, a sharp knot on each arm. My friend's boyfriend, a sophomore football player, used to call me "anorexic girl," not because I was thin, but because of the way my skeleton emerged under my skin.

I finished shading around my wrist and in the crevice between my thumb and index finger, and put down my pencil. I blew the eraser dust off the paper. It was as accurate as possible, I decided.

When I got the drawing back, the letter B was written in pencil and circled on the back. B? Impossible; this hand was nearly perfect. The next week at a parent/teacher conference, my mother asked Mrs. McElroy about the grade as they reviewed my sketches: "Now, why did she get a B on this one?"

"Well," she explained in the nasal voice I eventually learned to mock almost perfectly, "It's a lovely hand, except for this deformity here." She pointed to my wrist.

"No," my mother explained, "Her wrists are really like that. They've always been that way." My mom thought it was funny, and maybe I did, too. I felt gratified when the grade was changed, but what sticks in my mind is a keener understanding of the ways one can stand out at fourteen. It didn't matter if the drawing was faithful if the subject was awkward and graceless. Despite our best efforts, identity is determined by far more than what we do well.

The nave of the Chiesa di San Domenico was an open, quiet space with no pews or furnishings. On the wall of the chapel was a fresco of Ste. Catherine. She wore a white habit and black robe and carried lilies. Her head was angled so that she seemed neither old nor young, only pensive and peaceful. In her hands were small red holes, stigmata.

At first glance, there were no obvious signs of a head residing anywhere in the room. We began to explore, choosing opposite directions. Along the wall, on a small shelf under a glass globe, I found a thumb sitting inconspicuously among other relics. It was browned, aged, with paper-bag skin crumpled to the bone, the thumbnail like an almond slice. It was elegant and thin, standing erect as if it grew out of the brass candle stand in which it rested—a finger with the grace of an adolescent girl's, no longer bearing baby fat but still small and fragile. It was a timeless digit. I put my face as close to it as I could, wanting to savor it for a moment before calling Erin over to say, "Hey, I found one of her parts."

I am almost twenty-three and in love for the first time. Justin and I rode the Metro around Washington, D.C. for four days, sleeping late and exploring art museums. I watched him across the galleries at the Hirschorn. He is captivating when absorbed in the line and composition of a photograph.

I have just discovered, to my horror and delight, that we have a look. We can, without trying, isolate ourselves from everyone in the room in a glance. My college roommate and her fiancé used to do it, and I'd have to leave the room, unable to study or think in the intensity of their intimacy. And now I have a look; we have a look. I stare up at his irises in the center of the gallery for the ridiculous thrill of it, and I know that everyone else in the room can feel our stare radiating like a sidewalk heat lamp, and I do not care if they are appalled by our audacity.

When we are on the Metro, he whispers into my ear. He says things about my body that thrill and embarrass me. His whisper is loud, and I am afraid that the man to our right isn't reading his *Washington Post* but listening to muffled descriptions of my skin. But I do not stop Justin or tell him to speak more softly. I press my index finger into the center of his palm.

His favorite parts of my body are my hands. He makes fun of their disproportionately elongated "orangutan fingers," but they are graceful in a way I wish the rest of my body could be. He likes my particularly pronounced ulnas, my knots. The bones rise from the safety of each arm, stretching my skin thinner, but it is solid and sturdy. These pokey wrists have drawn attention for as long as I can remember, usually in the form of a question: "Did you break your arm?"

I have not in twenty-three years seen anything comparable to the size of my wrist bones. I've come to believe that no one's wrists obtrude as harshly as mine, but I have outgrown my self-consciousness. Now, for the first time, they are not mere oddities. They are sexy. When we are on the Metro, he slides his finger around and over that mound that pushes up from my arm like a singular mountain. He slides skin over bone, and I feel wanted in a way that is entirely new and consuming.

I spotted Erin in the crowd. "I found the thumb," I mouthed.

"Ooooh. Show me."

I led her to the thumb, which seemed to be of interest only to us. While other tourists examined tapestries and frescoes or meandered aimlessly, we examined the digit.

"It hardly looks real," Erin whispered. "She must've been so tiny."

The longer I stared at the thumb, the more it mesmerized me. I tried to imagine the owner of such a delicate form. Something about the way it was at once girlish and grotesque compelled me to find the head. I walked along the perimeter of the room. It must be here, I thought, maybe along the wall like the thumb, sitting without ostentation.

One would assume the head of a saint would be prominently positioned within the church, that people would be crowded around it in reverence or awe or in the silence of revolting shock that must come with seeing a human head that has been inanimate for more than six hundred years. I looked around—people must be staring somewhere, staring, staring, unable to look away because they were consumed by the sight I imagined in my mind.

I came across an iron helmet in a glass case, like one of a medieval knight, something that could probably house a small head under its dense metal. Maybe, I thought, the head is not something we get to see. Maybe we must have faith that it is here and feel its presence only. I glanced around for a metal plaque designating the helmet as somehow significant. Nothing. I continued along the wall, sure it would appear soon enough.

Then Erin grabbed my arm. "I bet it's there," she nodded toward an altar. It had to be there, where no one was speaking or moving. Where eight or ten people stared or kneeled or inhaled but were too removed from their bodies to even visibly expand their chests by taking in air.

Mystics experience a range of consciousness that is greater than that of the average person. This can include visions, distortion of time and space, access to memories and sensations beyond the self—so much so that in some cases the self is no longer distinguishable from the environment. It is an elusive condition that contemporary psychology often aligns with schizophrenia.

Ste. Catherine dedicated her life to Christ at age seven. As a teenager she scalded herself so that she might appear unattractive to potential suitors. At seventeen she received her habit, and at twenty she underwent a spiritual espousing to the infant Jesus. She had visions, ecstatic trances in which she dictated "The Dialogue of Divine Providence"; she underwent a mystical death and received stigmata on her hands and feet. She died at age thirty-three, the same as Christ.

These are extraordinary activities, even for a mystic. But to me, they sound like standard-issue saintly behavior, apart from the spiritual espousing. Many members of the Church commit their lives to, or "marry," Christ. Ste. Catherine is one of the few who actually had a vision of receiving a ring from Jesus—not the wise, patient pedagogue who spent his days with prostitutes and tax collectors, not the man who fed thousands with a few loaves and fish, but the infant we sing about in Christmas carols, the little lord Jesus. Catherine had a vision of the Virgin Mary holding her son, who extended a ring to her in his tiny, chubby hand. It was this union that was consecrated, this union that was consummated.

When I saw the head, I gasped—audibly. And then I stared. It was, technically speaking, what one would expect of an old, fairly well-preserved human head: grotesque. It was the same gray, paper-bag skin as the thumb. It had sinkhole eyes, deep indentations the size of small apples. Snaggled teeth poked out from where lips once parted. The distance between the hole of her nose and the hole of her mouth was unnaturally far. I squinted my eyes. It wore a white habit.

Ste. Catherine's head sat in an ornate glass box, under a high-watt bulb, behind brass bars, surrounded by an altar of stone guardian cherubs, in a recess of the church, behind another altar. Visitors to the relic could get no closer than thirty feet.

This was it, what we'd come to see. Erin began to giggle silently—or maybe it was me. We both giggled, shoulders shaking. I can't tell you now what was funny; I couldn't have told you then. But I was choking on laughter. The harder we laughed, the more blasphemous I felt, and the more difficult it became to stop laughing. My face was burning; my whole hung-over body was quaking in quiet, painful laughter.

I felt surprised and revolted. I felt disappointed. It was just a relic. I was ultimately unmoved, and my only response was laughter. I'd wanted more—to feel something, to question the nature of faith or to better understand what it meant to live only for the grace of Christ. The head did not speak of her life or love. It was lost in age and the burden of trying so vigorously to mean something to a hundred people each day.

The head was the anticlimax, the thing that meant she lived. The thumb, I realize in retrospect, meant she was alive. It modestly spoke to the fierce passion that allowed a woman to think holes into her wrists. It made me want to know incorruptible love.

The female body in motion, I have come to believe, is the most compelling form of God's creation. In repose, the flesh of the hips can settle, the breasts recline and separate, all of the softness of woman melting into the chaise lounge on which the artist has propped her.

But in motion, the female form is stunning under the command of its owner. Whether strolling, dancing, brushing her teeth, or writhing in spiritual ecstasy, it is the woman who is aware of every fold, every gathering of flesh, every freckle, cuticle, smooth or rough patch of skin who commands our attention across the room or street. And I want to be her, to be able to embrace the dimples on my pink bottom in bright daylight. I want to know each part—nipples, navel, irises, ankles, calves—to memorize the nuances of their structure, the breadth of their motion, to accept it all as integral to woman-ness.

I remember first seeing Rodin's *Eternal Idol* in Paris. It was one of the smaller sculptures in the collection. In it, a man and woman emerge from partly carved stone. She rests on her knees and gently arches her back, grabbing her feet with her hands, wrapping long fingers over her toes. He kneels below her, as if she is on a pedestal. With arms folded behind him, he leans quietly toward her, tilting his head so that his lips can graze the skin just below her breast. As I left the museum, I bought a postcard of the sculpture, which I used as a bookmark. I can recall winding through the Alps on an old train, staring into the depths of that 5 x 7 card, thinking, *This looks like love*. It wasn't the worshipful way he knelt in front of her but the precise tilt of his head, the downward slope of his jaw. I couldn't see his lips, but I knew where they were: not on her breast or thigh, but on the ribcage, a seemingly anonymous spot where he found beauty. This, I was sure, was the kind of touch that would make me beautiful.

Now, I look at Rodin's sculpture, Degas's dancers, and I am struck by their perfection and grace. Maybe it is because these bodies are fleshier, like mine. But that alone cannot make them immortal—it is because of the reverence for form, for woman-ness in physical embodiment. These limbs are alive. These bodies know what they are capable of.

And I have been, for almost a quarter century, in possession of this exquisite form. How fortunate for me. I am the stuff of art, yet, even as I write this, I do not quite believe it. But I am old enough now to start trying, really trying. Beauty, I have learned, can be in an inch of abdomen, the shape of a thumb, or the bend of a wrist.

I think of Catherine, who is not even of full body in death. In an attempt to appease the people of Siena, where Catherine spent most of her life, Blessed Raymond of Capua secretly sent her head to the city. After a few rainy weeks in the tomb in Rome (where she had died), her body had already begun to decompose, and the head was easy to remove. No information on the arrival of the thumb seems to exist. Though the practice of dismembering the bodies of the pious was not uncommon, there are still doubts as to whether the thumb and head truly are those of the saint. I find these debates irrelevant, amazed that the head and thumb of *any* woman exist in such reverence. No one considered how the desire to acquire her made her no longer herself. I like to imagine her, young and wrought with passion.

The thumb stands in my mind as fragile and graceful, with a joie de vivre that the head almost nullified. It was real, and it spoke to the life of a woman who could be enraptured most completely; someone who was unafraid to feel something so hard it levitated her fitfully into the air. I like to project my own life into that thumb.

Now I am apart from Justin. I am in Florida and he is in Virginia. Soon I will be in Virginia, and soon after, he will be in Thailand. This has been the constant in our relationship: living apart or in the anticipation of soon being apart. It is because we are young and have independent lives from which we cannot be kept, or that is at least what I tell myself when I ache to feel his skin on mine like heavy plaster. When he is beside me, I want to be pulled inside out so all of him can touch the inside of me at once. Apart from him, I long to expose those nerves at the base of my spine that send out radio waves, a frequency just from the memory of his chapped lips in the space between ear and hairline.

I wonder what must come with knowing divine love. Of course, in the delight of passion and youth I can say there is divinity in the union of bodies, our bodies, because when my hair falls into my face and I am looking into the creases that run under and out from his eyes, I see what makes me want to make him feel this way forever. Did Ste. Catherine long for Christ this way? Could she? He was her bridegroom, her soulmate, her life's love. When she walked down the street could she feel his fingers sliding in hers at the disparate rhythm of their steps? In her visions, did she try tirelessly to melt and be absorbed into his pores, to produce slick thin sweat at the intersection of their thighs so that they might find in one another that greater aesthetic: the beauty of sculpture, of captured motion, of fingers cradling the thin bulb of a wine glass, of that sentence that screams what she'd always wanted to say but never realized was on her tongue, of the iris which runs brown to olive from pupil outward, of the deep bass beat—the one that pounds through the bowels and pushes blood to the surface of the skin at the center of his body?

Did he hold that finger, compare the distance from tip to first knuckle to other lengths of space on her body? Did he whisper sweet nothings, or did he say, "Look at me. Look," and ravish her with the squeezing of his irises—contract, release, contract, release, contract—a tiny divine muscle showing her the way, the truth, and the light? I am walking the line of blasphemy with this line of questioning—I caution myself—or I have long since crossed it, but I cannot stop. It seems the deepest loves must comprise knowing the other in every capacity as thoroughly as possible. So why is it wrong to assume Catherine had some kind of metaphysical physical relationship with him—the son of God, God incarnate, carnal God? How far removed, really, are spiritual ecstasy and physical ecstasy?

Could Catherine give all of herself to Christ without giving her body, without running that thumb across the dent of his metaphysical hip? Though he was surely concerned with that plane of existence superior to the physical, did he not command Catherine to care for the sick, to nurture not only their spirits but their bodies? Did she ever doubt, could she, in his love, or was his love like a rock in a riverbed—utterly endurable and balanced? Was it like bread and wine, a grape juice and wafer; was it richness beyond egg yolks? Did she feel luxury in his love? Did he say to her, "I like the curve of your breasts just below your arms when you are at rest"? Did he say not "I love you," because Christ is love, but "I am love, and in me, you are also love"?

Serena Richardson

An Italian
Thanksgiving

The parents of my boyfriend, Luciano, had
never met an American before. And when I began my
new life in Northern Italy with the kind, loving man I had
met in California, his parents suddenly had to begin speaking a new
language: Italian. For in the in the rolling hills outside of Venice, the
dialect changes from village to village. And as I slowly and sometimes painfully learned Italian and their dialect, I found that they
were fascinated by tales of American life, especially Luciano's
mother, Anna Maria, who loved my story of Thanksgiving.

I told her that the Friday after Thanksgiving, "*tutti i tacchini
negli Stati Uniti sono morti*" (all the turkeys are dead).

"*Tutti morti?*" She thought that was so funny. They had only
seen one whole in the movies. So of course, I wanted to cook
Thanksgiving dinner for this family.

I discovered that it is very difficult to find a complete turkey in Italy, even in the larger town of Treviso, where I live and work as an English teacher. Turkeys are too big to stay in one piece. I could find legs and breasts, but not the whole bird. I thought, *No problem, I can ask the butcher across the street to order one.*

He is the classic butcher: round, bald, and with a little mustache. However, I should have expected trouble ever since the day he told me that *filetto al pepe verde* is always made with pork. "Pork! You use pork for *filetto al pepe verde.* Absolutely. How much do you want?" Well, now I know, as everyone else does, that it is always made with beef— but only after an attempt to amaze one of Luciano's friends, Massimo, for his birthday. While very appreciative of the meal, Massimo gently informed me of my mistake, and I made a mental note on the credibility of the butcher. This same butcher informed me sadly, a week before Thanksgiving, that turkeys are just not available *intero*, only in pieces. I could not believe this. Turkeys had to be in one piece at some point in their lives, especially in Italy, where I have seen them running around, blithely enjoying a Thanksgiving-free environment.

I consulted the food experts, Luciano's parents. They were endlessly amused by my predicament, which was discussed at length at the kitchen table.

"Why don't you buy a lot of turkey pieces and make a little mountain?" Giancarlo suggested. "You can sew the pieces together," Anna Marie recommended. Frankenstein's Turkey.

I asked my students about the mystery of the whole turkey as part of a classroom discussion on holidays. First, I told them all

about Thanksgiving, *Ringraziamento:* its history, that it is always on
the third Thursday in November, and that it is traditional to roast a
turkey. And then I mentioned my difficulties in finding one whole.
After taking this all in, the class was silent.

I imagined them all processing the concept of buying, cooking,
and then eating an *entire* turkey. Then they collected themselves, and
several suggested that I go to a very beautiful butcher shop near the
school. This particular shop is a temple to meat: glass, mirrors, cop-
per cases, and huge legs of prosciutto sticking in the air with bows on
their ankles. A heavy curtain is pulled over the window at the lunch
pausa so the meat is not disturbed.

Promptly, in I went and asked the butcher if I could order a
miniature but *complete* turkey to be picked up next week. With a
small smile he said, "Why yes, it can be done."

What a relief!

But he added that it was going to be a *tacchina,* not a *tacchino.* I
figured, girl or boy turkey, I didn't care, as long as it was small and
in one piece. To my dismay, the next day my students told me that
there was no such thing as a *tacchina.* I could have ordered a toad for
dinner, for all I knew. But it was ordered, and whatever it was, it was
going to get roasted whole.

Since I taught a class on Thursday nights, we decided to hold
the dinner on a Friday night. Luciano's parents and *la Nonna*—his
ninety-one-year-old grandmother, Italia—would arrive at my house
at 7:30 PM, and dinner would be served promptly at 7:45 PM.
Because I knew that this was a late night for them, I asked if we

should celebrate Thanksgiving on Sunday afternoon instead, but Giancarlo said, "No, we must follow tradition and come as close to the real day as possible."

All was set for dinner on the day after Thanksgiving, Friday, November 21. Thursday morning I went to my first meeting of the English Speaking Ladies Club, a group of ladies that strives to provide a tiny English-speaking world in the middle of the Veneto. The subject of Thanksgiving came up. One woman mentioned how one year she went to the butcher to pick up her turkey (the same place where I had placed my order) and was informed that there was no turkey for her because they had not been able to get it across the Piave (a very large river nearby), and she said that she'd had to settle for two ducks. I wanted to ask why the turkeys could not get across the Piave—I mean, there are bridges, of course—but I did not. I was distracted by the way they were referring to Thanksgiving in the future, as if it were next week, not today.

I offhandedly remarked, "Isn't today Thanksgiving?"

"No, no, Serena. Check your calendar," one woman offered.

"Oh," I said casually, hoping that I did not reveal my confusion.

The conversation moved on to something else, and I quietly snuck out and looked, for the first time, in my datebook. And there it was, in the front of the book, staring at me: THANKSGIVING, NOVEMBER 27, 2003.

No wonder the butcher had smiled at me. He knew it was on the 27th, not the 20th. I felt so disoriented, so embarrassed. I mean, this was *my* holiday. *I* was supposed to be the expert. I had wanted to impress the family. And I had gotten it wrong. By a whole week! I frantically called Luciano to see what we should do. No answer. I left a message.

Oh no! I had to teach on Friday the 28th. I dropped by the school to see if I could get a sub to teach the class. No way. So, literally pacing in front of the grocery store, I waited to hear from Luciano whether to go ahead with Thanksgiving a week early.

He called. "What do I do?" I pleaded.

"You know, Serena," Luciano said, "people pay a lot of money to go to funny movies or to see comedians, but I don't need to, I have you. Don't worry, you are in Italy . . . early or late, it does not matter. Besides, my parents will never know it is not really tomorrow." So it was decided to go ahead with the plan; we would tell them the truth later.

Friday morning I picked up the bird, ready to face the butcher, pretending as if I knew damn well that I was a week early. Maybe I was jetting off to Paris for the real Thanksgiving; *he* didn't know. I was in suspense about how big the turkey would be . . . and there it was, not too big, weighing in about thirteen or fourteen pounds. The clerk politely asked me if I wanted her to cut it into pieces. I almost leaped across the counter. Did she have any idea?

And so the turkey rode home with me, intact, bouncing across the cobblestones in the basket of my bicycle. Once home, I unwrapped it and discovered that he (she?) still needed a good deal of plucking. So there I stood in my kitchen, plucking a turkey with a pair of tweezers. I thought, *Oh my God, I really am an Italian housewife.*

But of course an Italian housewife would never be caught dead in such a predicament. Into the oven it went, where it just barely fit. I was so prepared for the day that I even had a few minutes to sit down and relax. Ready for a 7:45 seating.

But then the doorbell rang at 7:05. They were early! I jumped into action and got dinner on the table at 7:30.

Broiled almond-stuffed dates wrapped in pancetta

Cherry tomatoes stuffed with gorgonzola cream

Baked radicchio with casatella cheese and golden raisins

Herb-roasted turkey sausage and mushroom stuffing

Braised fennel

Oven-roasted potatoes with rosemary

Sautéed turnip greens with peperoncini

Hazelnut cake with chocolate ganache glaze

Coffee, grappa

Hah!

To a round of applause, I brought out their first whole turkey. *La Nonna* ate two helpings; Giancarlo, three. Giancarlo made a little speech as he sometimes does: "We would all like to thank La Serena for this wonderful dinner with the family and the *tacchino spet-ta-co-lo-so.*" He likes to draw out the syllables of words for dramatic affect, and it works.

The next day, there was turkey all over the place. I sent some home with Luciano's relatives, and I froze the rest. Luciano was already sick of it. Even I couldn't face it anymore. But friends looked at the family with new respect when someone would say, "Oh yes, we have had a whole turkey."

The next week, Luciano casually mentioned to the family that the real Thanksgiving was tomorrow, and that we had feasted a little early. There was a moment of silence. I held my breath. All eyes were on Giancarlo, who solemnly said, "The day is not important. What is important is that we celebrated it together."

He was right. It gave me goose bumps to hear him say this about a holiday that means absolutely nothing to Italians. In this simple sentence, he summed up the meaning of Thanksgiving, which has perhaps become lost to those of us who have celebrated it for years simply because it is on the calendar.

For a fleeting moment I thought, *Next year I will get it right. Next year I won't make the same mistake.* But then I corrected myself. We were early, so what? Maybe those ladies who are all celebrating tomorrow will have to cross the Piave to get their turkeys. We already had ours.

Natalie Galli

Black and Pink in Cefalù

In my dream, I stood twirling with my arms outstretched in the center of a red room with all the windows open; the curtains billowed luxuriantly, and a lantern flickered on and off. When I woke up groggy, displaced, and sticking to the sheets, it took me a minute. Blood had gushed out. Oh man, now what would I do? I couldn't leave this stain for the housekeeper; he shouldn't have to wash out a woman's blood. The blaze of red would surely offend him. Look at these pure white European sheets I had darkened! Mea culpa, mea maxi-pad culpa. I pulled off the bottom sheet and the mattress pad and carried them out of my door to the bathroom

My seventy-four-year-old cousin looked up from her newspaper. "But what are you doing, *cara?*"

"Good morning, Maia, I need to wash these out."

"No no, you mustn't do that, you're the guest. Primo will take care of it. Put them back."

I left a note on the bundled-up pile in the bedroom:

Dear Primo, I'm very, very sorry to inconvenience you.

The sheets need cleaning. Again, I am terribly sorry.

"Have some breakfast," said Maia. "What shall we do today, *tesoro?*"

"Uh, well . . ." I stood drinking the tea she had made for me and washing down two painkillers to avoid doubling over with cramps. My cycle must have been thrown off by the trans-Atlantic flight, because hadn't I bled only two or so weeks ago?

Maia jumped up from her armchair. "In that case, I want to show you part of the north coast and Cefalù. We'll be back by four. *Andiamo.*" In no time we were battling a monumental traffic jam along Palermo's waterfront. Only motor scooters moved forward, whining through the narrow openings. The rest of us sat stuck in a devastated neighborhood bombed by the Americans during World War II. Weeds sprouted from the gaping gray walls of former baroque palaces.

"Will it ever be rebuilt?" I felt ashamed for my country. They'd had no strategic reason to bomb Sicily in 1945.

"Ehh . . . " she trailed off, stalwart behind the wheel. My cousin carried her losses folded inside her. During the war she lost her mother; her brother was taken to Germany as a prisoner of war; I knew not to bring up either of them.

"Look at the nuns," she nodded to our left.

A Fiat, packed with five or six teeny sisters, revved. They had strapped a bundle of jumbo artichokes on long, leafy stalks to the roof like a bad green hairpiece. "Nuns with artichokes," my cousin deadpanned. "A good title for a still life."

With their hands, the sisters argued about something. The driver behind us leaned on his horn. "What do you think we can do about it?" Maia protested indignantly, lifting her palms heavenward for his benefit. We remained trapped like everyone else by rivers of vehicles and clouds of diesel. A St. Christopher medallion, dangling from his rear-view mirror, swung madly back and forth from constant stopping and starting. In fact, he appeared to be on the verge of achieving full apoplexy. *San Cristoforo, proteggemi.* St. Christopher, protect me.

"I wonder what they're talking about," I said. "Looks like a deep theological question—something profound."

Maia, always eager to engage with her fellow citizens, rolled the window down as soon as we came abreast of them. "Tell us, Sister, we would like to know, what recipe will you use for those beautiful *carciofi?* My cousin visiting from America is curious."

The nuns' level of animation rose to greater heights as word spread that an American asked, and they rolled down their windows and waved to me, grinning. I waved back, relieved that they didn't hate all Americans because of the bombing half a century ago.

"Fried in olive oil with a flour-and-egg batter, that's what I would do," Maia offered. "Of course, you would want to stuff each with a piece of pecorino beforehand, naturally."

This culinary suggestion was relayed throughout their car. The driver, barely visible above the dashboard, did not seem pleased, her hands slicing the air.

"Slivered thin, then layered with mushrooms and sauce and topped with mozzarella," came the decree from within. "Baked slowly. If God grants that we arrive back to the convent in time for lunch," the nun added under her breath. "Otherwise, it's bread soup again."

Maia translated for me rapidly, using her hands as well. Though I got the ingredients, she rightly worried that I wouldn't catch every verb: slivered, sliced, oven-baked. "Mmmm," I responded, searching my bag for the pocket-size dictionary. I'd forgotten to pack it in our rush to leave.

"How about roasted with crushed garlic, mint, olive oil, and breadcrumbs?" I contributed. I could still taste the Pasquetta (Little Easter) feast cooked in the coals. "Tell them, Maia."

"*Arrostiti*," Maia hollered to be heard in the din. "*Con aglio, menta, olio d'olive, e briciole di pane.* And don't forget to put an anchovy in the center."

Our back-and-forth had attracted the attention of other drivers, who were giving the topic serious consideration as well. A man in a business suit, a couple of cars over, actually got out (leaving his motor running; I could see the black smoke rising from the tailpipe), strolled over, and stood fingering the chokes, petting the silvery-green leaves. "It would be a shame to do anything but boil them whole because of their excellent size," he declaimed. "That way, you see, they retain all their flavor. If you start pulling off this leaf here and cutting that leaf there, you will destroy the integrity of the vegetable. Serve them simply with olive oil, warmed with some garlic and sprinkled with lemon. Imagine their hearts . . ." he paused to observe a moment of reverent silence. "You can't go wrong, I assure you."

"Lemon rind in the boiling water?" The spokesnun asked.

"*Beh* . . . I prefer after."

"Why not both?" Maia, ever the diplomat, suggested. "Is there such a thing as too much lemon?"

"Hey, move it, move it," yelled St. Christopher, "Go!" The traffic had suddenly opened up.

"*Buon appetito*, sisters," Maia saluted. "What is your order, by the way?"

"Convent of the Most Precious Blood."

By the time we made it out of the city, my cousin—my brave, pedal-happy Palermitana driver—seemed energized, even as I felt myself fading from all the exhaust. I cracked open my window and breathed in. We breezed through groves of aromatic lemon and orange.

"What sweet air," I said, rolling down my window farther. "Wow! I've never seen such enormous grapefruits." They tugged their branches toward the ground. My abdomen was tugging downward too—the pills had only worked about halfway.

"Citrons, not grapefruit."

"Another way to flavor artichokes, maybe?"

"They are quite strong and bitter. We don't use them much for savory cooking, but for sweets. We boil their rinds with sugar water until they have candied."

How Sicilian—the bitter and the sweet. We sped past villas. Wisteria graced the shuttered windows.

"Of course, these buildings are in a terrible state of neglect now, but you can imagine them in the eighteenth century."

Maia watched the road now and again. "While most Sicilians struggled to eat one meal a day, these aristocrats had so much wealth that they sent their laundry to Paris to be cleaned."

"No! What are you saying? They didn't have it done here?"

"And allow it to be touched by lower-class hands? Never." She made a mocking face.

"*Incredibile.*" What could I add about the very rich that hadn't been said before? Apropos of laundry, I should have insisted on soaking the sheets right away, I realized now. How could I have done that to poor Primo? I closed my eyes, just for a moment. I swore I still had jet lag ten days into the trip.

"There it is." Maia jingled her keys.

"Hmm?" My eyes flew open; I hid a yawn with my hand.

"*Cefalù.*" She pointed to a bulging granite cliff and a port clinging to its base. "Named for the hill, which, as you can see, looks something like a head, from the Greek cephalos."

I peeled myself out of her car. Soon she was guiding me

through the port, past moored boats painted bright blue and green and rose, past six little boys in shorts and sandals throwing rocks into the clear water and then taking turns holding one fishing rod. We ambled past neat piles of dripping fishnets, past wrought-iron streetlamps, past arched stone houses pressed together with balconies gazing waterward, past shutters of green and orange. Walking roused me. The fuzz in my head started to clear, and before my eyes, a fishing village came into focus—a real one, doing what it had always done.

"Thank you, Maia, for bringing me here." Spontaneously on this day, to stunning Cefalù, with glossy green water and a cathedral in the distance, my mood had shifted this exquisite afternoon. I liked a town with a brain, with some anatomy.

I trailed Maia across a sloping piazza dotted with palm trees and into the Norman cathedral to see the tremendous mosaic Christ in the apse. He was so kind looking, with deep, round, pensive eyes that followed us, each one of us at the same time, as we wandered through the echoing vault, watching Him watching us. He was so welcoming, His outstretched arms forever offering solace and acceptance as we approached Him down the aisle.

Outside on the piazza, Maia began to read from her guidebook: "The Cathedral, a splendid edifice begun by Roger II in 1131, is particularly effective owing to the formidable cliff immediately behind it. . . ."

I spotted him about twenty feet away, sitting on his motor scooter, hunched over just so. The gold crucifix hanging from his neck dangled in the air between his chest and the odometer. *Dio mio.* He wore a salmon-pink button-down shirt, pegged black pants, salmon-pink socks, and black shoes. Maybe he was nineteen, maybe twenty-two.

"The facade, a distinctive design by Giovanni Panettera, dates from 1240; it is flanked by two massive towers and enlivened by . . ."

He straddled his machine, fiddling a little with the handles, making a show of polishing the chrome, mere gratuitous activity. He was here for one purpose: to be gazed upon. Which was impossible not to do, since he had the face of this island, deep-lidded eyes to sink into, and a profile straight off an old Roman coin. In addition, he happened to have the body of *The Discus Thrower. Madonna mia.* So much antiquity wrapped up in one live person. I wished I could magically slip away for five minutes, hop onto the back of his *moto,* and have him drive around the bend; have him stop the engine and lean against a stone wall. Then I would kiss his eyelids—first one, then the other, then the one, then the other. Just kiss, that's all. Kiss only. Lid and lid. Then I could rejoin Maia, who would still be reading aloud and wouldn't have noticed my absence, and she and I would continue on our way, discussing Norman architecture.

"The exterior of the south side and transept and of the triple apse is well worth studying."

Well worth studying. A number of women, boys, men, girls, and stray cats were studying him as well. The star attraction, the chief entertainment, the major drama of Cefalù, a deity landed in the middle of the piazza, the Pink and Black Adonis. He'd perfected a kind of smoky glance, taking in the looks not only through his eyes, but also through the pores of his skin, the black curls of his head, then deflecting them, returning them. My eyes would not budge, and when he turned his attention to me for a moment, I nearly toppled off my cobblestone. He narrowed his black eyes and flared his nostrils. (Help me.) And to think that this was how some engagements used to be made—just by signaling, by a look.

"Hmm," Maia stood firmly planted in her walking shoes, glancing back and forth between Adonis and me. *"Proprio un fusto."* (A real good-looker.) "Hmmmm." A quarter-smile flitted across her face.

"Nice colors," I stammered.

"He's got something," she winked.

"Yes, something."

The church bells began to peal. As we turned to find the car, I narrowed my eyes back at Pink and Black. He was watching me—and everyone else—all at the same time.

Barbara Grizzuti Harrison

Rome,
the Art of Living

There is, sometimes, a bleeding, a time when by
some peculiar combination of elements all of Rome is flat
and overexposed, a time of light without shadows, a still white
light that is more like the seepage of light than light itself: a vam-
pire light. Rome is then breathless, withdrawn. If you are with a
Roman when this phenomenon occurs—everything against the
bleached and empty sky assumes a singularity and integrity, and
nothing trembles but the heart of things—you will hear him sigh;
an agitated fatalism like a little whirlwind will possess him, and—
Romans like to define themselves, it is a form of forgivable
narcissism in a city of regarded artifacts; his city is not only its
intimidating stones—perhaps he will choose the ephemeral occasion to tell you that Romans are a "meteorological" lot. And so they

are, like necromancers attuned to weather; perhaps it comes of growing up so intimately under the sign of the Cross, of pledging oneself in the name of the Holy Spirit, the Spirit of God that moves across the waters (as children blow bubbles, as angels blow clouds). The Romans profess themselves to be governed by the spirit of the winds that play across their sweet, grand city—the *ponentino*, a pet of a wind, the westerly sea breeze that cools that hottest August day on afternoons when help is needed and despaired of; the *tramontana*, the steely northerly winter wind that threads the air and stirs the palms with Alpine cold and searches into every place (the wind is *brutto*, it incites to murder); the *scirocco*, the siren wind of Africa, hot, suggestive, weakening.

One afternoon in May—Henry James says "there are days when the beauty of the climate of Rome alone suffices for happiness," and May is the loveliest month of all—I stood on a promontory overlooking the Forum in one of those reveries one is always falling into in Rome (a nourished melancholy), and a fierce hot wind sprang up like an assailant and slammed me. It ripped the glasses off my face and they flew high and landed on the lap of a souvenir hawker below me. "Ah, signora," he called out, looking complacently upon my distress, looking oracular, too (and also lecherous), "there must be an earthquake in Sicily." He made this sound like an invitation to licentiousness; and there was an earthquake, in Messina, I saw it in the paper the next day.

From the bluff upon which I stood, traitors had, in ancient times, been hurled to their death.

Mattina   *Morning*

Millumino   *On the edge of night*

d'immenso   *I fill with the light*

of Immensity.

—*Giuseppe Ungaretti*

I met Eva in a restaurant near the Piazza di Spagna. We were obliged to share a table. This did not suit her, for she has an icy Swedish reserve. But it is not worth the effort, in Rome, to hold on to an idea of oneself, and soon she was quite merry, and from time to time we saw each other; and she did brave things: She rode on Vespas with beautiful young strangers; she strode through the Borghese Gardens alone at night, never fearing the thieves who lurk in that once-malarial expanse ("where fever walks arm-in-arm with you, and death awaits you at the end of the dim vista"*). Every six months or so this Valkyrie sends me a card: "Have you caught the light? . . . Do you remember the light? . . . Will you write about the light?" She longs for that light. I do, too.

The light shatters reserve.

The skies are endless; the trees define them: "These trees are magnificent, but even more magnificent is the sublime and moving space between them, as though with their growth it too increased."[†] Solemn, ornamental, and eternal, the cypress and the umbrella pine enlarge the Roman sky.

From my balcony I see across the Tiber to the Aventine. There, in the Piazza dei Cavalieri di Malta, is a green door with a tiny keyhole, and through that keyhole one can see, at the end of a long avenue of mingling branches, the dome of St. Peter's. From the dome we should see the world; instead, from the keyhole we see the dome. The keyhole is bigger than we are; the large is contained in the small. This strange and wonderful inversion of perspective is magic—and a metaphor, perhaps, for Catholic Italy: "Experience," wrote Santayana, "is a mere peephole through which glimpses come down to us of eternal things." That is what Rome has been for many; and for me: a glimpse, an intimation, as glorious as the empty thrones that Giotto imagined in Paradise.

On the crest of the Aventine, umbrella pines frame the intimate immensity of sky, their graceful sobriety a necessary counterpoint to the wasted grandeur of Rome's ruins. Two decades ago it was feared that a blight might destroy them, and the cry went up that had been sounded so often before: Rome will be ruined!

"You'll like it," Henry James's Osmond says to Isabel. "They have spoiled it, but you'll like it."

"Ought I to dislike it, because it's spoiled?" she asks.

"No, I think not. It has been spoiled so often," he says.

James, who in 1869 reeled through Rome in a liberating fever of delight, three years later pronounced the city hopelessly modernized, and foretold that it would soon become "a lugubrious modern capital." Dickens, whose superstitious horror of relics often made him bellicose and cranky in Italy, fumed and called Rome "the Dead City . . . no more my Rome, [but] the Rome of anybody's fancy, man or boy: degraded and fallen and lying asleep in the sun among a heap of ruins." Hawthorne thought even the ruins were ruined.

We are all proprietary toward cities we love. "Ah, you should have seen her when I loved her!" we say, reciting glories since faded or defiled, trusting her to no one else; that others should know and love her in her present fallen state (for she must fall without our vigilant love) is a species of betrayal.

Rome seems perpetually perched on the very edge of ruin.

In the last century it was the Vittorio Emanuele Monument on the Piazza Venezia, silly and pompous, white as an operating room, bombastic and ridiculously at odds with its neighbors—a failed attempt, at the time of the unification of Italy, to reanimate the spirit of Imperial Rome—that was said to be emblematic of the decline of Rome. It hasn't worn well; it hasn't, in fact, worn at all. The distinguishing white Brescian marble of which it is made continues, unlike Rome's honey-colored travertine, to blind but not to dazzle. It refuses to be anything other than white. It is not a morally illuminating building.

Nineteenth-century writers invariably capitalized *Beauty*, and as in Rome Beauty is a boon companion, not abstract but corporeal, this was more than sentimentality. Rome, as one romantic traveler observed, not only cultivates Beauty as other countries cultivate corn but tolerates all things without defilement. (This is said of the Catholic Church, too: that it elevates, consecrates, and dedicates all things to God's glory. Rome, like the Church, is a living organism, an example of Darwinian principles at work.) It is now possible to regard the foolish Vittorio Emanuele almost with affection. That which makes it deplorable—its brazen conspicuousness—also works to redeem it: It serves as a landmark; if your path takes you, as mine often did, up the traffic-clogged Corso and beyond the Piazza Venezia to the Tiber and Trastevere, you find the sight of the funny old thing not only reassuring but bracing. Now, when I close my eyes to receive one of those lantern-slide memories that hold me in love with Rome, I see a grouping that has arranged itself without my advice and consent: I see, from a café on the Via del Teatro di Marcello, the dignified amber-brown brick Church of Santa Maria d'Aracoeli with its two Gothic rose windows, a building sensual in its severity; and Michelangelo's peach- and honey-colored Capitol buildings; and—it has become part of the landscape of memory—the Vittorio Emanuele, Rome's colossal "wedding cake."

More recently it was Mussolini who "ruined" Rome, not nearly so much by building (his sterile and spooky "garden suburb" built for an exposition that never happened—Esposizione Universale di Rome [EUR, pronounced "ay-ur"]—is too far south to impinge upon that part of Rome that we think of as Rome) as by excavating the odd Roman ruin, here a ruin, there a ruin, tearing down belonging buildings, peeling back visible layers of history to do so. Romans' respect for ruins is fabulous. When I entered Rome for the first time, years ago, by train, I practically swooned with gratitude when I saw that fragments of an Etruscan wall were an integral part of the structure of the railroad terminal. I immediately saw what the texture of Rome would be. Many of the landmarks of my youth were being torn down in an orgy of building that my own city, New York, was at that time undergoing, and having entered adulthood recently and tentatively enough to need all the outward and visible emblems of my childhood firmly in place, I was feeling like a displaced person. Rome is kind to its past; and to grow up in a city that reveres history must make one feel that history—the world's, and one's own—has a point.

In the Piazza Augusto Imperatore, Augustus Caesar's jostled bones lie buried near one of the restaurants that vie for the title of the "original Alfredo's," and next to the sunken ruins excavated by Mussolini is a fatuous Fascist building with this inscription: THE ITALIAN PEOPLE ARE THE PEOPLE IMMORTAL WHO FIND ALWAYS THE SPRINGTIME OF HOPE, OF PASSION, OF GRANDEUR (which springtime for Mussolini did not last long). It is a strange juxtaposition . . . but Rome is full of unexpected juxtapositions, most of them felicitous; this one is not.

While time has not effaced the architectural damage the Fascists inflicted upon Rome, time—helped along by the Romans— has softened it. The massive Fascist government building near the

Circus Maximus on what used to be called the Viale Adolfo Hitler now serves as offices for the United Nations Food and Agricultural Organization; the *viale* has been rechristened Viale delle Fosse Ardeatine, in memory of the 335 souls, including 100 Jews and a boy of fourteen, massacred in 1944 by the Nazis in the Ardeatine caves beyond the Catacombs.

Time has humanized ruins which somehow, under Mussolini's patronage, tended to look like visual aids for a dreary civics lesson. On the Piazza Fiume, for example—a busy piazza to which one goes for the pleasure of shopping at a Roman department store—there is an extrusion, perhaps once a fortification, from a Roman wall (and growing from the broken wall, a tree as ancient as the ruin). People, perhaps squatters, live here—their laundry proclaims their existence; they revivify the ruins. We are not far from the Baths of Diocletian, and in the neighborhood of the Porta Pia and the Porta Salaria, two of the fifteen gates that pierce the encircling Wall of Rome—a monument itself, though so much an integrated part of the landscape we don't see it in that light. Beyond these gates once lay the vast Campagna, miles and miles of waste and grass-covered ruins: "an undulating flat . . . where few people can live; and where, for miles and miles, there is nothing to relieve the terrible monotony and gloom . . . So sad, so quiet, so sullen; so secret in its covering up of great masses of ruin, and hiding them; so like the wasted places into which the men possessed with devils used to go and howl and rend themselves, in the old days of Jerusalem. . . . Nothing but now and then a lonely house, or a villainous-looking shepherd: with matted hair all over his face, and himself wrapped to the chin in a frowsy brown mantle, tending his sheep." This is not long ago as time is counted in Rome; Dickens wrote this of it.

There is not, on the other hand, much to be said for the Via della Conciliazione, the broad thoroughfare that leads to the Square of St. Peter's, or for the two raw-looking end buildings that link the thoroughfare to Bernini's colonnade. The Borgo is the area around St. Peter's; surrounded by Leonine walls, it is bordered by the Castel Sant'Angelo on the west and the Vatican on the east, two strongholds that are connected by a *passetto*, or fortified corridor, through which Clement VIII escaped during the Sack of Rome; its residents call the Via della Conciliazione "the gash," an ugly name. It was begun in 1936 and not finished until the Holy Year of 1950, and it replaced a cluster of medieval streets. God save Rome from reckless city planners who want to "open the city up." The beautiful *piazze* of Rome always take one by surprise, *especially* if one knows they are there; one comes from dark and narrow streets, hoarding and postponing pleasure, into a bath of always surprising light. Some liken the effect of this tunneling in the dark toward light to the Resurrection. The Via della Conciliazione, with its absurd obelisk lamps, its shops with their souvenirs poignant and execrable in equal part (*articoli religiosi, oggetti sacri*—pictures of Christ with tearful eyes that follow you lasciviously), robs the pilgrim of surprise. (And to add insult to injury, there is not even a good café or restaurant along this avenue, a most un-Roman state of affairs.)

Now it is the roisterous traffic or the proliferating American-style fast-food restaurants that will "ruin" Rome.

The fast-food restaurant near the Fountain of Trevi, where "in a narrow little throat of a street," Dickens saw "a booth, dressed out with flaring lamps, and boughs of trees . . . a group of sulky Romans round smoky coppers of hot broth and cauliflower stew; trays of dried fish and . . . flasks of wine," is of course not admirable. But Trevi, once a basin in which to rinse wool, a fountain that barely escapes lunacy to achieve an incarnation of joy, still shelters lovers in its hollows late at night. Poor Trevi; its water comes from Agrippa's aqueduct, Acqua Vergine, built nineteen years before the birth of Christ, but someone is always having a brand-new idea for this fantastic wall of sporting gods and goddesses and cascading water which is set, improbably, in the junction of the three tiny streets (hence, *tre vie*). When leaders of the Italian fashion industry wanted a removable Plexiglas walkway placed across the riotous fountain in order for models to parade the season's wares, the city said No, it would be unbecoming. And shortly after this contretemps a judge banned the use of ancient monuments for "cultural extravaganzas"; he suggested that even outdoor opera at the Baths of Caracalla might be illegal, and considered, in the interest of safeguarding the historical and artistic wealth of Italy, halting the sale of refreshments at the Colosseum. A former mayor of Rome called a city-sponsored circus at the Piazza Navona the "sign of a fallen civilization."

Quod non fecerunt barbari, fecerunt Barberini (What the barbarians didn't do, the Barberinis did): We can't reasonably expect to see the elevation, purification, and consecration of the sleazy fast-food restaurants near traffic-throttled Piazza Barberini (or, for that matter, the [discreetly archless] McDonald's near the Spanish Steps). The Barberinis, for their sins—they stripped the Pantheon of its bronze—gaze upward or downward, as the case may be, from the place assigned to them by God, to see that Bernini's lovely Triton Fountain and the piazza named for them has become a traffic rotary.

These new food establishments (of the one that faces the Pantheon it is too awful to speak), because they are less inexpensive than the unpretentious *rosticcerie* and *tavole calda* that have served Romans and visitors adequately and sometimes brilliantly for years with simple food (cold meats; roasted chicken; plain or grilled sandwiches [*panini*]; salads), are an affront to logic as well as to aesthetics. It's a shock to see a Benny Burger on the Viale di Trastevere; the Roman youngbloods on Vespas and on foot who frequent it look pleased with themselves and defiant (and Benny Burger as a consequence has a rakish, speakeasy air), which suggests that they are doing something naughty, as perhaps they are. . . . But no one is so beautiful, taking his ease, as a Roman; and at night, on the *viale*, it is lively and gay, and Rome is not "spoiled," only minimally altered, immensely lovable, pleasing not in every part but steadfastly beautiful as a whole. It remains in its essentials unalterable.

---

* Nathaniel Hawthorne, *The Marble Faun*

† Gaston Bachelard, *The Poetics of Space*

Julianne DiNenna

Back to
Nonna's Boot

"They riced me out like hard-boiled potatoes through a ricer," my Nonna told me, "mixed me with American wheat, and now you can call me 'gnocchi americani'." Her muscular hands kneaded the potato and flour dough into the shape of the Italian peninsula on the wooden pasta board. She joined the two ends of the dough, shaping, kneading, flattening, and kneading again, just as her parents had once kneaded and shaped her into a fusion of two cultures.

"We're from the boot" was my first geography lesson in relief from my Nonna, who had little education herself. I watched raptly as she twisted and convoluted gnocchi dough over the rough side of the pasta board, the cherry table trembling slightly at each fold. La Campania, the province of her birth, sounded mystical. Nonna promised to take me there as soon as she got enough money.

"Maria Angela," Poppie scolded her, "*non siamo più italiani, siamo americani adesso.* We're American now." This last part in perfect, Italian-accented English was for my benefit. "Why do you keep talking to our granddaughter about that place?! What do you want to go to Italy for? There's nothing there for us anymore!" His sputtering almost made him choke on his black coffee.

Nonna raised her ricer in defiance. She was a large woman for an Italian, six feet tall, astonishing considering living conditions in Southern Italy during her childhood.

"We will go," she insisted, "and they will call my granddaughter Giovannina, as she was supposed to be called—after my mother—until you Americanized her name!" Fortunately, the shaking cherry table stood between them or Poppie could have been hacked by Nonna's ricer. Poppie rolled his chestnut-brown eyes, leaving us alone in the kitchen that my mother later resurfaced in ceramic tiles from Italy.

As time passed, we lost Poppie, and Nonna's overpowering six-foot frame began to stoop, then hunch, then shrink. The more Nonna diminished, the more she spoke of la Campania in between her *Santa Marias* on her rosary.

By the time Nonna shrank down to my grand size of five towering feet, black night claimed her. Drifting away to return in spirit to la Campania, where Naples is the capital, she admonished me: "They say 'see Naples and die.' If you go to Italy, don't go to Naples. I want you to live a long life and have plenty of granddaughters on your own."

Nonna was the last survivor of the family members who had immigrated from the Old Country. She took with her my last connection to the language and heritage. After she was gone, the longing for homemade gnocchi or *pizzelle* or biscotti or cannoli or sweet ravioli pulled from my innards like a centripetal force.

So, while in college on an exchange program in Switzerland, I decided to make my way down to this bewildering Campania. At first vacation break, I hopped on a train down through the Alps and into my Nonna's cherished native land. I unwittingly asked a blond friend with ceramic skin and blue-green eyes to accompany me on my path of family discovery. With little money, I set off with Carole, who had a *Cheap Sleeps* guide.

As we began our journey, I tried to imagine what I would find: maybe tall old ladies like Nonna, who would gesticulate vivaciously at every other word. Maybe bright yellow and orange tiles in restaurants that smelled of fresh oregano and basil, maybe *spinaci con limone,* my favorite dish, heaped onto colorful, hand-painted pottery. With the rhythmic *click-clack* of locomotion, I slept lightly on our way down to Verona, recalling Nonna at her pasta board, kneading and folding thick, elastic gnocchi dough.

Hardly off the train in Verona, we heard "*Ciao, bella!*" sounding at every passage. The first time, we looked over our shoulders to see what all the fuss was about. I had little time to ponder if my ancestors ever walked down the sun-streamed, narrow cobblestone streets past Giulietta's balcony when, behold, one, then three, then a half-dozen dark-haired Romeos catcalled to my blond friend, following us throughout the tiny medieval town. *"Ciao, bella, vieni parlarci un po!"* (Hey, beautiful, come, let's talk for a while.)

Their number grew in size as our steps increased. Our every gesture and window-shopping stops solicited snickers from these uninvited spectators. Our ignoring tactics had minimal effect. As we walked we drew the attention of all passersby, who chuckled at the spectacle. No one took pity on us. None of the elderly men standing in shop doorways. None of the older women shopkeepers behind deli counters (all of whom were probably *nonne* themselves). Not the young waiters or waitresses. Not even the *pensione* managers. No one stepped in to shoo them away.

One Romeo even had the gall to stand next to my friend while she posed next to Giulietta's gray statue, awaiting the click on my camera. As I hid behind my Canon AE-1, I scrutinized the young man's face. His dark eyes were clouded by a lock of dark wavy hair. His wry smile boasted amusement at our expense. I took a while to click the shutter. The extra seconds gave me the time to size up those studs who seemed to want to taunt us rather than anything else.

Gazing through the viewfinder, I shuddered. I was staring into faces similar to my own. My legs trembled like those of the cherry kitchen table as Nonna kneaded pasta dough. For the first time in my life, I looked like the mass of people around me. In the United States as well as in Italy, blondness hailed as the standard of beauty. In Italy, however, my black hair, dark eyes, and olive skin did not stick out in the crowd. Unlike in the States, no one here was curious about where I came from.

The blond-gazing mob took all the taste out of our gelato, so we boarded the train early for Venice. I worried that the blond-gazers would board too, as they remained on the platform until the train departed, howling and catcalling all the while. The train finally pulled out, leaving behind the mob Romeos. Carole and I sighed in relief, settling back into the vinyl seats, quietly opening our paperbacks. I was barely into Macchiavelli's *The Prince* when our mutual intuition kicked in. Carole and I looked up at each other. There, just outside our cabin window in the narrow passageway, new Romeos had taken up post. Though fewer in number this time, they stared at Carole the entire trip to Venice, as if mesmerized by tropical fish in a northern-set aquarium.

From the Basilica di San Marco in Venice under pouring rain, to the beach in Rimini, to the Uffizi, in front of *David*, at Santa Croce in Florence, to the Piazza di Trevi in Rome, hordes of young Romeos gathered, gazed, and followed every footstep of my blond-haired, blue-eyed, ceramic-skinned friend. This scene repeated itself no matter where we went. Romeos appeared at big and small street corners, staying on our heels and treading our steps. Romeos eventually faded into other Romeos.

"Don't these guys have anything to do?" asked Carole.

Remembering Nonna's shimmering black hair, bushy black eyebrows, and rich, amber eyes, I wished she were there to raise her ricer at those youths. I tried to bail from my friend and that bleak blond hair, but she insisted on remaining with me. Maybe she relied on my broken Italian and my chaperonelike demeanor to keep her safe.

Despite my despair over the Romeo mobs, this land, from where my foremothers came, kept calling to me. I could not decide what was worse: the repeated requests back home for proof of American citizenship upon every job application or the tireless male trail during what was supposed to be a path along parental discovery. Equally unsettling was the fact that most of these fans of flaxen hair could have easily been mistaken for my brothers.

On our way south to Pompeii, we stopped at the Banca Nazionale to exchange some of our dwindling funds. Damning each strand of her yellow hair, I forced my friend into a parallel line to await another teller. Detecting my game, Carole butted in front of me in my line, as if she needed to show me up.

"You just wish you were Italian," I teased. I avoided a stir in the bank, but I was determined to dump Carole and be free of the burdensome boys. Carole completed her transaction and stepped to the side to count her money.

"*Vorrei cambiare cento franchi svizzeri, per favore,*" I said to the teller—I would like to change one hundred Swiss francs, please. I laid my final Thomas Cook on the granite counter like a bet.

The teller looked at me. "*Passaporto.*" I produced my passport as requested. He dragged it along the counter and drew it to his chest as if my document were his draw in a game of poker where he held all the chips. Staring me in the eye, he shuffled the pages until he came to the one bearing my picture. He studied my photo, then me, then my passport. The teller printed out our exchange on paper, pointing to his percentage, and placed a ballpoint pen on the counter for me to sign. He was as poised as Mona Lisa with his eyes transfixed as he handed me my "winnings." Was he contemplating how lucky I was to have blond friends?

"Hey," cried Carole, who had remained glued to me during the transaction, "he's giving you one percent more!" I tried to move her away from the counter as soon as I grabbed my last lira.

"The rate just changed," replied the teller.

He swiftly disappeared behind his CHIUSO (closed) sign, successfully thwarting further protests.

"That is not fair! He gave you a better deal!"

"Go complain to the bank manager," I shot back, consoled that some things even blond hair couldn't buy. Her heels skidded on the marble floor as she rotated them, probably seeking refuge among the Romeos, leaving me alone in the center of the rotunda. Alone, I recounted my lire, then studied the bank's ornate vaulted ceiling, painted a sky blue with half-naked women who had flowing hair—blond, of course, an orange-blond—that floated like leaves around their chests.

Outside the bank, Carole stood alone next to a white marble pillar. *No more blond-worshipers?* Finally freed from Romeos, we ran to catch our bus.

Outside of Rome, I observed women dressed in black as they worked in the fields. *Women in black working in the fields?* I strained my eyes to witness a scene familiar to me but taking place some five thousand miles away from home. *They're not working the fields! They're picking dandelions! They'll make their grandkids eat that stuff, telling them it's* cicoria—*chicory—and good for them!* Instinctively I knew that we had crossed over into la Campania, where Naples lay just some kilometers ahead. Memories of my father scolding Nonna for picking and then actually cooking dandelions in her big white porcelain pot whizzed me back to the States. "You're not poor anymore! What will the neighbors think?!" My brothers would chime in, "Aren't dandelions weeds?" "Didn't Poppie spray weed-killer just last week?"

We spent our day of respite from blond-gazers alongside other travelers, exclaiming at the contrast between the earth-born beige and orange terra-cotta bricks of various Italian towns to the exhumed town of Pompeii. Pompeii boasted lava-laden passageways and centuries-old stones, once covered in gray molten ash. Formerly a thriving city, Pompeii had fallen prey to its tumultuous history and the earth's revenge. Excavation was still taking place during our visit. Uncovered treasures—such as vivid frescoes, bronze pots and pans, silver spoons, and even a wooden cradle—hinted at other artifacts that lay engulfed in volcanic rock. Italians were also still trying to understand their own lineage, their own past.

Touring the museum of excavated artifacts, we saw in a glass tomb the body of a small man encased in lava. His legs were bent as if running. The guide explained that people at that time were probably much shorter, probably due to poor nutrition and drought. "According to our measurements and taking into account how his body was calcined by lava, we calculate that this man was about . . . let's say . . . no more than . . . five feet." The granddaughter of a six-foot

woman born not far from Pompeii straightened her back while trying to find her footing on the ancient stones. I pulled Carole with
me out into the open stone walkway to get some fresh air. Had
Nonna's *nonne,* or Nonna's people, lived in Pompeii, Nonna would
never have lived, I marveled.

Walking through the volcanic ruins of Pompeii, we stopped in
front of an ancient villa under restoration. I wondered how many
women had given birth in that villa and from where Nonna's *nonne*
had emanated. The women from whom I descended may have come
from somewhere else—where exactly I am not sure. But it wasn't
Pompeii, where molten lava from Mt. Vesuvius would have put an
abrupt end to their story. History suddenly felt oppressive while
walking on ancestral soil.

Recalling Nonna's final imperative, I insisted that Carole and I
take the bus back to Rome instead of following our previously
planned itinerary onward to Naples.

"Already tired of your country of origin?" Carole sniffed.

"My wallet is nearly empty," I pleaded.

When we got into Rome, night had already fallen. Carole's hair
gleamed less in the evening and fortunately did not stir up a crowd of
Romeos. On our way to find a *pensione,* we stopped in a clothing
shop of the latest Italian mode. High-fashion jeans, t-shirts, and
sweaters glittered in the store showcase. My mind was still oscillating
to and from Pompeii and thoughts of babies—maybe one of my
Nonna's ancestors—being born in that ancient, now-crumbled villa.

"Can I help you?" asked the saleswoman, slightly older and

taller than me, with medium-length, thick, frosted-yellow and brown hair and large hoop earrings. She wore bell-bottom pants that showed off black high-heeled boots. I jolted back to the present.

"Oh, no . . . no thank you. I am just looking. . . ." I stammered.

"Then go look in the window!" she snapped.

"You must be Sicilian," I retorted, heading toward the door. *My other grandmother is from Sicily, and she orders everybody around, just like you.*

To console myself, I directed Carole into the *pasticceria*, a sweet shop, on the same street. She ordered cappuccino. I had a cannoli, which reminded me of Mt. Vesuvius. The first bite caused the cylindrical pastry to erupt its sweetened ricotta cheese and chocolate bits onto an unsuspecting saucer underneath.

That night I dreamed that Nonna and Poppie were running to board a dinghy to escape hot, flowing cappuccino. Spewing milk-chocolate chunks the size of solid, massive rocks chased them from their barber and shoe-making shops. Naples spilled its inhabitants along bristling beaches as fluffy white ricotta lava engulfed them, encapsulating them in running motion. Nonna's black hair appeared a floating dandelion-orange color as she murmured, "Better bits and ricotta from home over there. . . . " The next morning I awoke in a huff.

"I have to go," slipped from my lips as I realized I had just enough money to make it back to Switzerland. Pushing Carole out of the room, it struck me as ironic that my *nonna* had left her homeland because of money, too.

"I would like to check out," I said to the clerk.

"*Sì*, Signorina Giovannina. *Eccole*," replied the clerk as he handed me the remainder of my lire in change.

I stared at him, stupefied. He called me by the name that Nonna always said Italians would call me. *Nonna must be near*, I grinned to myself.

Turning the corner from the *pensione*, a few blond-admirers gathered and followed Carole and me to the railway station. With my Eurail Pass in hand, I smiled at them and even waved goodbye as I boarded the train heading north. *No more looking in the window for me; I will be back for a longer stay very soon!*

Linda Watanabe McFerrin

A Hunger for Monica's Mascarpone

Lawrence and I had sampled only a small part of
Venice before our dear friend Monica arrived fresh from her
travels elsewhere. We had disembarked at Piazza San Marco and
crossed it, noting the Duomo's landmark rotunda and the rows of
apostles draped in scaffold and net; then we checked into our hotel,
the Panada, at 5:00 and had a very light dinner several hours later at
the Pescatore Conte.

The next morning, dawn awakened us, weaseling its way in
through the casements, creeping down draperies, columning them
in substance. The scent of baking bread trailed the light and was followed by the clatter of pots and pans and children's voices rising
from the street below.

When Monica disembarked, we were seated at a sidewalk café

on the perimeter of Piazza San Marco. Across the wide, noon-bright circle of the piazza, she progressed—a scintillating clove-brown figure, an exotic and imperious Cleopatra clad in a saffron blouse and billowing peasant skirt—preceded by a porter carting her enormous black suitcase and a few smaller bags. Her head was uncovered, scarfed only in the straight black fall of her hair. She seemed made for the heat. Her Italian movie-star carriage had the usual grand and eye-stopping effect. Pigeons scattered. Heads turned. Men's hands reached involuntarily out toward her as she passed, thumbs and forefingers kissing in empty pinches that would never be consummated.

At that moment, I realized that I loved Monica in the same way that I loved my Barbie dolls as a child, with the passionate attachment one feels toward an ideal shimmering on the distant, never-to-be-attained horizon. Men also had this feeling for her.

Lawrence and I pushed back our chairs, threw our napkins down next to our plates, and advanced toward her with the well-choreographed precision of two chorus-line extras supporting the principal dancer.

She rewarded us with a white flash of smile.

"Ciao," she sang out to us. "When did you get here?"

"Last night," we answered in unison.

"Don't you love it?" Monica crooned, echoing the plump pigeons that cooed, pecked, and preened around our ankles and feet, their feathered bodies pressing carelessly up against us.

"More so now because you are here," we responded.

"Well, I have to get rid of this luggage," she confided with well-practiced urgency. "Then, I will show you my Venice."

I've always felt very small next to Monica, petite and childlike, like a pawn. My adoration only increases when I see the impact she has on everyone else. On her ample bosom, Lawrence's head had found a place to come, metaphorically, to rest. At least I hoped it was metaphorical. I watched the two walk arm in arm ahead of me while I dawdled on bridges. The chipped, gap-toothed buildings leaned toward us, leering like doddering courtiers drunk on the sunlight.

"Where did you eat last night?" Monica asked as we walked past a series of portside cafés on the Canale Della Giudecca.

"At the Pescatore Conte," Lawrence replied.

"Hmmm," she said thoughtfully, as if trying it out in her mind. "I've never eaten there." Monica was a connoisseur of both food and men. She paused for a moment considering the place. "Well, tonight," she said with a long, slow smile, "we will dine at the Bai Barbacani. It is better even than that one, Au Pied du Cochon, in Paris, remember? You will love it. I'll introduce you to Aldo, the owner. I wonder if he will remember me."

There was no doubt in my mind about this.

We expected other friends to join us in the afternoon, but they arrived exhausted and ill. Dinner with them was out of the question.

Night had pitched its black tent over the city. Monica, in her sunflower-yellow dress, gleamed like a beacon beneath the lanterns that lined the narrow alleyways near the canal. On the marled stone walls that rose from the shadows on the opposite bank, small windows opened like the tiny doors in an advent calendar, torch lit, adventures seeming to smolder within their confines. The entrance to the Bai Barbacani was behind one of these windows.

We crossed a narrow bridge to Calle del Paradiso, on the other side of the canal. At the portals of the Bai Barbacani, we were greeted by a slender, tuxedoed waiter who escorted us into the cavelike interior and to a round white-clothed table, where the candlelight danced over crystal, china, and silver.

Light flooded across Monica's shoulders, pooling gracefully at the juncture of her breasts. Her eyelashes cast shadows on the rise of her cheeks. Lawrence's hair glinted fiery.

Our waiter seemed adequate, but Monica was still restless, her eyes on a tall, broad-shouldered man impeccably dressed in a double-breasted blue jacket cut to enhance a narrow waist.

He was making his way across the room, stopping at each of the tables and chatting with guests. His progress was arrested at the table next to ours, for he seemed to have found among these diners several dear friends.

"Aldo?" I asked.

"No," said Monica.

"Aldo is not here," she added with just a soupçon of petulance. I noticed that the slightest of pouts had settled upon her carnation-red lips. She seemed dismayed that the restaurant had changed, had been rearranged. Gone was Aldo. Gone were the dusty bottles of homemade fragolino that Monica had raved about. The broad-shouldered man was laughing, leaning into the table right next to us, ignoring our table completely. He summoned a waiter, who disappeared into the back of the restaurant and returned with what must have been a very special bottle of wine. It was uncorked with great ritual. The diner who sampled it nodded his head furiously. The broad-shouldered man squeezed his arm and moved on to us. His dark hair was thin and cut very short. He had eaglelike features. "Welcome to the Bai Barbacani," he said, in musically accented English.

"Where's Aldo?" Monica demanded in response.

"He is gone," said our host.

Monica let him know that Aldo was missed.

"I was here before Aldo," the man replied simply. "I went away and now I am back. Aldo is gone." He said this with the finality of a man who is used to fitting his confreres with shoes of cement.

"I don't believe you," Monica whispered tauntingly. "I think you have Aldo locked up in the basement."

"So," the man said, looking down at Monica, noticing appreciatively the way the darkness gathered at the top of her breasts like a pendant of jet and, sliding between them, disappeared into the soft yellow fabric of her bodice.

He looked up at us and smiled.

Monica told the man that Aldo had promised her certain secrets—"secret recipes"—when she returned, and she wasn't pleased to find him no longer there. Our new host was given to understand that she liked him less.

He asked her, "You don't like me as much?"

Monica shrugged and smiled. "I miss Aldo," she said.

It was a challenge, a gauntlet thrown down. Then it began—the wooing. Perhaps it was the candlelight that bathed everything in a kind of fairytale beauty, perhaps it was the desire to best the chivalrous Aldo, or maybe it was the Circean net that Monica carried for occasions like this one. Whatever the cause, though the waiter returned and was very solicitous, the man could not seem to stay away from our table.

"Come, come back to the kitchen with me. I can show you how to stir the risotto," he said archly. We had visions of Monica being abducted into the back, into the restaurant's nether regions, or into the basement where Aldo was most certainly buried.

Monica laughed. "Maybe," she said. "Maybe later."

For an appetizer Monica ordered a bowl full of mussels, and our host nearly swallowed his tongue. Piled high on their perfect white china bowl, each glistening shell held the tiny mollusk that has been compared to that most delicate part of a woman's anatomy. Pry open the shell, shut tight as a virgin's thighs, and you feast on the sweet mound of flesh in its own fragrant liquor. Dress them with wine or eat them undressed—either way, to consume them is heaven.

Roberto (by this time we knew his name) leaned over Monica's shoulder and asked, not so innocently, if she'd like him to put a little lemon on them. Monica said yes, so he called over the waiter, who arrived with the proper tools: a silver plate holding a gauze-wrapped half lemon and a small silver spoon. Roberto expertly disrobed the lemon and took firm hold of the spoon. He aggressively screwed his small spoon into the lemon, dribbling its juices all over Monica's mussels. Monica watched him. He continued to screw away, eyes upon hers, really building up a sweat in the process. It seemed to go on forever. I was amazed. I'm sure none of us thought there could be that much juice in a single lemon. But Roberto was determined to lemon up the mussels to Monica's satisfaction or knock himself out trying. It was pathetic.

"Monica," I wanted to plead, "make him stop."

"That's enough," Monica said, as if reading my mind. "Thank you," she purred demurely. Imaginary handkerchiefs went to three foreheads: Lawrence's, Roberto's, and mine.

I had ordered sweet and sour sardines for an appetizer. (I do not want to speculate upon their metaphorical value.) Lawrence had ordered mussels as well, but all he got were a few cursory twists of lemon from the waiter.

Monica consumed her mussels with incredible gusto and even offered a few to me, though she knows that I'm allergic to shellfish. It's an allergy I developed recently and one that I never manage to recollect without a puritanical pang.

The appetizers had nearly exhausted us. I wasn't sure we were ready to deal with our entrées. To calm my nerves, I ordered risotto: a sweet, pearly mixture, perfectly flavored and designed to comfort the taker. Lawrence had scampi: meaty pink prawns. He separated them from their wafer-thin jackets of exoskeleton with fingers perfumed in lemon water.

Monica ordered gnocchi, a regional favorite: satiny black

pillows colored with cuttlefish ink and bathed in a fragrant salmon-red sauce. Before us, the simple potato dumplings lay transformed into something incredibly sexy.

"Round two," I thought. "Victoria's Secret. Frederick's of Hollywood."

Roberto appeared again, along with the entrées.

"This is the perfect choice for you," he said to Monica, his hand, braceleted at the wrist, gesturing toward her plate.

"I love those colors," giggled Monica.

"Come to the kitchen with me," Robert challenged with a canine grin. "I will show you how it is done."

Monica laughed, "I'll bet," she said, and bit into one of the little black pillows. Her sharp teeth cut a tiny half moon out of one side. I'd swear Roberto was salivating.

"Do you know," he asked, warming to the subject of food as he watched Monica eat, "do you know how I like to eat spaghetti?"

"No, how?" asked Monica.

"I float a wooden bowl of spaghetti in my swimming pool." His large hands placed an imaginary bowl upon the cobalt-blue waters shimmering in front of him.

"Then I float up to it."

We could now picture him in swim trunks, approaching the spaghetti that bobbed in its big wooden bowl on the water's flickering surface.

"Then I suck the spaghetti slowly out of the bowl," he said, looking down at Monica. He was grinning from ear to ear.

"Oh, that sounds wonderful," Monica responded, placing her napkin beside her plate and gazing up into his dark brown eyes.

"You could try it," he said, raising an eyebrow.

"Do you know what my favorite food is?" Monica countered. "It is mascarpone. Do you know how to make mascarpone?"

"Yes," said Roberto. "This cheese takes a long time."

"It does," agreed Monica. "I make fabulous mascarpone. I can teach you to make it my way."

"I would love to make mascarpone with you," said Roberto formally. I half expected him to salute.

"*La vie est belle,*" Monica laughed.

"*Toujours l'amour,*" Roberto chimed back.

The clichés began flying back and forth like shuttlecocks. Roberto would not leave our table. He catered to us to the point of neglecting the rest of his clientele. Diners ordered desserts and after-dinner drinks. He ignored them. Regulars paid bills and left the restaurant. He ignored them.

We struggled through apple strudels and tortes and polished things off with homemade fragolino, a strawberry liqueur more fragrant, Monica declared, than Aldo's.

"This is my fragolino," Roberto said with great pride.

It was like perfume, really, a dark, beautiful perfume. We chuckled and whispered that he probably had Aldo locked up in the basement making the stuff. Hours had passed. Candles had burned down to mere stumps. All of the other diners were gone.

"Will you come again tomorrow night?" Roberto asked

Monica, leaning over her chair, his mouth close to her ear.

"No," Monica said, turning her face to his, her nose nearly touching the sharp beak that was his. "No, but I'm here every year."

"Well," he said, as she rose from the table, "you must come again next year."

He took Monica's arm and escorted her gallantly back to the restaurant's threshold. "I will give you the secret then, to the fragolino," Roberto said solemnly exchanging cards with Monica, promising her the recipe "next year," if she came, just as Aldo once had.

Lawrence and I knew better, of course. We had seen this happen before. We knew that the meal most longed for is the meal not yet eaten. We knew that Roberto's appetite had been aroused. And we knew, for certain, that sometime—long before the promised next year—there'd be a knock on Monica's door, and there he would be—the man with a hunger for mascarpone.

Jennifer Sexton

Sexing the Eggplant

Quannu lassi a vecchia pa nova,

sai chi lassi ma non sai chi trovi.

When you leave the old for the new, you know

what you are leaving but not what you will find.

—Sicilian proverb

I'm not Italian. At least, I wasn't born Italian. So stop asking.

Thanks to my dramatic coloring and temperamental hair, I've been mistaken for an Italian all my life. There's also my love of food. And the hand gestures. To be honest, I encourage the assumption by collecting phrases and profanities from my Italian-born friend, Carolina, and sprinkling them liberally through my conversation like salt on a ripe tomato, to punch up the flavor. I like being a pseudo-Italiana. I love Italians and all things Italian—how could I not? Italians have made the most beautiful, playful, sexy, delicious things in the world. The most elegant shoes. The Vespa scooter. The films of Fellini. The works of Michelangelo. The cannoli. The alchemy of tomato and cheese. The olive. The eggplant. Venus herself was borne across the waves on her scallop shell to land on the sands of Sicily, her blond ropes of hair notwithstanding, as Botticelli himself was Sicilian. I may live in rainy Seattle, but I have the sun-drenched Mediterranean flowing in my veins. In spirit, anyway. That's what makes it so hard to tell the truth when someone comes right out and asks me point blank.

"Not Italian? What are you then, Greek?"

No.

"Spanish?"

Nope.

"Portuguese-Dominican Gypsy with a Cherokee grandma on your mother's side?"

No. I'm Swedish.

My mom is 100 percent Scandinavian. She's a cheekboned, pert-nosed, green-eyed, pale, Nordic, nutmeg and herring–snarfing Scandy, from the top of her blond head to the wooden soles of her— I'm not kidding—clogs. Well, then, my father's ethnicity must explain my appearance and Mediterranean tendencies, right? Well, kind of. See that dusky-skinned gentleman over there, hovering over a steaming crock of corned beef and cabbage? Yes, the one with the kinky hair, generous mouth, and decidedly un-Anglo nose. Ask him what his nationality is. He'll tell you that he's Irish. Irish? I know, I know. He's not exactly the typical freckled or ruddy-faced Irishman with a shock of coppery hair falling rakishly over one fiery eye, but my dad is a wearer of the green in earnest, a lover of all things Irish, and as far as he's concerned, he's a true son of Eire. He's Irish, damnit. I'd love to prove him wrong and explain everything about his origins and mine by reaching into a closet and marching out some Sicilian or Moroccan ancestor, complete with a name and date of emigration to Ireland, to explain all of this swarthiness and curl, but I can't. Alas, the church that supposedly housed the birth records of the Sexton family clan in County Clare burned to the ground under murky circumstances many years ago, forever shrouding my true heritage and all of its curl and melanin in a dark, kinky cloud of mystery. Pity.

Anyway, here I am with my riddles of impossible hair, indignant eyebrows like black horsehairs sprouting over my eyes, and aquiline nose. Fortunately, I have grown into my nose over the years, which was a process quite a bit less revolting than it sounds.

My mother loves my dark complexion. As a young woman, she always wished for more Sophia Loren in her mirror but got double doses of Sonja Henie instead. Thrilled with a brunette baby daughter to dress, she clothed me in all of the colors she insists she "can't" wear. Turquoise. Fuchsia. Scarlet. Shocking pink. Electric blue. Colors whose very names sizzle and pop. Colors that she insists "make her into a ghost." She thrills when I wear lipstick shades like Rage, Catwalk, Raven. Her purse rattles with meek tubes of Petal and Honey Blush. And the money I must save on eyebrow pencil! she crows. Little does she imagine the furtive plucking I inflict on myself, let alone the mental gymnastics I perform in order to reconcile such foolishness with my feminist stance in other, more socially visible areas of my life. Like my perverse love of 1940s cookbooks, I keep this to myself.

Last year I Italicized myself in a big way: I married a Sicilian. A passionate cook, he seduced me with eggplant in a divine sauce, his family recipe; it simmered morning to dusk in his spotless bachelor's kitchen. When I gushed to my Italian girlfriend that the first meal he made for me was eggplant, her eyes widened in alarm. "Eggplant! Oh, *Madonna*, watch out! The *melanzana* is the food of love! *Attenzione*, be careful of that one!"

"Don't be silly, Carolina! It was just dinner, that's all!"

"It is never just dinner when a Sicilian man cooks."

Three weeks later, I was pregnant. Finally, I had a little Italian in me!

As I contemplated my changing shape in the mirror, I remembered and updated Sophia Loren's famous quote about spaghetti: "Everything you see," I said, stroking my round belly, "I owe to eggplant."

U signuri chiudi na porta e nni apri nautra.

God closes one door and opens another.

—*Sicilian proverb*

Engaged and housing a tiny Sicilian in my ever-growing abdomen, I faced a new reality. With the bright pink line (Shocking pink? Definitely.) indicating a positive result and the pregnancy test still in hand, my life as a single girl came to a screeching close. Now I was in a sort of no-woman's land, a limbo between my simple, spacious life and a dark, rich, unknown future of marriage and motherhood. When God closes one door, He opens another, as the saying goes. Here I was, waiting nervously in the hallway with a pregnancy test in my hand.

In addition to a new Sicilian husband and baby-to-be, I was soon to be on the receiving end of a creature the likes of which I desperately imagined, worrying myself into a frazzle: a Sicilian mother-in-law. Sure, she lived in Ohio, several thousand miles away from our home in Seattle. But I had to meet her. Would she recognize my innate pseudo-Italianness and embrace me as one of her own? Or would this be the end of my beloved Mediterranean delusion once and for all? Would I have to fess up to my Nordic roots; develop a cool affinity for wool cardigans with chilly silver buttons and pickled herring in cream sauce instead of sleek cashmere pullovers and eggplant crisped and kissed with tomato? It was one thing to love all things Italian and try to train myself to instinctively swear in a long bouncy stream when stubbing my toe, to always keep a gallon of the best olive oil in the kitchen, to watch unsubtitled films with a minidictionary clutched in my hands, to pore over issues of Italian *Vogue*. That was fine, and possibly even kind of cute. But this was different. Dangerous. My new mother-in-law's maiden name translates to "the mallet." Of all the Romance languages, only Italian could soften and curl a word so beautifully around the unyielding concept of a hammer meant to strike and shape raw materials without marring their surfaces. I began scrutinizing my fiancé, searching for evidence of a hard maternal hand, an Old World, don't-spare-the-rod kind of upbringing so I could brace myself for future poundings of my own. I was marrying this woman's son, carrying her grandchild. And this was bound to be a woman who wore scarlet and fuchsia—I couldn't imagine a Sicilian mother-in-law being made into a ghost by a color, like my pastel-hued Mom. I had to prepare. I became determined to learn about Sicily, about cooking, about eggplant. Maybe I can't be Italian, I reasoned. But by God, I can come close.

I learned that the eggplant is a member of the nightshade family, which I find tremendously sexy and vampirish. It has fallen victim to many misunderstandings over the centuries, from rumors of its fatally poisonous nature (untrue but nevertheless responsible for the tragic waste of thousands of eggplants senselessly uneaten throughout the Dark Ages) to its rather adorable sound-alike nickname, *mela insana*, "insanity apple," a simple mistake arising from a flub of the eggplant's Italian name, *melanzana*. A mistake that gave rise to the myth that the eggplant causes insanity. Ecstasy? Of course. Euphoria? Yes! Insanity? That seems a bit harsh. And then there's my friend Carolina's warning about the eggplant, the dangerous *alimento di amore*, food of love. A powerful aphrodisiac and booster of fertility, combined into one big, delicious, baby-making speedball. I heartily endorse that particular belief, and my midwife will back me up on that opinion.

To determine the gender of the eggplant, look at the indentation at the bottom. If it is deep and shaped like a dash, the eggplant is female. If it is shallow and round, it is a male. Great, great, I thought to myself, lifting the glossy dark shapes and turning them over and over in my hands at the market. Some people feel that bitterness is best drawn out before cooking by soaking the slices in salted water. Others feel that the issue of bitterness can be avoided by selecting the eggplants by sex. But which one was supposed to be the bitter one, male or female? I couldn't remember. I hadn't noticed my husband soaking the eggplant before rolling the slices in his special mixture and frying them in the mellow green olive oil. So he must know the correct gender to buy.

"Honey? Can you help me sex these eggplants?" He looked up, alarmed, from the other side of a mountain of pineapples and mangoes, as the heads of many other shoppers turned to gaze with puzzled expressions at the crazy perverted pregnant woman, smiling and holding aloft a shining dark vegetable.

Tantu va a cottara o puzzu finu ca si rumpi.

The pot goes down into the well so many times

and then it finally breaks.

—Sicilian proverb

We flew to Ohio to meet the mallet-in-law when I was seven months pregnant, one month into our marriage. Our wedding photographs feature a very pregnant me in the maternity wedding dress I created for myself out of necessity. I am an empire-waisted, eggplant-shaped vision in ivory embroidered silk and satin, which ends above the knee to show off my garnet-stockinged legs, the only part of my body that I could still recognize as mine. I flipped through the stack of photos on the plane, imagining them through the eyes of my husband's mother. She hadn't attended our hastily planned Seattle wedding, as the date coincided with the long-planned, elaborate, and equally distant marriage of her older daughter on the East Coast. I reasoned that my mother-in-law could hardly view these photos of me, grinning in the sunshine over my bouquet of scarlet and white gerbera daisies, snuggling up to her son and raising a glass of sparkling cider to toast against his champagne, without recognizing me as feisty, passionate, and deserving of all the heady emotion and spice that an Italian family would provide. I was certainly Italian enough in spirit to raise her future granddaughter to be a minisensualist, a drooling little brown-eyed girly-putto, toddling after the good things in life. Wasn't I?

When I finally met my mother-in-law, I was completely unprepared. As we parked our rental car in the driveway of my husband's immaculately kept childhood home, I took a few deep breaths. I stroked the dome of my pregnant belly. *This is it, kid. Let's go captivate ourselves a Sicilian grandma.* She emerged smiling from the cool depths of the garage. "Nonna!" I cried, quite sure that my accent was perfect.

Sexing the Eggplant

"Call me Helen, dear. Oh, you called me Nonna! That's sweet, but I like Grandma better. It's so nice to finally meet you." She embraced me lightly and gazed at me through her glasses, sometimes adjusting them on her face or fiddling self-consciously with her wristwatch. She was shy! I had expected running; outbursts; tears of joy; a stifling, perfumed squeeze in jeweled arms; a smear of fiery lipstick on my cheek. Instead, her hair was a quiet silvery puff, and she approached silently in soft-soled, ivory-colored shoes. I had expected a brightly dressed lady with an outrageous laugh and music spilling out into her kitchen garden, overgrown with unruly sweet basil and heavy with tomatoes. My new mother-in-law was welcoming but quiet. Measured. Modulated. Like the expanse of her front lawn, she was soft, close clipped, without a weed in sight.

Helen made an enormous batch of her special eggplant in honor of our arrival. Eggplant! My husband's magical eggplant, which was directly responsible for my pregnancy, had been but a preview of this, the original eggplant straight from Nonna's—I mean Helen's—kitchen! But instead of serving the slices piled on rough pieces torn from some crusty artisan loaf, it was pillowed between Midwestern white slices from a plastic bag. I was ready to debate the virtues of white eggplant as opposed to purple or striped, the ingredients of the perfect caponata, the value of the *melanzana* for bringing prosperity and spirituality into a household. As was my habit in college before a big exam, I did myself in by overstudying. If I concentrated any harder on things *siciliano*, the traditional three-legged, Medusa-faced *Trinacria* banner of Sicily might appear emblazoned on my forehead; a miracle. But something was wrong. My new mother-in-law was no mallet at all. She was warm, but quietly so. A wonderful cook, yet somehow too tidy, too tame, too many startlingly white dishtowels and no marinara splatters. There was more of manicured, suburban Ohio in my mother-in-law than Sicily.

As we sat around her table, she talked about what the neighbors' grown children were up to. About the new people next door who let their lawn grow thick with dandelions. Small-town talk that never ventured more than a few streets over. When I steered the conversation toward Sicily, eager to show off my depth of knowledge, she faded back still more and became wistful. Her parents spoke no English at home. They left their ancestral village behind to raise their many children here in the States, where they would have endless opportunities. She missed her parents. The memories were bittersweet. She had never seen Sicily. As we finished eating, I felt pangs of loss. Why? She certainly could have traveled to Sicily as an adult if she wanted to. But she married young and soon had five children of her own to raise, a household to run, dinners to prepare. Maybe her Sicilian childhood hadn't been all garlic perfume and bursts of song that pulled her heart inexorably back to the Old Country. Maybe life had been challenging with her house full of siblings and the difficulties of plain old family living, which are the same in any language. She found genuine comfort in the humble, Midwestern neighborhood life she had created here. I was completely unprepared for this possibility.

In my heart I had made space for a fiery, unreasonable, unsat-isfiable, frightening Sicilian mother-in-law and her beloved country, my new country. I was aching for a lifeline to passion, a direct con-nection to the original spicy meatball, and the hormones racing around in my now seven-months-pregnant body were blowing everything out of proportion, twisting it out of shape. "Your mom," I stammered to my husband as we turned back the flowered bed-spread in one of the spotless upstairs guestrooms. "She's sweet. But she's so . . . quiet. So reserved. She's not quite what I imagined. I had built up an expectation . . . that she'd be more . . . Sicilian."

"Ohio can drain the fire out of a Sicilian like olive oil into a slice of white bread," he said, shaking his head.

Mangiati quattru figatedd'I muschi arrustitti.

Go and eat four roasted flies' livers.

—Sicilian insult

Today I am mother to an eleven-month-old Sicilian daughter who has never lived in Ohio, and it shows. She was born with a cloud of dark curls that has only grown longer, higher, wider and more unruly with each day. Her dark eyes radiate warmth when she smiles and splinter the air with black light when she cries. She gesticulates wildly, hurling *ma-ma-mas* and *da-da-das* toward her parents, toward the houseplants, toward the furniture. And she has inherited, by some mysterious genetic choreography, her grandmother's sole Sicilian trait: a dismissive and vicious-sounding hiss issued forth between snarling teeth, an instinctive expression of derision that goes beyond words. My mother-in-law uses this to show her disdain for the neighbors who never cut their grass; for the road work between her house and the grocery store, which never seems to progress; for the family who stopped going to her church because they didn't like the new pews. Our baby somehow manages this hiss despite her toothless gums, and the accompanying sweeping back-handed gesture has sent many a bowl of offending oatmeal flying. This passionate little *bambina* has contributed more to my adopted Italianness by natural example than years of watching Fellini films and quizzing Carolina about the meanings of gestures. When she grows a bit older, my husband and I are planning a trip to Sicily to show her the family's village of origin. Maybe I will feel prepared for the experience and maybe I won't. Maybe it will feel like a home-coming to me as well as to my husband and daughter, and maybe not, but one thing is guaranteed: I will go as a Sicilian wife and mother, if only by association, and I'd rather be a Sicilian by virtue of context than no Sicilian at all. I may be genetically Swedish, but *Madonna*, I can sex an eggplant.

Acknowledgments

I would like to thank all the many women (and one man who wrote of getting married in Rome) who sent me their wonderful personal essays on Italy to read and enjoy. I regret not being able to include more of them here. The reading experience was more edifying than I have space to say. I also thank the writers whose work appears in this book, who were willing to tweak, rework, rewrite, and do all the tedious things to their precious words that an editor asks—for the greater good, I hope, of the entire collection. I am grateful to Seal Press for being such noteworthy champions of women's writing—we still need such champions, I believe. And in particular, I'm thankful to have an editor like Marisa Solís to work with at Seal Press. Her high standards and sense of excellence and ability to communicate them clearly to me are not taken for granted. Having worked in publishing for twenty-seven years, I know how painful it is when those attributes are missing. Finally, thanks to Dan for his support.

About the Contributors

Kate Adamek is a social worker and writer whose travels have taken her to Europe, India, and Nepal. She has lived abroad in Austria, France, England, Scotland, Sri Lanka, Tanzania, and, of course, her beloved Italy. She has contributed to Seal Press's anthology *France, A Love Story*. She continues to write as she works among the Yup'ik people in the Kuskokwim Delta of southwestern Alaska and looks forward to writing about her love of "the last frontier."

Elizabeth Asdorian is a freelance copywriter in San Francisco. Her work has appeared in *Print*, *Creativity*, and *Archive*, as well as in the Travelers' Tales anthology *Whose Panties Are These?* She is currently traveling extensively—around the living room, dining room, and playground, chasing a rambunctious one-year-old and dreaming of *brodo con stracciatella*.

Amanda Castleman returned to Seattle after eight years in England, Italy, Greece, and Cyprus. An Italian American travel writer, she has contributed to the *International Herald Tribune*, the *Daily Mail*, *MSNBC*, *Salon*, *Wired*, and *Italy Daily*. Her guidebook credits include *Time Out Athens*, *The Rough Guide to Italy*, and the *Rome and Central Italy Adventure Guide*. She holds a degree in Latin and teaches travel writing. Amanda misses her mod moped and her stint as a Visiting Writer at the American Academy in Rome. Her website is at www.amandacastleman.com.

Mandy Catron is studying writing at American University in Washington, D.C. When she's not reading or writing, she drinks too much espresso and eats oranges. On sunny days, she rides her bike to her favorite art museums.

Rachel Dacus is from the Southern California community of San Pedro, where the population includes many sons and daughters of Italy. She is the author of two poetry books, *Femme au Chapeau* and *Earth Lessons*, and two poetry CDs, *A God You Can Dance* and *Singing in the Pandaleshwar Caves*. Writing in the San Francisco area, she is working on essays about Italy, India, and Northern California. She has just finished writing *Rocket Lessons*, her memoir of growing up with a rocket scientist father. She can be found on the web at www.dacushome.com.

About the Contributors

Deana David is a freelance writer whose fiction and nonfiction work has appeared in a number of national publications and literary journals. She is completing her first novel, which she hopes will be the first in a series of literary travelogues. She is a devoted traveler who pets animals in the street, kisses statues, and perpetually has cobwebby hands and grass-stained knees.

Fran Davis lives in Summerland, California. Her essays, short stories, and poems have appeared in *Calyx*, the *Chattahoochee Review*, *Vincent Brothers Review*, *Acorn*, *Reed* magazine, *Passager*, and several anthologies and newspapers. She is a winner of the Lamar York Prize for nonfiction and is a Pushcart Prize nominee. She writes a column for the *South Coast News* and is currently working on a nonfiction book on the third age.

Holly Smith Dinbergs lives in Switzerland and has contributed to a new series of books for girls called *Girlz Rock!*, scheduled for publication in 2005 in the United Kingdom, Australia, and the United States. She's currently writing a novel entitled *Joyful Noisemakers*.

Julianne DiNenna is an Italian American who lives outside of Geneva and works for a humanitarian organization. She is a member of the Geneva Writers' Group and has published poems in literary journals, including *Offshoots VII*, *Grasslands Review*, the *Swiss American Review*, *Explorer* magazine, and *Melting Trees Review*. She also writes fiction for adults as well as for children and travels to Italy at every vacation break.

Laura Fraser is a San Francisco–based journalist and author of the best-selling travel memoir *An Italian Affair*. You can read her Italian recipes, travel tips, and handy romantic phrases at www.laurafraser.com.

Natalie Galli lives in San Rafael, California. She writes, edits, and does acupressure. Her articles have appeared in the *San Francisco Chronicle* and the (Berkeley) *Monthly*. She wrote *Three-Cornered Island*, a story about her search for a Sicilian woman who resisted the custom of forcible marriage; an excerpt of this piece was published in the Travelers' Tales anthology *Italy*. She is also the writer of *Sabina Pokes Around*, a children's book, which was illustrated by her sister.

Constance Hale grew up speaking Hawaiian Creole in school, Standard English at home, and French with her mother. But on the day she arrived in Tuscany, she knew only four words of Italian. She has worked as an editor at the *San Francisco Examiner*, *Wired*, and *Health*, and as a writer for *Honolulu*, the *Los Angeles Times*, and the *Atlantic Monthly*. Stories of her adventures abroad have appeared in *Provence, A Woman's Europe*, and *France, A Love Story*. Her two books on language, *Sin and Syntax* and *Wired Style*, have gotten her dubbed "Marian the Librarian on a Harley."

About the Contributors

Barbara Grizzuti Harrison grew up in Bensonhurst, Brooklyn. Her work *Visions of Glory: A History and a Memory of Jehovah's Witnesses* brought her national renown. In 1969 she published *Unlearning the Lie: Sexism in School*, a work about children's experience of sexism at a school in Brooklyn. Her book *Italian Days*, a literary work on her travels in Italy, won the American Book Award. She is also the author of a novel called *Foreign Bodies*. She died in 2002 at the age of 67.

Ann Lindsay returned from Italy in 1969 to open a kitchenware store with her husband, David, in London, Ontario. She is the author of *The Cookshop Cookbook* (illustrated by David), a book on specialty kitchen equipment. She has written about street markets for *City Life* magazine, a chapter on the historic Covent Garden Market in the book *London Downtown, Layers of Time*, and an introduction to the market cookbook, *Cooking with the Seasons*. She currently writes a column for *Canadian Home Style* magazine on trends in houseware design and food-related travel. "Italy of the Poets" is a chapter from her manuscript *Traveling Business Class*, a recently completed account of a year's journey that changed her from a teacher to a retailer.

Mardith J. Louisell is a child welfare consultant whose essays and book reviews have been published in *The House on Via Gombito Street*, *The Best American Erotica*, and *Poets & Writers* magazine. She has just completed her memoir, *A Blossom in the Brain*.

Linda Watanabe McFerrin has been traveling since she was two and writing about it since she was six. She is a poet, travel writer, novelist, and contributor to numerous journals, newspapers, magazines, anthologies, and online publications and is the author of two novels, an award-winning short story collection, and two poetry collections. She has edited two anthologies and a guidebook to Northern California. Her work has also appeared in *In Search of Adventure: A Wild Travel Anthology,* and *American Fiction.* Other book-length works include a novel, *Namako: Sea Cucumber,* and an award-winning short story collection, *The Hand of Buddha.* Her website is at www.lwmcferrin.com.

Rachel Hosein Nisbet moved from her native England to work on a doctorate at University of Neuchâtel in Switzerland. During her studies she began classical singing lessons, which fostered her interest in Italy. She now lives in France, where she has written a play, *Christmas Present,* and a series of poems to accompany Gilbert Paquet's photographs of Disco Bay, Greenland. She attends the Geneva Writers' Conference.

Anita Olachea is originally from Philadelphia, where she wrote for city publications and sourcebooks. A resident of Italy for more than thirty-five years, she lives in Parma—staying in Tuscany during time off—and works as a translator of literary and scientific texts, among them *The Dynamics of Ambiguity.* Her poetry and prose have appeared in literary magazines such as the *Atlanta Review, Treasure*

House, the Malahat Review, Prism International, and *New Grains,* as well as in the anthology *The Party Train.* Writing with a foot in two cultures, she tries to explore significant moments of each for the human concerns that are common to both.

Nora Pierce is a Wallace Stegner Fellow in Fiction Writing at Stanford University. She has been a Rosenthal Fellow in the PEN Center Emerging Voices Program and is the recipient of numerous awards for her writing, including a grant from the Maryland State Arts Council. Her fiction, essays, and articles have appeared in the *Baltimore Sun, Travel Magazine, Hampton Shorts, SOMA,* and many other publications. She is a Writer-in-Residence at the Headlands Center for the Arts in Marin County, California. She has lived in Rome, where she fell in love with both Italy and her husband, painter Michael Stevenson.

Serena Richardson arrived in Treviso, Italy in June 2003 with her Wüsthof knives, English textbooks, an exercise ball, and absolutely no preparation for her new life with her Italian fiancé and future in-laws. Since then, she has been teaching English, learning Italian, and trying to fit in. She has been writing stories of her adventures, and misadventures, one of which appeared in the *San Francisco Chronicle Magazine.* She is currently compiling a collection of her essays and continues to teach English, study Italian, and search for a way to fit into her two cultures.

Marguerite Rigoglioso is a freelance writer, university lecturer, and doctoral student at the California Institute of Integral Studies in San Francisco, and is a pioneer in the field of women's spirituality. Her research and nonfiction writings on goddesses, priestesses, and her ancestors of Sicily, Italy, and North Africa have been published in several anthologies, magazines, and academic journals. Her book about the religion sacred to Demeter and Persephone at Lake Pergusa and Enna in Sicily is forthcoming.

Terez Rose has written for numerous publications, including the *San Jose Mercury News*, the *Milwaukee Journal Sentinel*, *Literary Mama*, and the anthologies *Women Who Eat: A New Generation on the Glory of Food* and *A Woman's Europe*. A European expatriate assignment for her husband gave her the opportunity to tag along on business trips and visit Italy jet lag–free for two years. She now makes her home with husband and son in the Santa Cruz mountains.

Beth Schommer, born and raised in America's Dairyland, has long followed an imprecise desire for Italy, perhaps due to a trace amount of Italian blood. Upon completing a *summa cum laude* bachelor's degree in Italian Area Studies, punctuated by a year abroad in Milan, Beth moved permanently to Italy in 1993. Her writing has appeared in the literary collections *The Yellow Room* and *New Grains*. In addition to writing essays, creative nonfiction, and short stories, she directs an Italian program that promotes scientific research for sustainable development in the mountains of Nepal and Pakistan.

Melissa Secola earned her bachelor's degree in cinema from the University of Southern California's world-renowned School of Cinema. She went on to study modernist fiction at the University of Cambridge's International Summer School English Literature Program. Her essay "Kimiko" appears in the anthology *Waking Up American*. She lives in California.

Jennifer Sexton lives in Seattle with her husband, their baby daughter, and a garden full of eggplants and tomatoes—which are very difficult to grow in the Pacific Northwest but definitely worth the trouble. Her work has appeared in *Women's Work, Synapse, 4th Street Press,* and *Red-Headed Stepchild.*

Susan M. Tiberghien, an American living in Switzerland, has published three memoirs, *Looking for Gold, Circling to the Center,* and *Footsteps, A European Journal,* as well as shorter work in journals and anthologies. She teaches writing workshops in the United States and in Europe for the International Women's Writing Guild, for C. G. Jung Centers, and for the Geneva Writers' Group, where she directs the biennial Geneva Writers' Conference.

Ronna Welsh has cooked professionally for more than ten years as both executive and pastry chef in a number of New York City restaurants, as well as in restaurants, at pastry shops, on farms, and in homes in France, Spain, Greece, and Sicily. She has written articles and developed recipes for the Food TV Network, *Saveur, Time Out*

New York, Martha Stewart Living, and others. Her culinary work has been featured in *Diario de Alto Aragón,* a Spanish regional newspaper. Ronna is an advocate for sustainable farming and cooking causes and is active in numerous organizations, including the Chef's Collaborative, Women Chefs and Restaurateurs, Slow Food, and the Philosophy of Food Convivium. She is currently writing a book about her travels cooking abroad.

Wallis Wilde-Menozzi is the author of *Mother Tongue: An American Life in Italy.* Her work, essays, stories, poems, and translations have appeared widely in journals, including *Granta, Kenyon Review, Agni, Southwest Review,* and *The Best Spiritual Writing.* She runs writers workshops in Parma, Italy, where she lives and publishes a magazine of crosscultural writing, *New Grains.* A version of this essay appeared in the *Informer,* a Milan journal, where she had a bimonthly column.

About the Editor

Camille Cusumano is an editor at *VIA* magazine in San Francisco. She is the author of many food and travel articles, several food books, and *The Last Cannoli*, a novel about a Sicilian American family in New Jersey. She is the editor of *France, A Love Story*.

Selected Titles from Seal Press

For more than twenty-five years, Seal Press has published ground-breaking books. By women. For women. Visit our website at www.sealpress.com.

France, A Love Story: Women Write about the French Experience edited by Camille Cusumano. $15.95, 1-58005-115-4. Twenty-eight women describe the country they love and why they fell under its spell.

Solo: On Her Own Adventure edited by Susan Fox Rogers. $15.95, 1-58005-137-5. The second edition of this collection describes the inspiring challenges and exhilarating rewards of going it alone.

The Risks of Sunbathing Topless: And Other Funny Stories from the Road edited by Kate Chynoweth. $15.95, 1-58005-141-3. These wry, amusing, and insightful stories capture the comical essence of bad travel, and the uniquely female experience on the road.

The Unsavvy Traveler: Women's Comic Tales of Catastrophe edited by Rosemary Caperton, Anne Mathews, and Lucie Ocenas. $15.95, 1-58005-058-1. Thirty gut-wrenchingly funny responses to the question: What happens when trips go wrong?

I'll Know It When I See It: A Daughter's Search for Home In Ireland by Alice Carey. $12.95, 1-58005-132-4. This lyrically written memoir of a young New Yorker's ties to Ireland also shares her eventual move to the country as an adult.

Lost on Purpose
ited by Amy Prior. $13.95, 1-58005-120-0. This vibrant collection
ort fiction by women features characters held in thrall by an
xistence.

Selected Titles from Seal Press

For more than twenty-five years, Seal Press has published ground-breaking books. By women. For women. Visit our website at www.sealpress.com.

France, A Love Story: Women Write about the French Experience edited by Camille Cusumano. $15.95, 1-58005-115-4. Twenty-eight women describe the country they love and why they fell under its spell.

Solo: On Her Own Adventure edited by Susan Fox Rogers. $15.95, 1-58005-137-5. The second edition of this collection describes the inspiring challenges and exhilarating rewards of going it alone.

The Risks of Sunbathing Topless: And Other Funny Stories from the Road edited by Kate Chynoweth. $15.95, 1-58005-141-3. These wry, amusing, and insightful stories capture the comical essence of bad travel, and the uniquely female experience on the road.

The Unsavvy Traveler: Women's Comic Tales of Catastrophe edited by Rosemary Caperton, Anne Mathews, and Lucie Ocenas. $15.95, 1-58005-058-1. Thirty gut-wrenchingly funny responses to the question: What happens when trips go wrong?

I'll Know It When I See It: A Daughter's Search for Home In Ireland by Alice Carey. $12.95, 1-58005-132-4. This lyrically written memoir of a young New Yorker's ties to Ireland also shares her eventual move to the country as an adult.

Lost on Purpose edited by Amy Prior. $13.95, 1-58005-120-0. This vibrant collection of short fiction by women features characters held in thrall by an urban existence.